AFRICAN ENERGY WORLDS
IN FILM AND MEDIA

NEW DIRECTIONS IN NATIONAL CINEMAS
Robert Rushing, editor

AFRICAN ENERGY WORLDS
IN FILM AND MEDIA

Carmela Garritano

INDIANA UNIVERSITY PRESS

This book is a publication of

Indiana University Press
Office of Scholarly Publishing
Herman B Wells Library 350
1320 East 10th Street
Bloomington, Indiana 47405 USA

iupress.org

© 2025 by Carmela Garritano

The author and publisher acknowledge permission to use the following materials:
Excerpts from chapter one appeared in
Garritano, Carmela. "Waiting on the Past: African Uranium Futures in Arlit, Deuxième Paris." *MFS Modern Fiction Studies* 66, no. 1 (March 2020): 122–140. doi:10.1353/mfs.2020.0005.

Excerpts from chapter two appeared in
Garritano, Carmela. "Living Precariously in the African Postcolony: Debt and Labor Relations in the Films of Mahamat-Saleh Haroun." *JCMS: Journal of Cinema and Media Studies* 58, no. 2 (January 2019).

All rights reserved
No part of this book may be reproduced or utilized in any form or by any means, electronic or mechanical, including photocopying and recording, or by any information storage and retrieval system, without permission in writing from the publisher.

First Printing 2025

Cataloging information is available from the Library of Congress.

ISBN 978-0-253-07227-6 (hardcover)
ISBN 978-0-253-07228-3 (paperback)
ISBN 978-0-253-07230-6 (ebook)

For Kenneth W. Harrow

CONTENTS

Acknowledgments ix

Introduction: African Energy Worlds in Cinema 1

1. Global Time and Planetary Violence in African Films about Energy Extraction 17
2. Oil Pipelines and Debt Relations 47
3. Energy Infrastructures and Petronoir Sensibilities in African Cinema 80
4. Electrifying Movies in Northern Ghana 105
5. Sustainability, Ecological Thought, and Ghanaian Plastic Waste in Film and Art 129

Conclusion: Reading for Renewable Futures 157

Filmography 165
Bibliography 167
Index 181

ACKNOWLEDGMENTS

I DEDICATE THIS BOOK TO my PhD advisor, mentor, collaborator, and dear, dear friend, the late Ken Harrow. Ken opened a door into a scholarly life for me, a first-gen MA student who stumbled into his African literature class at Michigan State University and really had no idea what it might mean to study and write about Africa professionally. Ken made me, and all his students, feel like we had valuable contributions to make to the study of African film and literature. I love the academic life and will be forever grateful to Ken for his example. I am thankful beyond measure for the many years of reading, writing, watching, and learning beside and with him. Rest in perfect peace, sweet Dr. Harrow.

This book benefited from the support of several units at Texas A&M: I received a three-year Arts and Humanities Fellowship (2020–2023) that funded research in Ghana. The Glasscock Humanities Center provided support for an Energy Humanities reading group and the Energy Humanities and the Global South research cluster, initiatives that helped me develop expertise in energy humanities and locate a community of colleagues, both essential to writing this book. I joined the Department of International Affairs at the Bush School of Government and Public Service in 2022, and the support of the Bush School, in particular school, Dr. Steve Oberhelmen, Senior Associate Dean for Faculty Affairs, and Dr. David Bearce, my department head, made it possible for me to complete this project and include color images.

In Tamale, tremendous thanks to OBL, Rasheed, Fatawu, Nash, and all the young creatives at OBL Studios as well as to Jon Gil. Research in Takoradi was made possible by the generosity of Moyo Okediji, Rikki Wemega-Kwawu,

Patrick Tagoe-Turkson, and Elijah Sofo. My sincere thanks to my old friends Arcton, Safo, Elijah, Vero, and JoAnn, who have supported me during my research in Accra since 1999. More recently, I have benefited from spending time with Kofi Asamoah, Kwame Boateng, Serge Attukwei Clottey, Joseph Frimpong, Juliette Asante, and Salimata Sadisu.

There is no group of scholars like those who study Africa. Over the years, at the African Studies Association and African Literature Association conferences, I have been inspired by conversations with Moradewun Adejunmobi, Akin Adesokan, Lade Adunbi, Karen Bouwer, Matt Brown, Esther de Bruijn, Carli Coetzee, Vlad Dima, Rachel Gabara, Simon Gikandi, Lindsey Green-Simms, Jon Haynes, Olabode Ibironke, Cajetan Iheka, Cilas Kemedijo, Rita Keresztesi, Hilary Kowino Carmen McCain, John Metzler Cara Moyer-Duncan, Akinloye Ojo, Dayna Oscherwitz, Victoria Pasley, Ato Quayson, Connor Ryan, Phyllis Taoua, Alexie Tcheuyap, Olivier-Jean Tchouaffe, Steven Thomas, Paul Ugor, and Joya Uraizee. I am especially thankful for the friendship of Ellie Higgins, with whom I have been discussing African cinema, and other stimulating topics, for many years.

Thanks to Danya Abt, OBL, Patrick Tagoe-Turkson, and Serge Clottey for providing images from and of your work and giving me permission to include them in this book. Working with Allison Chaplin at Indiana University Press was an absolute pleasure. Thank you, Allison, for shepherding this project through the publication process. Full-throated thanks to the two anonymous readers whose critical insights and generosity made this a much better book.

I appreciate colleagues and friends in Texas who have encouraged me with their friendship, brilliance, home-cooked meals, bottles of wine, and laughter: Grace Adinku, Michael Alvard, Maddalena Cerrato, Michael Collins, David Donkor, Ira Dworkin, Dinah Hannaford, Rebecca Hankins, Silva Hamie, Violet Johnson, Ruth Larson, Alain Lawo-Sukam, Portia Owusu, Leslie Ruyle, Al Saenz, Bob Shandley, and Niki Shea. For cat and plant care while I was away doing research, I am indebted to Melinda Alvarado, Teresa Luck, and Hannah Alvard. Mel and Tea deserve special recognition for the love and support they have shown me and Mikołaj throughout the long process of writing this book. I owe deep gratitude to Bartek Plichta and our son Mikołaj, for patience and love.

AFRICAN ENERGY WORLDS
IN FILM AND MEDIA

Introduction

African Energy Worlds in Cinema

AFRICA IS AN ENERGY PARADOX. Uniquely vulnerable to sea level rise, drought, and other extreme weather events produced by global warming, the continent supplies a sizable percentage of the fossil fuels responsible for that very warming. In the twenty-first century, international investment in the extraction of African oil and natural gas has grown exponentially; in the United States alone, oil imports from Africa have increased by more than 40 percent.[1] Although most of the hydrocarbons extracted from African countries are exported, Degani, Chalfin, and Cross note in their introduction to a special issue of the *Cambridge Journal of Anthropology* on energy capture that Africa has become "a crucial planetary energy *source* and, increasingly, an energy *sink*."[2] Here, *sink* refers to the energy consumption of an increasing number of African consumers, who are releasing ever-larger amounts of carbon into the atmosphere. At the same time, these developing energy markets have positioned Africa as a frontier for small-scale and other renewable energy projects, which will be crucial to meeting growing energy demands in the Anthropocene. African entrepreneurs and governments across the continent—in some cases with support from international financial institutions and international nongovernmental organizations—are investing large sums of money in developing energy systems powered by solar, wind, and biofuels. This multifaceted and complex energy-scape shows that the planet's energy future is unfolding in Africa.[3]

Despite Africa's centrality to energy in the twenty-first century, the continent has only recently begun to attract the notice of scholars working in the field of energy humanities. Common across this deeply interdisciplinary formation is the key role of humanities-based research in addressing anthropogenic climate catastrophe and facilitating the considerable ideological and political transformations required to transition to greener and more sustainable energy systems. The earliest research in energy humanities has stressed the role of hydrocarbons in shaping modern life in the global North. This is perhaps best stated by Stephanie LeMenager: "We experience ourselves, as moderns and most especially as modern Americans, every day in oil, living within oil, breathing it and registering it with our senses."[4] Complementing this work, scholars have detailed the history of Western petrocapitalism and the imbrication of carbon-based fuels and politics. Energy humanists have tracked the deep imprint of energy on cultural products like literature and film and have examined the ontologies and ethics of hydrocarbons.[5] Exciting new research challenges the utopian discourses that renewable energy sources generate by examining the actual political and economic relations produced, for instance, by wind-energy projects in Mexico or an energy currency in Abu Dhabi.[6]

Africanists, not surprisingly, have taken the lead in the study of African energy infrastructures and commodity chains, mapping the global distribution of wealth and risk produced by resource extraction and the exploitation of hydro-energy sources.[7] They have advocated for the communities and ecologies imperiled by petrocapitalism, particularly in the Niger Delta, and written detailed ethnographies of energy enclaves in Africa and unpacked the discourses that sustain them.[8] Given Africa's significance to the future of energy, however, there is still much scholarly work to be done. *African Energy Worlds in Film and Media*, situated at the intersection of African studies, energy humanities, and film studies, analyzes the political, social, and economic dimensions of global energy forms and systems as depicted in African cinema and highlights African demands for radically just processes of energy transition.

AN AFRICAN ANTHROPOCENE

The idea of the Anthropocene has provoked a series of ethical and political questions of particular urgency for the global South. Defining the current geological epoch as the one in which humans act as a planetary force makes us recognize the harm caused by depending on fossil fuels to build and maintain modern energy systems. And yet, as Ian Baucom explains, anthropogenic global warming places postcolonial Africa in a singular position, "merging the long-visibly global politics of centers and peripheries with a newly visible geological exacerbation and intensification of that still unpassed and human-organized distribution of harms, vulnerabilities, and unfreedoms so fundamentally constitutive to the making of the modern world."[9] In this book, I use the term *Anthropocene* both to signal a political position attuned to the magnitude of human-induced planetary crisis and as a challenge. I examine African film, media, and art to understand the Anthropocene from African perspectives. I ask how we might use the term to account for the grossly uneven distribution of ecological risk among humans, how it might be helpful to acknowledge that the energy consumption of the wealthiest humans has caused the greatest harm to the earth and its biosphere—the worst effects of which are suffered by people experiencing poverty, especially those of the global South.

Baucom's book *History 4° Celsius* offers one approach to thinking about climate crisis from the African postcolony. A photograph series by Ghanaian photographer Nyani Quarmyne, "We Were Once Three Miles from the Sea," provides an African foundation for Baucom's book. The photographs feature people and landscapes in and around Totope, a small village on the coast of the Gulf of Guinea in the Western Region of Ghana, which is being "reconstitut[ed] by the forcings of climate change."[10] Baucom reprints several photos from the series. In one, a small boy, Collins Kusietey, stands in the ruins of a house that a rising ocean has claimed for its shore. He looks into the camera, serious and steadfast. In another, a man and a woman, identified by Baucom as Anikor Adjawutor and Miyorhokpor Anikor, lean on a window frame from inside an eroding dwelling on the same beach; their eyes, too, gaze directly into the camera. The man wears a T-shirt emblazoned with the image of Nana Addo Dankwa Akufo-Addo, Ghana's president since 2017. Baucom sees in Quarmyne's photographs a provocation. The images call on us, he argues, to develop methods of humanistic research that seek "to understand how the prior and enduring conditions of unfreedom" that originated in the slave factories along the West African coast "are now being exacerbated and intensified, slowly and explosively, by the forcings of the Anthropocene."[11] Baucom's method, sketched out in the book, looks to the philosophical dispute between Claude Lévi-Strauss and Jean-Paul Sartre about the capacity of historical analysis to understand human experience. I take no issue with Baucom's careful and close attention to the writings of these thinkers to theorize a dialectical relationship between planetary temporality and human conceptions of time, nor of his turn to Walter Benjamin and Dipesh Chakrabarty to refine his outline of an approach adequate to the multiple time scales at which humans experience the Anthropocene. Instead, I want to enlarge the lens through which Baucom views the African imaginary of the Anthropocene. I ask what it would mean to widen the scope of the analysis to account for the Jubilee Oil Fields and ultradeep oil-drilling infrastructure about thirty-seven miles beyond the Ghanaian shore where, in 2007, American oil company Kosmos Energy verified abundant reserves of high-quality crude. The Ghana National Petroleum Company shares ownership of the deep-sea oil with three transnational firms, and the Ghanaian government regulates its extraction and processes of revenue disbursement. Production began in 2010 and averages approximately 150,000 barrels per day. Since this discovery, oil has been a large part of Ghana's gross domestic product and its publicly expressed imaginary, especially in the southern regions of the country. The photograph mentioned above, the one in which a man wears a shirt with the image of Ghana's president, indexes this period and invites us to think through traces not only of the transatlantic history of slavery and colonialism, as Baucom does, but also to reflect on the local and national histories of the picture's production, which are shaped by debates about oil, development, and the future.

According to Baucom, African art primarily provides a way through which we might understand the "exorbitantly vulnerable citizen of the Anthropocene."[12] But the energy context outside the frame of Quarmyne's ten images, which includes Ghanaians who participate in and expect to benefit from the extraction of carbon-based resources, requires us to ask if vulnerability is the only theme expressed in African arts of the Anthropocene. African cinema, I argue, brings into visibility features of African subjects' multilayered and complex energy worldliness. Here, I follow Edward Said's concept of "worldliness" to refer to the material as well as the political and economic conditions texts originate from and seek to intervene in.[13] Energy worldliness, more specifically, describes the energy forms, systems, and infrastructures that are portrayed in and support the production and circulation of African cinema, but it also includes energy as intertwined with the relations of power challenged by the films and art examined in this book. African cinema, across forms and genres, asserts the call for energy justice made by postcolonial citizens of the Anthropocene, a call that must be central to our attempts to imagine the immense transformations required to disentangle ourselves from fossil fuels. The films articulate African claims to what James Ferguson calls "modern" life, lives of security made possible by affordable and reliable access to energy;

they remind us that Africans, as agents, are part of energy-intensive projects and processes and are also among those who advocate for the preservation of life on Earth and promote more sustainable ecological relations; and they signal a future focused on anticolonial energy policies that prioritize shared and equivalent opportunity and risk.[14]

To use the term *Anthropocene* to describe our current geological age is to insist that we think beyond humans to acknowledge nonhuman life in the context of the almost incomprehensible vastness of the planet's geological past and future. Rhetorical and descriptive, the concept of the Anthropocene, Dipesh Chakrabarty notes, "requires us to think on the two vastly different scales of time that earth history and world history respectively involve."[15] This book conceptualizes energy as a resource created from a variety of interactions between the human and nonhuman across various time frames. Humans mine the planet to extract crude, natural gas, and coal, tapping into the deep time of compressed solar energy to generate electricity and heat in the present and setting in motion planetary changes that ripple far into the future. My approach to African cinema aligns with Gabrielle Hecht's "interscalar analysis." For Hecht, a historian, to be attentive to expanding temporal and spatial scales requires that we grapple with "the political and ethical work accomplished by scalar choices and claims."[16] This means calibrating the scales of our scholarship self-reflexively, and, to this end, Hecht proposes the metaphor of "interscalar vehicles," objects that, through analysis, bring together "stories and scales usually kept apart." Her method follows rocks of uranium from their origins in mines in a small town in Gabon to eventually become the focus of transnational debates about uranium and toxicity.[17] I understand African cinematic texts as vehicles that allow us, through close reading, to cross and connect scales of space and time. Like Hecht, I use the idea of an *African* Anthropocene to emphasize my commitment to approaching the Anthropocene and its effects from locations in Africa. Interpreting African cinematic arts in relation to the energy worlds they project offers us "a means of holding *the planet* and *a place on the planet* on the same analytic plane."[18] The films studied in this book bring to light the energetic aspects of life in the ecological mesh that is planet Earth, grounding us in the everyday realities of postcolonial Africa.

In the last two decades, African literary ecocriticism has demonstrated that attending to cultural forms about and by Africans is fundamental to addressing some of the Anthropocene's most urgent issues. William Slaymaker, Byron Santangelo, and Cajetan Iheka, engaging with postcolonial ecocritics, have promoted African environmental literature and brought attention to the history of colonial and postcolonial regimes of resource capture and dispossession found in colonial discourse, Euro-American travel writing, and, most importantly, African literature.[19] They have also looked to African cosmologies and lifeworlds for the "agentic possibilities of the nonhuman world" in order to dismantle the humancentric ideologies of modernity.[20] *African Energy Worlds in Film and Media*, inspired by this work, endeavors to extend our response to the ever-more dire climate crisis by, first and most obviously, deliberately centering energy and African energy humanities because, as Jennifer Wenzel remarks, energy humanities and environmental humanities "are complementary *but not identical*" (emphasis mine).[21] When African literary ecocriticism addresses energy, it tends to focus exclusively on literary works that speak out against petrocapitalism and its exploitation, victimization, and degradation of African ecologies.[22] This attention to the extraction of fossil fuels remains vital given the seemingly intractable global dominance of carbon-intensive industries and ways of life, and in this book, I devote one chapter to extractive violence. Nonetheless, that focus has tended to shrink the spectrum of energy relations emergent in Africa under late capitalism and emphasized the suffering and deprivation that oil has brought to bear on African people and environments. *African Energy Worlds in Film and Media* follows films and media produced by Africans to other energy sites, including those involved in energy production and distribution as well as to sources and forms of energy that are not carbon based. It stresses the agency of Africans as expressed cinematically in their claims to the modest amounts of energy required for social reproduction and in their efforts to pirate, reroute, and attach to energy infrastructures. A comparative analysis of art made from and about energy waste—namely plastic—near the book's end stresses that petroculture ensnares Africans in oil as manufacturers and consumers, not only as those subjected to its waste and toxicity.

Cajetan Iheka's *African Ecomedia* deserves mention here because it is the first monograph to explore screen media by and about Africans through the lens of environmental studies. Iheka's book, drawing on the work of John Durham Peters, uses a broad definition of media that includes not only traditional media, such as video and photography, but also art and even "oil, uranium, coltan, and bananas" as well as water, fire, and earth.[23] This book interfaces with Iheka's pioneering analyses of media and in particular, media about the slow violence unleashed by energy extraction and electronic trash. *African Energy Worlds*, however, avoids a similar flattening of media types and forms

Introduction 7

and is firmly grounded in film studies and the material, sensory, technological, and historical particularities of African film. While Iheka centers on narrative (and the ideological positions expressed there), this book does more. It examines how film and video perform cultural work as film and video, how they produce multidimensional sensoria, how they provoke both affective and ideological responses in viewers, and how they move through the world as art objects and commodities within distinct networks.

ENERGY ANALYTICS

In recent years, established African film scholars such as Moradewun Adejunmobi, Akin Adesokan, Vlad Dima, Kenneth Harrow, Mary Ellen Higgins, and Alexis Tcheauyap have called for critical approaches aligned with the changes that have diversified and expanded the field of African film and screen media in the twenty-first century.[24] By looking at energy as portrayed in, but also crucial to the production and distribution of, twenty-first-century African cinema, *African Energy World* takes up this challenge. The book proposes a novel approach to interpreting African cinema: an energy analytics that highlights energy in interpretations of documentaries, commercial feature films, art films, and hybrid cinematic forms by Africans. I discuss films made in Cameroon, Chad, Congo, Ghana, Niger, Nigeria, Malawi, Mali, and Senegal, all of which come from distinct transnational and local production and distribution processes. This broad generic and geographical scope guides readers to a new way of approaching African films, stressing energy and its significance in relation to various cinematic forms across multiple registers.

In her introduction to the volume *Fueling Culture: 101 Words for Energy and Environment*, Jennifer Wenzel describes the value of "protocols of reading and modes of inquiry that can perceive the pressure that energy exerts on cultures, even and especially when energy is not-said: invisible, erased, elided ... and so ubiquitous so as to elude representation and critical attention."[25] Wenzel emphasizes the importance of locating energy in the absence of "the hook of the thematic: texts and other cultural objects about energy or where energy regimes become unmistakably manifest."[26] To understand the strong connection between modern life and energy, she suggests that we recognize energy's presence especially when it seems to be absent. This book grabs the hook, to borrow Wenzel's term, and analyzes films that directly address the extraction of uranium and carbon-based resources as well as films about pipelines, gas stations, petrol smuggling, and electricity. But I move beyond the thematic to incorporate energetic objects like light bulbs, batteries, power lines, and cell phones into narrative space. I analyze interactions between plot and setting, people and things to demonstrate that "props" function as more than inert features of a static background; they provoke and direct action and also actively generate the film's sensorium. Finally, *African Energy Worlds* uncovers the energopolitics behind the history indexed in the films to bring energy into visibility. Dominic Boyer invented the term *energopolitics* to denote the "energo-material contributions" of energy to political power and as a shorthand for the "massive, hidden influence" that energy exerts "over political and economic systems."[27] Tuning into energopolitics, this book demonstrates that African cinema offers a powerful reflection on energy's imbrication with capital accumulation and African underdevelopment. I also argue that sovereign debt as experienced by citizens of many African countries manifests the energopower regime that became dominant globally after the 1970s oil crisis. African films that critique life lived under sovereign debt, I suggest, challenge this regime, even when they never mention energy.

TWENTY-FIRST-CENTURY AFRICAN CINEMA

The collection of film texts in this book offers nonspecialist readers a glimpse of the rich cultural assemblage that is African cinema since the 1990s, a decade that brought massive structural and technological changes to cinema production and distribution worldwide. Recent African films emerge from and participate in vastly different historical circumstances than those of earlier generations and circulate through dramatically altered transnational networks of production and distribution. Under globalization, media and movies, like capital, flow more easily across borders but in grossly asymmetrical patterns, and the result is a major shift in the films and media viewers have access to, in how viewers watch content, in who makes movies, and even in what counts as cinema. In Africa, the liberalization of national economies and the imposition of structural adjustment policies, the opening-up of media environments, and the widespread availability of video technologies have transformed production, viewing, and distribution and initiated an unprecedented broadening of the field of African cinema. The appearance and growth of transnational, commercial movie industries in Ghana and Nigeria, which are often lumped loosely together under the label "Nollywood," represent the most obvious example of these transformations, but Nollywood "video films" are only one manifestation of many. As Kenneth Harrow and I write: "If 'video films' had typically been associated with greater commercial cinematic values, they now have begun to include 'transnational films,' typically associated with greater post-production values, 'experimental' or 'innovative' New Nollywood styles and genres, . . . as might be seen in Djo Munga's dystopic *Viva Riva!* (2011)."[28] To represent this range, I discuss energy in features from Nollywood and the films of African auteurs. I revisit canonical films by Ousmane Sembène and Djibril Diop Mambety and introduce an experimental film by young director Nelson Makengo. The book analyzes documentaries about extractive energy industries in Africa as well as transnational "hybrid" films that straddle genre and art film classifications, including *Viva Riva!* (2011), a feature about petroleum smugglers.

Manthia Diawara's study of African cinema, *African Film: New Forms of Aesthetics and Politics* (2010), pays special attention to new art categories of African cinemas, the originality of which is found in "their mastery of the modern grammar of world cinemas." These filmmakers include Mahamat-Saleh Haroun and Abderrahmane Sissako, who receive special consideration in this book. Diawara compares their attention to artistic style and "the poetics of the image" to the political and ideological issues that historically have driven developments in African cinema.[29] Other critics have tried to locate the singularity of this wave of recent African filmmaking in the balance it achieves between ideological content and a formal attention to poetics, or what we might think of as a balance between the imperatives of Third Cinema and Second Cinema.[30] As Philip Rosen explains, art cinema and African cinema appeared at around the same time in the post–World War II period of African decolonization and political independence, and the two movements shared a mode of production structured around the figure of the auteur. African film lacked independent exhibition and distribution systems, and "the art cinema system, which was at its apogee in the 1960s and 1970s, offered a venue for films emerging from the contexts of a newly postcolonial Africa." Bound to European structures of distribution, African filmmakers have adopted "a double address." They have "had to make films for an international audience in the art cinema tradition, while simultaneously aiming at an African audience." So on the one hand, their films are "self-consciously African," and on the other, they cultivate an extroverted, global orientation.[31]

In the past twenty years, a proliferation of film festivals and domestic and on-demand viewing services have disrupted the structures of distinction and distribution to which Rosen refers. Lúcia Nagib notes that many independent and art films "can now bypass the intricate and selective networks of distribution and exhibition" for art and other festival films.[32] The films of the new African auteurs, such as Sissako and Haroun, still circulate through the conventional and prestigious African cinema venues—like the FESPACO film festival—and also move through the now-expansive networks of world cinema. Numerous factors have facilitated this convergence of African and world cinemas, including an increase in transnational cooperation across the Eurozone, which has led to more coproductions between European financiers and less prosperous countries in the global South. This has also reduced France's dominance as the main financial supporter of African cinema.[33] Films by Haroun, for instance, were among the 350 transnational productions launched by Pierre Chevalier between 1991 and 2003, while he was head of the fiction department at Arte, the Franco-German TV Network, and were subsequently incorporated into world cinema circuits with films by Laurent Cantet and Claire Denis (France) as well as Chantal Akerman (Belgium), Tsai Ming-liang (Taiwan), and Lars von Trier (Denmark).[34]

The films of Sissako and Haroun interest me because they exploit cinema's ability to represent the real, especially the material and sensory features of energy and its entanglements with human and nonhuman life. Following Nagib and Tiago de Luca, I find that for Haroun and Sissako, both of whom conceptualize realism as foundational to their aesthetics and politics, "the world is not a mere construct or discourse, but made of people, animals, plants, and objects that physically exist, thrive, suffer, and die. They feel part of, and responsible for, this material world and want to change it for the better."[35] I consider realism, after Nagib, as a mode of production that leaves its imprint on the text. Real locations, nonprofessional actors playing themselves, improvised dialogue and movement, and unscripted performances incorporate the material and sensory dimensions of the real into the diegetic world of their films. Stressing duration, using long takes, and rendering affective relations in film form, Haroun and Sissako achieve cinematically and formally what might be called a hyperrealism that emphasizes materiality. This commitment to the material world, as Nagib has noted, is attuned to the speculative realism of ecological thinkers like Timothy Morton. Morton suggests that the climate crisis and everything we know and feel about it necessitate new ways of thinking, interacting, making art, and being. He asks us to open our minds to "the ecological thought," the radical coexistence and radical intimacy that erase distinctions between nature and culture, human and animal, living and nonliving things. Radical coexistence, he explains, "must challenge our sense of what is real and what is unreal, what counts as existence and what counts as nonexistence."[36] It eliminates the foreground-background binary and the hierarchies that place humans over and above other forms of life and matter.

Morton uses the metaphor of "mesh" to understand the interconnectedness and interdependence of everything on our planet. In his book *The Ecological Thought* (2010), Morton explores various metaphors and examples to illustrate what he means by "mesh": "The ecological thought permits no distance. Thinking interdependence involves dissolving the barrier between 'over here' and 'over there,' and more fundamentally, the metaphysical illusion of rigid, narrow boundaries between inside and outside."[37] Art that stresses the material, Morton suggests, might be regarded as ecological in that it disturbs our sense of what is static and what is vibrant, what is natural and what is artificial, and of human agents and the locations and objects on which they act. Attention to the materiality of energy sources, like hydrocarbons and wind, and forms of energy, like electricity, in African cinema and art helps us understand agency as relational and distributed, disturbing the extractive, colonial mindset of modernity.

African cinema does more than stimulate our ability to imagine radical coexistence and energopolitical futures. The films examined here demonstrate Kathryn Yusoff's point that Black bodies bear a vastly disproportionate share of the burdens of the Anthropocene.[38] In the uranium mines in Arlit, Niger, and the enclaves of extraction in the Niger Delta, Africans absorb the toxic by-products of energy-intensive modernity. African films depict what Thom Davies in his research on Louisiana's Cancer Alley describes as "toxic biographies" to make slow violence "noticeable, vital, and manifest."[39] Going further, the focus on the uneven global distribution of machine power and embodied energy—industrialization and muscularity—extends Yusoff's argument into twenty-first-century regimes of labor and highlights the enduring "anti-Black biopolitics," which—within the neoliberal energy-capital nexus—overlay the histories of slavery and colonialism that Yusoff places at the heart of her book.[40] The African films featured in this book, set in underindustrialized cities and villages with no electricity, draw viewers into the lives of the people who do the work of machines, men and women whose physical energy draws water from wells, washes laundry, transports fuel, plants and harvests crops, spins cotton into yarn, and bakes bread. African feature and documentary films expose energy poverty as energy underdevelopment and assert political claims to safe and secure lives made possible by electricity and fuel.

CHAPTERS

The book comprises six chapters and is loosely organized to track the energy commodity chain, starting with sites of extraction and ending with plastic and electronic waste. The first chapter focuses on understanding the time frames of ecological violence. The chapter also compares the strategies used by auteur and commercial (Nollywood) filmmakers to manage the representational challenges created by what Rob Nixon describes as "slow violence."[41] I build on Nixon's literary analyses to explore how African cinema reveals the various temporal aspects of violence caused by resource extraction (uranium and crude). In this case, film form works as a kind of interscalar vehicle by producing temporality at different scales. Paying close attention to the time people spend waiting, Idrissou Mora-Kpai's poetic documentary *Arlit, Deuxième Paris* (2005) is an artistic and activist endeavor to bring understanding to the prolonged and elongated impacts of uranium mining through cinema. Mora-Kpai uses cinematic devices like duration and long takes to give time structure and uncover evidence of deep planetary history in human and nonhuman matter damaged by nuclear radiation.

Produced and released in 2015, the Nollywood movies *Black November* and *Blood and Oil* use the cinematic and narrative conventions of action films to portray the intensity of the lived destruction that characterizes the extractive zones of the Delta region. These genre films struggle to represent the Niger Delta as a site where the imperceptible, slow violence of environmental degradation interacts with the high-speed and visceral violence of armed conflict. In the last section of this chapter, I show how the Niger Delta movies provide an opportunity to question Nixon's reservations about the capacity of genre films that participate in "dominant structures of perception" to "rouse public sentiment" on behalf of ecologies afflicted by energy-related violence at multiple temporalities.[42]

In chapter 2, "Oil Pipelines and Debt Relations," I consider indebtedness in the films of Chadian director Mahamat Saleh-Haroun within the context of the Chad-Cameroon Petroleum Development and Pipeline Project. Since at least the oil crisis of the 1970s, which plunged many African nations into economic collapse, oil has been fundamental to postcolonial debt relations with international financial institutions. It is not surprising, then, that African films, from Djibril Diop Mambety's *Hyenas* (1992) to Abderrahmane Sissako's *Bamako* (2006), have agitated against energy-resource extraction and sovereign indebtedness. In recent years, Haroun's films have deepened cinema's exploration of African indebtedness, exposing the interplay of sovereign and subjective debt as experienced by those who live in Chad where oil reserves have guaranteed the debt incurred to support the three-billion-dollar Chad-Cameroon pipeline. Taking place during the same time as the immense extraction project, Haroun's films center on African men who struggle to manage personal debts and everyday precarity, conditions caused by the sovereign indebtedness of postcolonial countries in what Timothy Mitchell calls "the postwar petroleum order."[43] This chapter expands on the historical and political context of Haroun's films to include oil wells and pipelines and asks if these cinematic investigations of debt relations might also help us imagine an energopolitics that advances energy and climate justice on a planetary scale.

The third chapter, "Energy Infrastructures and Petronoir Sensibilities," introduces the term *petronoir* to describe prestige and art films from Africa that retool the narrative and formal conventions of film noir to denounce the endlessly deferred promises of oil-based national development and infrastructural modernity. Except for the first, *Faat Kiné* (Senegal, 1999 the films analyzed in this chapter—*Up at Night* (DRC, 2020), *Viva Riva!* (DRC, 2011), and *Grigris* (Chad, 2013)—detail incomplete, failed, or underdeveloped energy infrastructures across several African cities and closely examine the novel forms of labor and sociality that emerge in response to energy shortage. The figure of the petroleum smuggler is depicted in a number of these recent African films as a fuel transport apparatus who takes advantage of breakdown to participate in the "prevailing modes of accumulation" dominant in African frontier zones.[44] The smuggler's work brings him in contact with the materiality and toxicity of petroleum and produces a dangerous, type of human-nonhuman interconnectedness experienced by those who are excluded from networks that transport oil around the globe. Petronoir films stress the dark dimensions of human proximity to vital matter.

Chapter 4, "Electrifying Movies in Northern Ghana," maps a group of Dagbani-language video production and exhibition in and around Tamale, Ghana, in relation to the country's National Electrification Program (NEP) and the subsequent Self-Help Electrification Programme (SHEP). In this chapter, I examine the kinds of cultural productions that materialize around energy and technological infrastructures, in this case, electricity and the internet, in northern Ghana. The broadening network of electricity around Tamale coupled with the slow expansion of telecommunications and media infrastructures have created conditions that support a small, informal straight-to-video distribution circuit. With limited competition from television and YouTube, Dagbani-language moviemakers, unlike their counterparts making movies in English in Accra and Lagos, make and circulate their movies in large numbers for consumers throughout the northern region. I discuss a selection of Dagbani movies produced by OBL Studios in Tamale, in particular, *Piele: Rise of Montana* (2017), a film that depends on electricity for its production and the computer-generated and enhanced sounds, movement, and images that make tangible the key elements of Dagbon origin narratives and drum histories. These energetic elements make the mythic real to the senses and alive in the present.

Chapter 5, "Visual Arts of Energy Ruins," compares the ecological politics enacted by a documentary and a series of art installations about energy waste (plastic and electronic) in Ghana. The documentary *Welcome to Sodom* (2019), set in an electronic waste dump in Accra, and the plastic-art installations of Ghanaian artists Serge Attukwei Clottey and Patrick Tagoe-Turkson, explore human energy consumption through their close attention to the waste generated from energy's commodity forms, byproducts, politics, regimes of labor, and social life. Taking on plastic waste as their material and theme, these artworks deal with human and nonhuman relationships in the age of climate catastrophe more explicitly than the African films analyzed in earlier sections of the book. As presented in the documentary and installations, waste commands attention in its liveliness and vibrancy and raises crucial questions about plasticity as a condition of life in the global South. The reach of plastic waste, its pervasiveness and persistence, is planetary in scale; however, the expressive forms discussed here reflect on the deeply historical patterns through which energy waste circulates and accumulates. *Welcome to Sodom* stages revolting and shocking images of African trash and trash workers to incite viewers in the global North to limit their consumption, and analyzing the political aesthetics of the documentary reveals the limits of sustainability discourse. In contrast, Clottey's Afrogallonism, the creation of art with recycled jerry cans, and Tagoe-Turkson's repurposed sculptures invite people to feel part of plasticity in its vastness across time and space and in its intimate and ordinary relations with human bodies.

At the most general level, *African Energy Worlds* demonstrates the critical role of humanities-based research by showing the extent to which modern human life is enmeshed with energy and calling out the enduring legacies of racism and colonialism that unevenly distribute the benefits of energetic modernity and energy-related violence and risk. This book stands beside novelist Amitav Ghosh, who states that the "worldwide adoption of colonial methods of extraction and consumption" is responsible for the great acceleration of carbon emissions into the atmosphere and for the cascade of devastating effects now upon us. Just as crucially, energy humanities helps us to imagine and theorize what Ghosh calls a vitalist politics, which, like Morton's ecological thought and Wangari Mataai's interconnectedness, dismantles the "old mechanistic ideologies of conquest" that undergird modernity so that we might build ways of living that recognize the deep interconnectedness of all life and matter on our planet without, however and crucially, disregarding the enduring legacies of human histories of unfreedom and exploitation.[45]

NOTES

1. Bassey, *To Cook a Continent*, 27; Wengraf, *Extracting Profit*, 137.
2. Degani, Chalfin, and Cross, "Introduction: Fueling Capture," 2.
3. Readers might recognize that last sentence as a riff off Achille Mbembe's claim that "our planet's destiny might be played out in Africa." See *Out of the Dark Night*.
4. LeMenager, *Living Oil*, 6.
5. For energy and politics, see Adunbi, *Oil Wealth and Insurgency in Nigeria*; Boyer, *Energopolitics*; Huber, *Lifeblood*; Mitchell, *Carbon Democracy*. For energy in literature and film, see DeLoughrey, *Allegories of the Anthropocene*; Ghosh, *Great Derangement, Nutmeg's Curse*; LeMenager, *Living Oil*; Szeman and Boyer, *Energy Humanities*; Szeman, Wenzel, and Yaeger, *Fueling Culture*; Wilson, Carlson, and Szemen, *Petrocultures*; Wenzel, "Petro-Magic-Realism," *The Disposition of Nature*; Yeager et al., "Editor's Column: Literature in the Ages of Wood."
6. See Hitchcock, "Velocity and Viscosity"; Jamieson, *Ethics for the Anthropocene*; Morton, *Dark Ecology, The Ecological Thought, Hyperobjects*. On cultures of renewable energy, see Boyer, *Energopolitics*; Howe, *Ecologics*; Günel, *Spaceship in the Desert*.
7. Gore, *Electricity in Africa*; Miescher, *A Dam for Africa*; Osseo-Asare, *Atomic Junction*; Tsikata, *Living in the Shadow of the Large Dams*; Watts, "Frontiers," "Righteous Oil?," "There Will Be Blood."
8. Appel, *The Licit Life of Capitalism*; Wenzel, *The Disposition of Nature*; Leonard, *Life in the Time of Oil*.
9. Baucom, *History 4° Celsius*, 81.
10. Baucom, *History 4° Celsius*, 3.
11. Baucom, *History 4° Celsius*, 17.
12. Baucom, *History 4° Celsius*, 74.
13. Said, *The World, the Text and the Critic*.

14. Ferguson, *Global Shadows*.
15. Chakrabarty, *The Climate of History*, 156.
16. Hecht, "Interscalar Vehicles for an African Anthropocene," 111.
17. Hecht, "Interscalar Vehicles for an African Anthropocene," 115.
18. Hecht, "Interscalar Vehicles for an African Anthropocene," 112.
19. Caminero-Santangelo, *Different Shades of Green*; See Iheka, *Naturalizing Africa*; Slaymaker, "Ecoing the Other(s)."
20. Iheka, *Naturalizing Africa*, 58.
21. Wenzel, "Introduction," 15.
22. See Caminero-Santangelo and Meyers, eds., *Environment at the Margins*; Caminero-Santangelo, *Different Shades of Green*; Iheka, *Naturalizing Africa*; Egya, *Nature, Environment, and Activism in Nigerian Literature*; and Ogude and Tafadzwa, eds., *Environmental Humanities of Extraction in Africa*.
23. Iheka, *African Ecomedia*, 4.
24. See, for example, Dovey, *Curating Africa*; Harrow, *Trash*; Harrow and Garritano, *A Companion to African Cinema*; Higgins, "Winds of African Cinema"; Tcheuyap *Postnationalist African Cinema*.
25. Wenzel, "Introduction," 11.
26. Wenzel, "Introduction," 11.
27. Boyer, *Energopolitics*, 5; 15.
28. Harrow and Garritano, *A Companion to African Cinema*, 7.
29. Diawara, *African Film*, 100.
30. See Gabara, "Abderrahmane Sissako: Second and Third Cinema in the First Person."
31. Rosen, "Notes on Art Cinema," 254–260.
32. Nagib, *Realist Cinema as World Cinema*, 16.
33. See Farahmand, "Disentangling the International Festival Circuit"; and Halle, "Offering Tales They Want to Hear." I also write more about this in "Living Precariously in the African Postcolony."
34. Diawara, *African Film*, 94.
35. Nagib, *Realist Cinema as World Cinema*, 15.
36. Morton, *The Ecological Thought*, 10.
37. Morton, *The Ecological Thought*, 20.
38. Yusoff, *A Billion Black Anthropocenes*, 15.
39. Davies, "Slow Violence and Toxic Geographies," 419.
40. Yusoff, *A Billion Black Anthropocenes*, 40.
41. Nixon, *Slow Violence*.
42. Nixon, *Slow Violence*, 20.
43. Mitchell, *Carbon Democracy*.
44. Roitman, *Fiscal Disobedience*, 264.
45. Ghosh, *The Nutmeg's Curse*, 243.

ONE

Global Time and Planetary Violence in African Films about Energy Extraction

INTRODUCTION

THE FILMS DISCUSSED IN THIS chapter—poetic documentary *Arlit, deuxième Paris* (2004) and Nollywood movies *Black November* (2015) and *Blood and Oil* (2015)—belong to a long tradition of engaged African artistic practice. As is well known, the articulation of anticolonialism and the promotion of African identity and culture were among the founding objectives of the African cinematic tradition, guiding African filmmaking and its criticism for decades. Today in African screen media, despite massive transformations in modes of production and distribution and the diversity of cinema and media forms and styles, activism continues to motivate many filmmakers across auteur and commercial registers. In this chapter, I discuss three films that demonstrate cinema's capacity to represent and denounce the ecological devastation of landscapes and living things caused by extractive energy industries in Arlit, Niger, and the Niger Delta region of Nigeria. These films invite readings aligned with what I refer to in the introduction as an energy analytics, a method of cinematic interpretation centered on the material and ideological dimensions of particular energy systems as well as the economic, social, and temporal relations associated with specific sources and forms of energy. Standing beside communities ravaged by ecological violence, the filmmakers speak out against the processes used to extract uranium and crude oil and the risk and corruption generated by these exploitative energy industries. Idrissou Mora Kpai's *Arlit, deuxième Paris* takes place in Arlit, Niger, a small northern town dependent on and devastated by the mining of uranium ore.

Moving between the testimonies of villagers who live near the uranium mine and images of a desolate place littered with abandoned and contaminated machinery, the film shows the effects of uranium mining's radioactive toxicity on people and the environment. The Nigerian coproductions *Black November* and *Blood and Oil* leverage star power and a Hollywood genre on behalf of minority communities in the Niger Delta. Working with limited resources and narrow profit margins, commercial directors Jeta Amata and Curtis Graham rely on the conventions of action cinema to depict the struggles of marginalized communities caught between the competing interests of oil companies and the state and local militants. Strikingly dissimilar in form and style, these films nonetheless, I argue, contend with similar representational challenges. Namely, the three films must find a cinematic way of expressing the temporal qualities of ecological and extractive violence.

Rob Nixon's outstanding book *Slow Violence and the Environmentalism of the Poor* has become something of a touchstone for scholars interested in literary representations of environmental violence, in part because Nixon explains the difficulties of conveying the effects of violence that "occurs gradually and out of sight" and is "neither spectacular nor instantaneous, but rather incremental and accretive, its calamitous repercussions playing out across a range of temporal scales."[1] Delayed and often invisible, the slow violence of "climate change, radioactive aftermath of wars, acidifying oceans, and a host of other slowly unfolding catastrophes," Nixon explains, defies literary and cinematic expression.[2] Nixon's description of ecological violence echoes Ulrich Beck's definition of risk as theorized in his important book *Risk Society: Towards a New Modernity*. For Beck, risks are distinct from personal dangers or accidents because they are products of the technologies and industries—the advances—of late modernity and include global perils like radioactivity, pollutants in food and air, climate warming, and other kinds of environmental devastation. Risks and risk fallout are distributed unequally. They "accumulate at the bottom," while wealth, of course, collects at the top, and internationally, risks are "transferred to the poor countries of the periphery."[3] Beck also elaborates on the perceptual and temporal characteristics of risk, explaining that risks are often invisible and latent and therefore "only exist in terms of the (scientific or antiscientific) *knowledge* about them."[4] Risks engender time; they "express a future component," promising "destruction that has not yet happened."[5] Beck emphasizes that because they are imperceptible and anticipated, risks must be defined and legitimized to be recognized as risk, so in what Beck refers to as a "world risk" society, "knowledge gains a new political significance."[6] This claim is supported in Nixon's book, which outlines the strategies used by writer-activists from the global South to describe the temporal and invisible dimensions of certain forms of ecological risk in politically compelling ways.

Nixon, a literary scholar, says very little about cinema. He mentions Hollywood if possible. and mainstream media without citing specific films or programs to suggest that an entire commercial media apparatus plays a role in conditioning our imaginations toward high-speed, "spectacle-driven" violence, which, he argues, diminishes our ability to grapple with "the slow erosion of environmental justice."[7] Cinema scholars have questioned Nixon's characterization of the dominant representational mode of cinematic violence as visual and spectacular and have challenged his somewhat reductive description of "the relationship of cinematic spectacle and imagination."[8] In this chapter, I build on Nixon's literary analysis to carefully explore African cinema's facility in demonstrating the various temporal dimensions of energy-related violence. The films discussed in this chapter are involved in risk definition. Their goal is to make people aware of the risks off-loaded to the global South and to make visible the anticipated and invisible forms of violence produced by energy-resource extraction. Deeply attentive to time subjects in Arlit spend waiting, Idrissou Mora-Kpai's poetic documentary *Arlit, deuxième Paris* is an artistic and activistic attempt at making uranium extraction's delayed and elongated violence sensible through cinema. The film depicts time as experienced by those who live in the grip of slow violence. Mora-Kpai is an artist interested in the creative and political potential of slowness, much like the writers whose work Nixon promotes. The first section of this chapter interprets Mora-Kpai's documentary as a cinematic exploration of the materiality of slow time. Produced and released in 2015, the Nollywood movies *Black November* and *Blood and Oil* use the cinematic and narrative conventions of action films to portray the lived violence, environmental and cultural degradation, exploitation, and corruption that characterize the Delta region.[9] These genre films struggle to represent the Niger Delta as an area where the imperceptible, slow violence of environmental degradation exists with the high-speed and visceral violence of resource wars. In the final pages of this chapter, the Niger Delta movies provide an opportunity to revisit Nixon's reservations about the capacity of films that participate in what he calls "dominant structures of perception" to "rouse public sentiment" on behalf of ecologies afflicted by slow violence.[10] Imperfect and problematic in ways that are easily identified by the "enlightened" film critic or literary scholar, these commercial films nonetheless highlight the complex political and ecological terrain of the Niger Delta. They seem to make the point that such a setting warrants different types of films that appeal to mainstream and art cinema audiences, at home and abroad, to support and amplify communities' calls for justice.

URANIUM FUTURES IN ARLIT, DEUXIÈME PARIS

Cinematic duration has been of interest to African filmmakers and those of other developing countries for decades. In his canonical essay "Towards a Critical Theory of Third World Films," Teshome Gabriel describes slowness as a distinctive feature of films from the Third World. He argues that "the slow, leisurely pacing" of Third World cinema "approximates the viewer's sense of time and rhythm of life."[11] Gabriel's piece, widely criticized for its reliance on cultural essentialism, points effectively at cinema's formal and narrative capacities to express time. More recently, film scholars have created the category of slow cinema to describe the work of auteurs such as Béla Tarr, Pedro Costa, Abbas Kiarostami, Wang Bing, and Kelly Reichardt, among others. These slow films adopt "extended temporal structures" to create a "durational aesthetic" that deemphasizes the plot.[12] They favor long takes, unbroken shots, and quiet, meditative images. As Song Hwee Lim shows in an analysis of Tsai Ming-liang's films, a cinema of slowness "comprises aesthetic acts that promote new modes of temporal awareness."[13] Time, in slow cinema, is given shape; it is not merely an invisible narrative frame that structures events, nor is it a problem to be resolved. Mora-Kpai's interest in temporalities of slowness coordinates, too, with a growing body of Africanist scholarship on time and uncertainty. Some of this work has been inspired by Jane Guyer's thoughts on the near future and prophetic time as well as Achille Mbembe's call for attention to time as lived.[14] Jacques de Villiers summarizes this trend as follows: "Both the understanding and experience of temporality are being urgently reformulated on a continent where a proliferation of widespread factors—the dynamics of mass migration; interstate conflict; the global neoliberal turn and its attendant structural adjustment"—have normalized radical social and economic uncertainty.[15] A major contribution to film and African studies, Mora-Kpai's *Arlit, Deuxième Paris* gives time as experienced within a context of slow violence and radical uncertainty cinematic form and feeling.

Poetic and observational, Mora-Kpai's one-hour documentary is structured loosely in three broad thematic segments. The first section of the film explores Arlit's location at the margins of the global uranium economy and depicts residents remembering a prosperous past when work and opportunities were plentiful. The next section reflects on the harrowing journeys of new immigrants to Arlit, and in the final segment, several speakers, including former employees of the French parastatal mining company AREVA, testify to the extent of radiation exposure and poisoning they suffered. Their bodies provide evidence of the sickness and death caused by working in the uranium mines, even as the mining company doctor denies any connection between mining and incidents of asthma, silicosis, and cancer. The documentary features interviews with Arlit residents but rejects conventions associated with documentary objectivity and truth telling. Mora-Kpai makes no attempt to document the history or process of uranium extraction in Niger. There is no authorial voiceover to contextualize what viewers see and why it matters. No intertitles explain when uranium deposits were discovered by the French or detail the course of radioactive breakdown. Instead, Mora-Kpai positions his interlocutors, whom he does not label or name, as witnesses and experts who speak for themselves. *Arlit*'s message is expressed mainly through testimony by the people of Arlit, who narrate the story of uranium in Niger. Each section of the film supplements these testimonies with sequences of contemplative images of the mining town's landscape and spaces of labor and leisure. These self-conscious, extended shots and sequences establish Mora-Kpai's presence as filmmaker; as Sheila Petty suggests, Mora-Kpai's visual motifs "replace the role of the narrator."[16] I would further add that Mora-Kpai's artfully composed extended shots give expression to the different modalities of waiting experienced in Arlit. The documentary itself takes shape in these spaces of waiting. Mora-Kpai's conversations and interviews with those who appear in the film—all of whom he finds waiting—reflect on and are products of suspended labor and stalled mobility.

In Arlit, Niger, time no longer advances; it is warped and stretched. Indeed, Mora-Kpai's documentary extends time to follow the drawn-out temporality of uranium's decay. During the chain-like process of radioactive breakdown, atoms explode to release bursts of energy as they transform into different radioactive substances that continue to erode and reconstitute for thousands, millions, and even billions of years. The by-products of uranium disintegration include thorium, radium, radon gas, and, finally, lead, all of which over many years cause critical damage to living things and landscapes. In a description of radioactive contamination caused by the detonation of nuclear bombs, Karen Barad describes the entangled temporality of uranium breakdown: "Radioactive decay elongates, disperses, and exponentially frays time's coherence. Time is unstable, continually leaking away from itself."[17] Mora-Kpai's film bends time in similar ways, denaturalizing the linear temporalities of development and modernity. For those who live in Arlit, the temporal atmosphere of the present derives from nonevents that reach across days, weeks, and years. The residents describe time as suspended; for many, this suspension exists between a prosperous past and the hope that things will return to the way they were, while others tread in place to hold off death or in anticipation of a better future.

The first part of the film describes "the geographies of exploitation" sustained by ore extraction in the isolated outpost of Arlit.[18] It draws attention to the geography of power that demarcates this extraction enclave; the first shots of the film reveal that Arlit is a space carved out of the desert by transnational capital. Mora-Kpai's camera plots Arlit's location at the start of the uranium commodity chain, emphasizing the town's detachment from the technologies and circuits of knowledge and commerce that add value to the ore mined there. The film opens on an empty desert landscape as seen by a static camera positioned behind and inside the gateway entrance to Arlit. The gateway features an arch, constructed from two tall poles supported by low brick walls on each side, displaying a banner that reads "Welcome to Arlit" (*Bienvenue A Arlit*). The entrance seems arbitrarily dropped into place, a flimsy frame erected over a narrow road that disappears into the desert sand. In real time, the extreme long shot captures the slow movement of a bus, the only vehicle on the road, as it approaches the town entrance across the vast and empty desert. The viewer takes several seconds to register that the bus is in fact moving, and as the vehicle nears the camera, extradiegetic music plays over the ambient sound of the wind, seeming to fill what had been a depopulated sound space. The entire shot lasts for more than thirty seconds, and the duration adds to the visual impression of Arlit as an outpost at the edge of the uranium frontier.

The road traveled by the bus is the *route de l'uranium*, but Mora-Kpai does not name the road or explain that since 1982, it has enabled the transport of uranium yellowcake, a semiprocessed form of uranium, from the northernmost tip of Arlit to the edge of the Sahel.[19] The image of this uranium road signals Arlit's tenuous attachment to the networks of exchange where uranium is processed and priced. It functions as a visual representation of a distant connection, one theme introduced in the documentary's first segment. Movement is another significant topic in the opening: the movement of the workers as they disembark and line up at the security gate into the mining site, moving away from the camera. These opening shots might represent a reversal of the Lumière actualité *Workers Leaving the Lumière Factory* (*Sortie des Usines Lumière à Lyon*, 1895). In Mora-Kpai's documentary, we are at the start, not the end, of the workday. Yet, like Lumière's camera, which never enters the factory, Mora-Kpai, with few exceptions, stays outside the open-pit and underground mines and the mill. Throughout the film, we see little of the actual work of extracting uranium. Instead, the documentary explores the social and environmental relationships associated with the mine in northern Niger. The movement of the distant camera maps the environment, first panning right across a canyon of gouged-out earth before cutting to another extreme long shot of the enormous uranium-processing apparatus. The camera pans left to take in the size of the industrial site and, at its edge, an enormous pool of a yellowish substance, perhaps sulfuric acid, inside of which sits a semitruck that looks as tiny as a toy. Finally, the music fades and the camera cuts to a long shot from outside the site and just beyond Arlit, highlighting the proximity of the mine and mill to the cluster of small mud-brick buildings that make up the town.[20]

This segment of the documentary shows the spatial dimensions of uranium extraction and the forms of governmentality this geography supports in Arlit, a town far removed from the state's protection and detached from the knowledge systems and market mechanisms that set uranium's value. In 2012, almost ten years after Mora-Kpai's film was released, the International Monetary Fund identified Niger as one of twenty-nine "resource-rich developing countries."[21] That year, mining accounted for 13 percent of government income. Three years later, that figure rose to 26 percent.[22] Despite its resource wealth, Niger has remained one of the world's poorest countries. The intensification and expansion of mining activity in Niger since 2003 is part of what Lee Wengraf has described as "a new scramble for Africa" that builds on a long history of slavery and resource theft but differs significantly from economic exploitation in earlier times.[23] The export of raw materials such as palm oil, gold, and ivory drove the colonial scramble for Africa, but today, Wengraf explains, it is the extraction of crude, metals, and minerals that has attracted massive foreign investment to Africa. The immense energy needs of developed nations as well as the escalating demands for electricity in rapidly developing countries such as China, India, and Brazil, power this new hunt for resources. Within a global dynamic enabled by neoliberal economic policies, Niger has become a vital source of uranium for the global North. France, for example, the largest consumer of uranium for energy after the United States, "relies on the mineral for a full three-quarters of its electrical production," and a great deal of this ore is mined from Niger.[24] As of 2012, thirty-four African countries had granted exploration licenses to mining firms; Niger alone had issued over one hundred exploration permits.[25]

The shift of mining activities to poorer countries in the global South has led to a global uranium rush[26] and a "nuclear renaissance,"[27] demonstrating the relevance of Beck's theorizing on late modernity and the world risk society to the global uranium trade.[28] For Beck, our current era is marked by the systemic production and distribution of risk and a proliferation of discourses and competing claims that seek to define and delineate it. Risk positions map onto low points on global wealth maps, clustering within "low-wage countries" and areas of "extreme poverty."[29] Confronted with strict regulatory environments in the West, which have made uranium mining economically impractical in many places, transnational mining companies have exported environmental and health risks produced by energy consumption in the developed world to remote, sparsely populated locations in Africa and other parts of the global South. Here, relaxed regulatory settings and local workers desperate to escape poverty facilitate virtually unregulated extraction and the accumulation of huge profits.[30] Mora-Kpai's documentary provides little evidence of the presence of the Nigerian state in Arlit. Its responsibilities appear to have been absorbed by the mining companies, who run the clinic, provide electricity where it is available, and maintain the roads its buses and equipment travel. Positioning the camera from within what Beck calls a "loser region" of the global economy, Mora-Kpai seeks to amplify the testimonies of those citizens and migrants forced to absorb the hazards produced by late industrial society.[31]

The testimonies of residents of this northern Nigerien town evidence the uneven allocation of risk and the technologies and discourses that identify it. A Tuareg man looks into the camera and says: "We don't know what they find in [the mine], or how it's done." He adds: "Nothing comes back to the people. No profits." A tall and lean older man, referred to by his friends as Alhadji, identifies himself as a former mineworker who came to Niger from Benin when the mines opened in the late 1960s. He is a key figure in the film. Mora-Kpai interviews him several times and visits his home, and Alhadji participates in interviews with other retired miners and his son, Amadou, who works as a mechanic in town. In this initial encounter, Alhadji blames a recent collapse in the price of uranium for Arlit's current depressed state. A third man, who we come to learn is a local environmental activist, states emphatically that "the mine is too close to the town.... We can't move Arlit, but I've got to say, it's shocking for a town to be located only a few miles from a mining operation.... It's not right to mine uranium in Niger so recklessly."[32] These men, who are not connected to the centers that produce knowledge about and profit from uranium but who are exposed to the risks associated with its extraction, criticize the global spatial arrangements that sustain uranium mining under neoliberalism.

The material processes of locating uranium deposits and extracting uranium ore from rock require an enormous investment in technology, expertise, transport, and machinery. The capital-intensive methods used to detect, extract, and process uranium put newly independent African countries like Niger at an insurmountable disadvantage in navigating what Gabrielle Hecht calls "the technopolitical systems" that turn resources into commodities. As Hecht explains in her historical study of uranium mining in Africa, *Being Nuclear: Africans and the Global Uranium Trade*, "Rocks and fluids and plants didn't become resources until technological processes identified, extracted, refined and exported them—all of which shape their 'value.' And resources didn't become commodities without trucks, ships, airplanes, processing plants, accounting systems, and myriad market devices that enable their commercial circulation."[33] Hecht's book details the uneven and exploitative terms that regulated the uranium business conducted between Niger and France in the aftermath of World War II, terms that were incorporated into decolonization treaties, which "gave the former colonizer privileged access to uranium and other strategic raw materials."[34] For leaders of France, nuclearity "would substitute for colonialism as an instrument of global power," and to achieve its nuclear ambitions, France needed the stores of uranium detected in its colonies.[35] Access to uranium strengthened the former colonial power's privileged place in "the new global order," and for the leaders of newly independent Niger, it provided "military security, guaranteed product markets, and offered development aid."[36] For both states, Hecht shows, uranium became a means "of expressing postcolonial sovereignty."[37]

In a twenty-first-century African extraction zone, sovereignty operates through techniques of power that are more diffuse than those deployed by colonial or national leaders who negotiated the price for uranium or secured commitments to development projects. Mora-Kpai depicts Arlit as what Achille Mbembe calls "an enclave economy" defined by "the concentration of activities connected with the extraction of valuable resources," especially "the controlled inflow and the fixing of movements of money."[38] Mbembe's description of the enclave centers on "militia economies" and "war machines" as technologies of power that govern "broad areas no longer contained by the boundaries of a territorial state."[39] Mora-Kpai's documentary, however, portrays a different dimension of the enclave economy, at least as it functioned in Niger in 2005. The film reveals a space governed not through war or armed conflict but through the biopolitics of precarity. This mode of governing is described by Isabel Lorey as "balancing a maximum of precarization ... with a minimum of safeguarding" so that populations are held in place at "the threshold" of social rupture or violence.[40] In Arlit, the maintenance of this threshold secures labor for capital, holding pools of surplus labor in reserve to meet the unpredictable needs of a fluctuating uranium market. Ghassan Hage uses the term "stuckedness" to describe a generalized sense that one is socially and existentially held in place. Hage argues that the conditions of permeant crisis in which many live "have led to a proliferation and intensification of ... stuckedness."[41] The widespread condition of being stuck has become ordinary, and therefore, "rather than being perceived as something one needs to get out of at any cost, it is now also experienced, ambivalently, as an inevitable pathological state which has to be endured."[42] Stuckedness, I suggest, is a fitting description of the particular experience of waiting found in *Arlit, Deuxième Paris*; it is a type of waiting that is imposed by structural conditions and that remains "just tolerable" amid normalized uncertainty in employment, health, and safety.[43]

For Mora-Kpai's interlocutors, better days, long past, drag down the present and contribute to the stasis that keeps people in place. They explain that they are waiting for the prosperity of the past to return to Arlit. It was, of course, uranium extraction that powered the economic growth residents remember with nostalgia. Alhadji and a former coworker, elderly men whose bodies have been depleted by work in the mines, tell Mora-Kpai that in the early days, Arlit was "an empty plain." They both found work with mining companies: "We removed stones from the sand. We dug it out with big Caterpillar machinery. They told us there was wealth underground. And when we'd got it out, Niger would be rich.... With tarred streets like in France. Not a grain of sand would be left." The two men laugh, presumably at the absurdity of these promises. In another interview, a man sits on a bench outside the deserted Tamesna café and explains that he used to work as a "researcher," finding cars, parts, or services for tourists and other foreigners who traveled to Arlit. He says of Arlit: "We used to call it the second Paris. Now it's the second dump. Nothing to do but wait. We're patient, we're used to it. We're here. But if a new door opens up for us, we'll rush through it." Interwoven with the interview are several uncut shots taken in the courtyard of the café. Devoid of people, these brief scenes of ruin evoke feelings of loss. The camera pauses on faded signs scarred by chipped paint, an empty water bottle, chairs and tables upturned. It is as if the spaces are waiting, too. The café, like these men, seems, in the words of the researcher, to "just watch time go by, with nothing to do."

Arlit's former prosperity was revealed in the availability of energy, namely in electricity to illuminate streets and homes and gasoline to power the cars and airplanes that brought goods and people to and from the town. Movement and mobility again surface as key themes in this first part of the film, which opens with a series of shots of a main street laced with wires strung across parallel lines of electrical poles. Various residents describe how the city used to be and return to the themes of electricity and movement again and again. Mora-Kpai interviews Amadou, Alhadji's son, who explains that Arlit was once famous. He boasts that it "was always on the move, day and night." He describes the coming and going of airplanes, the arrival of tourists, and the popularity of car rallies. "You should have seen it." Here, as in most of the interviews, Mora-Kpai captures the speaker in a conventional talking-head style, centered and from a middle distance. Significantly, an electrical pole appears in the corner of the frame, a reminder of the infrastructure that created work and wealth and powered modernization. A photographer, sitting in his studio and positioned next to his camera, explains that once "people from all over Africa lived here. People from the Ivory Coast, Senegal, Arabs, whites too." The mine, he continues, hired as many as twenty-five thousand workers "because there was building work, electrical work, maintenance work, plumbing." Amid these reminiscences, Mora-Kpai introduces a visual motif that contrasts with residents' memories of the past, highlighting the current state of stalled mobility: extended shots of parked cars in Amadou's mechanics yard being mined for parts, a car without wheels hauled on a cart by three men, and men gathered around a car with its hood open. These shots evidence the idle time that flattens out life for most Arlit residents, especially the young men who cannot find work.

Two narrative lines emerge in the second part of the documentary that further emphasize the juxtaposition between mobility and waiting. The interviewees talk about migrating to find work and better lives, but Mora-Kpai films them fixed in place and killing time. The extended long shots of their stationary bodies, which interrupt and pause the interviewees' stories, call attention to the nonproductive time they endure. A shot of a young Cameroonian man sitting in a doorway that opens onto a common courtyard, for example, enacts a sense of stuckedness. With his folded arms resting on bent knees, he looks blankly at the opposite wall. Except for a plastic bag and a few pieces of trash scattered on the ground at the man's feet, the yard is bare, and this spatial emptiness gives expression to hollowed-out time. The montage cuts to a small group of young people, two men and one woman, entering the compound. Mora-Kpai speaks with the men, both migrants from elsewhere in Africa stranded in Arlit on their way to Europe. One of them speaks English and tells Mora-Kpai that his time in Arlit has been "very rough ... either I die here or I pursue my journey. By God's grace. No one can help me." The man from Cameroon explains in French that his money and documents were stolen in Nigeria and now, with no money, his journey has come to a halt, and he can only wait. These men, economic refugees moored in place by poverty and uncertainty, might be considered "surplus people," a phrase deployed by Nixon to describe those "deemed superfluous to the labor market and to the idea of national development."[44] Although first applied to resettled populations in South Africa during apartheid, Nixon notes that the term *surplus people* can be repurposed to make visible the "ghosted communities" produced by narratives and processes of development during the era of late capitalism.[45] The men in Mora-Kpai's documentary move across national borders like ghosts, without identity or attachment, lured to Arlit's "exploitative center of gravity" by the promise of work in the mines.[46] They address the camera directly and speak of the extreme precarity they endure, and in these gestures, refuse to be invisible or silent.

Thematically linked to these immigration stories is a conversation that takes place in Amadou's mechanic shop yard. Mora-Kpai interviews a Tuareg man who works as a human smuggler, transporting people across the desert to Libya or Algeria. Sitting and waiting on a bench with two other men, his legs crossed and holding a cigarette, the man tells Mora-Kpai that "in the old days, people said Arlit was a prosperous place, where you could make money, where you could get rich." Today, however, there is no work: "People hear about Europe, Asia, or other places where there's money. They think they'll find work there and earn big money. It's better than being jobless for years. In our country, there's no work. Generations before you had none, nor will the next ones. Better than to sit around here, waiting for death, you might as well go elsewhere and die on your feet." He later adds that transporting human cargo is very dangerous, "but we make these runs out of necessity because we have no work. If you find a way to make a living, you must do it."[47] Nearby, groups of boys and young men assemble, gathering around a huge engine as it is hoisted to the ground from a truck bed. They linger and look absentmindedly into the camera. Like the figure of the unemployed kòbòlò in Accra, they also seem "burdened by free time," and they, too, "cluster around certain economically active hubs."[48] Ato Quayson describes kòbòlòi as "a sociological category that encapsulates a transitional state of urban experience at the intersecting vectors of space, time, and longing."[49] These young men exist on the margins of adulthood and stable employment. Like the men in Mora-Kpai's film, they represent a wider "culture of masculine waiting" experienced by men throughout the global South.[50] As detailed by Adeline Masquelier in her ethnography of male teatime in Niger, these jobless youth look for places where they can socialize and move around freely because, "trapped within the dull time of waiting," they feel left behind by the flow of an advancing life.[51]

In a comparative reading of Luc and Jean Pierre Dardenne's film *Rosetta* and Kelly Reichardt's *Wendy and Lucy*, Elena Gorfinkel uses the term *enduration* to capture "the cinema's capacity to make perceptible otherwise imperceptible experiences of the ordinary endurance of bodies on the margins."[52] Gorfinkel asserts that in these films, "tiredness," unlike boredom or inertia, "is a problem of work expended and strain made manifest, a bending under weight, a bulging distension, a flexing shape. It is a question of endurance, how much a body can endure as a condition of its continuous survival."[53] A correlative to Gorfinkel's enduration is found in *Arlit, deuxième Paris* when Mora-Kpai interviews two young women who came to Arlit from Togo because they heard there is work in town. A long shot places the women alone inside a run-down bar, waiting. One woman sits on a stool; the other is asleep in a chair, her feet propped up on a small table. The interview that follows positions the women side-by-side and behind the tall bar counter on which they wearily lean. For the first and only time in the documentary, Mora-Kpai questions his interviewees directly, out of frame and from behind the camera. The women respond reluctantly and without elaboration, and it is clear that the director's interjections were intended to encourage them to speak. There are no customers in the bar; the only ambient noise seems to be the whirring of a fan, which sounds eerily similar to the ticking of a clock and gives the impression of heaviness, of time having weight. The dilapidated bar seems utterly abandoned, which Mora-Kpai underscores with a cutaway shot of a small bird perched on the blade of a ceiling fan that does not turn. Throughout, the women seem too tired to gather the energy to respond to Mora-Kpai, whose disembodied voice prods them to speak.[54] When asked about the children she left behind, one woman says only that "it is better this way." She can send them money and clothes. "Do you miss them?" Mora-Kpai asks. "All we can do is wait," she answers. "They are waiting, like me." Here, waiting is not the opposite of work or even its threshold but a type of labor that makes demands on these bodies and takes effort. These young women expend energy to remain in place, to not give in to despair, to bear sadness and loss, to find ways to make money to send home, and to not think about the children left behind.

The film's final interviews document the long-term dangers of radiation exposure to the human body. A tracking shot across several large pieces of discarded machinery strewn over an empty stretch of sand hints at the focus of this last episode, in which several former mine workers, now retired, recount their maladies and the drawn-out deaths of their friends and brothers. Mora-Kpai continues to insert depopulated landscape scenes in and between his interviews, and by doing so, he makes visible the industrial processes involved in extracting uranium. From a long distance, he records a huge explosion at the bottom of the open-pit mine, then moves his camera along a conveyor belt that heaps radioactive mining waste, or tailings, into small hills. Gusts of dust and dirt blow continuously. Giant excavators pile dirt and sand into even larger banks, and at the mill, a massive rotating drum dries the ore that finally is rolled out into a shiny sheet of yellowcake. These images challenge the claim that nuclear power is a cleaner, more efficient alternative to carbon-based energy sources by showing the stores of energy required to power the fuel-hungry machines that extract ore from the ground and prepare it for transport.

The retired mine laborers describe their exposure to deadly risks they knew nothing about. One older man tells Mora-Kpai: "When we started work, we were told we'd be extracting something called 'uranium.' We didn't know what it was ... we didn't know if it caused illness or not." They explain that they had no idea that radiation exposure was dangerous. They "came home wearing the same clothes" they had worn to work, and in those clothes, "our children would play with us." Alhadji adds that the workers had annual checkups at the company clinic. "The results of the check-ups were always AOK. 'Everything's fine.'" But people started to get sick and die. "That means they lied to us, right?" he asks Mora-Kpai. He continues to describe the prolonged duration of his radiation sickness. "Going back to Benin, I hoped to be safely away from the radiation. But in fact my leaving only slowed the sickness. I was fine for five years back in my country. But in the sixth year, I developed asthma. I can't speak loudly or walk far. For four years, I haven't been able to ride a bike."

Hecht's history of uranium mining in Africa, cited previously, explains that miners become sick because they inhale radon and other elements that result from uranium decay. These microparticles "lodge in the lungs and bombard soft tissue with alpha particles."[55] Exposure of this kind can take from ten to thirty years to cause illness.[56]

The miners remember their many coworkers who died of radiation poisoning. "Of those who retired between 1999 and now, I know of seven who have died... all seven of them had liver cancer." Still, AREVA denies any link between work in the mines and cancer. At the company clinic, Mora-Kpai interviews a doctor who assures the filmmaker that 99 percent of cancer cases among those in Arlit are "due to smoking." The documentary refutes this claim by showing that the radiological impacts of uranium mining, as stated by activist Almoustapha Alhacen, extend far beyond the health risks faced by those who work in the mines. In *Arlit*'s final scenes, Alhacen presents a powerful, alternative account of risk. Positioned as an expert, he shows Mora-Kpai contaminated metal parts, some of which the mining company had presented to their workers as bonuses. To support Alhacen's testimony, Mora-Kpai cuts to piles of metal parts and broken and rusted machinery littered carelessly near homes and scattered across a soccer field where young boys play. Alhacen insists that people "should be informed." Even today, he adds, the residents use mining scrap to make kitchen utensils and building materials. Here the documentary makes visible the unjust "ecological expropriation" of radiological risk to the uranium frontier, where the labor generated by uranium extraction is doubly precarious.[57] The availability of this work and, subsequently, the community's development, is uncertain because it depends on the value of uranium, which is contingent on energy demands and economic calculations of the global North and is entirely detached from its production site in Niger. It also makes the miners and residents sick. Mora-Kpai's interlocutors witness and suffer from various lung and liver ailments linked to radioactive toxicity. In a very real sense, their bodies, have been made to take in the toxicity left over from global economic growth.

Idrissou Mora-Kpai's documentary *Arlit, deuxième Paris* invites viewers to "dwell in crisis."[58] The metaphor of dwelling in crisis, borrowed from Frederick Buell, functions to reject responses to ecological crisis that involve "turning over responsibility to distant authority, and deciding that one's environment is terminal." It also captures something of the experience of watching this film. Mora-Kpai invites viewers to use their imaginations and "dwell in their senses and with crisis" rather than "accommodating" or translating it.[59] The slow and invisible ecological violence offloaded to places like Arlit is not, for Mora-Kpai, a formal or narrative difficulty to be overcome. As I try to show, the film's durational aesthetic, which slows time, and its portrayal of emotions and sensory experiences through film techniques suggest and perhaps even re-create the temporal and affective aspects of life in Arlit. In its narrative and form, Mora-Kpai's documentary elicits what Rob Nixon calls an "ethical attention span" attuned to ecological time.[60] Form and duration give expression to waiting as experienced by people whose bodies and lives have been damaged by uranium extraction and then discarded, like the rusted machine parts that litter the town. Mora-Kpai's film asks that we not only hear and see the impacts of slow violence in the global South but that we also open up to "a new economy of feeling" that might help us imagine new "possibilities for care, commitment, and doing all one can."[61] The Nollywood movies in the following section make few demands of their viewers and instead aspire to entertain and educate.

NOLLYWOOD'S NIGER DELTA

Video technologies, new sources of global media, economic liberalization, and opportunities created within the state's depleted television environment provided the conditions for Nollywood, the English-language commercial movie industry in Nigeria, to emerge in the late 1980s. In its early years, this straight-to-video movie industry based in the capital city of Lagos mostly sought local audiences. It became one of the largest film production centers in the world by offering urban Nigerian audiences affordable and seemingly unlimited local content: low-budget genre movies that moved quickly through the loose arrangement of distribution circuits. In the last two decades, Nollywood has undergone a series of radical transformations that have enabled transnational coproductions like *Black November* and *Blood and Oil*. These higher-quality movies meant for international distribution are called "New Nollywood." Jonathan Haynes explains that around 2010, New Nollywood producers, exhausted by the oversaturated straight-to-DVD Nigerian market, began to make fewer top-tier films suitable for cinema release and competition at international film festivals.[62] They showed and promoted their films at the new multiplex cinemas that opened in Lagos and other large African cities, including Accra. More recently, New Nollywood producers have taken advantage of major global developments in cinema and media production and distribution. The surge in film festivals across the world and the availability of new forms of transnational collaboration and funding have created unprecedented opportunities for the exchange of capital, ideas, and expertise. An explosion of global outlets for media, including cable and satellite television and internet-based channels, has opened huge and hungry new markets for media products, while affordable digital production technologies have facilitated top-tier independent filmmaking based in Africa and other regions of the global South.

Detached from the artistic and institutional networks (and sources of funding) that support serious African cinema—a category into which Mora-Kpai's documentary can be placed—Nollywood, in its old and new incarnations, strives to become a major commercial cinema industry alongside Hollywood and Bollywood. As Haynes points out, the designation *New Nollywood* "names an aspiration."[63] Nollywood has always been and steadfastly remains a commercial creative practice, and its producers have tended to avoid political and other sensitive topics that might dissuade paying viewers and negatively impact return on investment. Nollywood moviemakers cannot afford artistic experimentation and instead hustle for scarce resources to make the star-studded genre films that will please audiences. Transnational productions with large budgets that are streamed on global media platforms (Amazon Prime and Netflix), *Black November* and *Blood and Oil* offer audiences the visceral and spectacular thrills that Nixon warns against, but they also try to do more. The films are imperfect acts of "political pedagogy," a term used by Imre Szeman to describe oil documentaries that seek to inform audiences and "generate political and ecological responses that otherwise would not occur."[64] Ambitious and at times overextended, the Nollywood films aim for big-budget action adventure, drawing from anticolonial, feminist, and environmental justice discourses to highlight ecological degradation and political unrest in the Niger Delta. In the final pages of this chapter, I explore how the pressure of genre, in terms of form and financial investment, impacts Nollywood's representations of the slow and spectacular violence of oil capitalism in the Niger Delta.

Different sources and types of energy materialize and generate different temporalities. Oil time, as others have noted, is complex and contradictory. The life of oil, writes Tim Kaposy, "from extraction and refinement to trade and emission, creates temporal circumstances at odds with one another."[65] Oil formed over hundreds of thousands of years. As a substance, it amasses "great quantities of space and time."[66] To quote Andrew Pendakis: "Oil is very literally time materialized, time that has pooled in the form of a liquid."[67] Yet oil's viscosity brings both movement and speed. Oil's substance, what Kaposy calls "its molecular *flow*,"[68] gushes and runs, and over time, burned oil emits carbon that accumulates, gradually and imperceptibly, in our atmosphere, warming the earth, acidifying oceans, and damaging the planet now and into the future. Immediate and anticipated, "oil propels daily activity into a rapid pace (e.g., travel, meals, communications) while simultaneously incurring effects that are understandable only after decades of study."[69]

The scholars quoted here theorize the temporalities of oil on a planetary scale and generalize across oil's geological chronology, making implicit scalar claims about the complexity of oil time.[70] Much like the Anthropocene itself, however, oil is lived in particular, localized, and highly uneven ways, and its violence is "not merely planetary—it also has particular, differential manifestations." This quote from Gabrielle Hecht's reflection on the scales of Anthropocenic violence also relates to oil.[71] In the oil-producing frontier that is the Niger Delta, it is the processes and products of petroleum extraction that generate oil's multifaceted temporality.[72] Oil lets loose harmful agents and violent effects over wide-ranging and overlapping time scales. Pumped to the surface, oil stagnates. The Niger Delta has been described as one of the most polluted regions of the world.[73] Oil leaks and spills, pooling in polluted rivers and sludge-soaked soil. Oil flares burn continually, emitting toxic by-products that hover in the atmosphere and settle in the lungs. Oil companies flare around twenty-three billion cubic meters of natural gas, released during the drilling process, in Nigeria per year; the fumes corrode zinc roofs, kill trees and shrubs, and cause asthma, bronchitis, and cancer.[74] In an ethnographic study of conflicts in Niger Delta communities, Omolade Adunbi uses the phrase "duality of violence" to describe "the violence that oil pipelines, flow stations, and oil wells inflict on the land as well as the violence orchestrated by militants in an attempt to reclaim lands and livelihoods."[75] Adunbi's study shows that oil, as a natural resource and commodity, instigates conflicts that erupt instantaneously and also seem to go on endlessly. Unlike Mora-Kpai's *Arlit*, which gives duration presence, the Nollywood movies analyzed here attempt to compress the multiple time scales generated by oil's duality of violence into the narrative and formal conventions of the two-hour action thriller.

A twenty-two-million-dollar budget supported the US-Nigeria coproduction *Black November*, making it an extraordinarily well-financed project by Nollywood's standards.[76] The film features big-name Hollywood and Nollywood stars and an international crew and cast. Its fast-paced plot moves between the United States and Nigeria, beginning in Los Angeles when a group of Niger Delta insurgents successfully carry out its plan to trigger a traffic pile-up and kidnap an American oil company executive. The film's opening is nothing short of spectacular. Giant SUVs screech and slide into a heap. Helicopters fly over the city in search of the kidnappers, and a SWAT team backed by officers from the LAPD surrounds the bridge where the kidnappers hold their target and a large group of innocent bystanders. Media producer Kristy Maine (Kim Basinger) is interviewing Tamuno (Enyinna Nwigwe), the spokesperson for the United People's Front for the Emancipation of the Niger Delta People when the plot erupts and she invites Tamuno "to tell [his] story" to the world. (It was Tamuno's plan to involve her in the plot for the media coverage it guaranteed.) Tamuno agrees to release the hostages, Tom Hudson (Mickey Rourke), CEO of Western Oil, and his daughter, if Hudson negotiates the release of Ebiere Perema (Mbong Amata). Ebiere is a Niger Delta activist unjustly tried and charged with murder and awaiting execution in a prison in Warri State, in the Niger Delta. Pointing his AK-47 at Tom Hudson's face, Tamuno shouts, "This is the only language the West understands." That language is the language of violence, the violence of guns and of action movies. The line is intended to explain why the United People's Front, a group the audience is expected to sympathize with, has had to resort to armed kidnapping to save Ebiere, but it also reflects the motives of the filmmakers who direct hard-won resources and expertise to the production of a violent action film to highlight the exploitation of the Niger Delta.

The suspenseful LA segments of the movie, which take place in the fictional present, frame an extended backstory set in the Niger Delta. Ebiere has been part of a nonviolent insurgency movement organized to protest oil companies' and the Nigerian state's abuse of the region and to make a claim on behalf of the people for greater control of its petroleum resources. The opening scenes of the Nigeria segments of *Black November*, like parallel scenes in *Blood and Oil*, represent ecological violence as the backdrop against which explosive and gripping armed conflict between militants on one side, and oil companies and the Nigerian military on the other, plays out. Early in the film, the audience sees images of environmental ruin and poverty in the Delta: gas flares burning against a darkening horizon, dead fish floating in pools of oily water, and clusters of fishing boats near small shacks on stilts. These types of images are somewhat common in nonfiction, visual representations of the Delta, appearing in documentaries such as *Delta Force*, *Daughters of the Niger Delta*, and *Sweet Crude* as well as in the art photography of Ed Kashi. A localized archive of a larger "image world" of oil, described by Hannah Appel, Arthur Mason, and Michaels Watts in the introduction to their edited collection *Subterranean Estates*, these images place us in the singular oil ecology of the Niger Delta.[77] The landscape montage signifies the real, giving the fictional narratives the imprint of truth. The films use intertitles similarly. White text scrolls across the black screen in *Black November* to explain that 90 percent of the Nigerian population "lives on less than $2 a day" and that the country is the "world's fifth largest exporter of oil." The film concludes with two haunting statements of fact: "Continuous oil spills make it the most environmentally devastated land in the world" and "Average life expectancy: 47." This background provides viewers with basic information about Nigeria and the Delta region and contextualizes the fictional narratives about the actions taken by activists and militants against the Nigerian state and the oil companies. It is intended to convince viewers of the legitimacy of calls for resource and environmental justice. But there also is a temporality implied in these "contextual" images, the framing and establishing shots that situate us in a particular place. These images ask us to accept the conditions they depict as ambient and ordinary features of the everyday. They mark out the ongoing time of lived experience. This signaling of the oil context demonstrates that the Nollywood movies do not merely convert the slow violence of ecological damage into the spectacle of an armed insurgency, nor do they erase it. Rather, the films expect viewers to understand that the pollution and poverty indexed in establishing shots and intertitles continue to play out under the action.

Black November, more stridently than *Blood and Oil*, articulates a strong critique of the Nigerian petrostate's contortion of the rules of citizenship and sovereignty to exploit the commodification of oil, what Jennifer Wenzel describes as "the nation-state repurposed for neoliberal globalization's international division of nature."[78] A short montage, which compresses Ebiere's childhood into a series of scenes from her youth, ends with the young woman winning a scholarship from Western Oil (not the Nigerian government) and leaving the country to attend university in the United States (not in Nigeria). The plot of the backstory formally begins on the day of Ebiere's return to Nigeria when she witnesses an explosion at a leaking oil pipe near her village. Thousands of people, including Ebiere's mother, who had been "bunkering" crude spilling from the pipe, are killed when a Nigerian police officer at the scene drops his smoldering cigarette carelessly to the ground. Before the blast is ignited, the "Anti-Crime Patrol" officers charge the large crowd of women and children with stealing fuel that is "the property of the Federal Republic of Nigeria." Ebiere's mother demands to know where the government is when leaked and dumped oil spoils their land and when no fuel is made available to them for purchase. She rallies the crowd by reminding the officers that the oil belongs to the people of the Delta. At this and other pivotal moments, the film gives voice to Delta communities' demands that the Nigerian state fulfill its obligations to citizens. After the explosion, Ebiere reluctantly assumes the role of representative of her Warri community in the protests that follow. She stands up to the male elders who warn her that "this is not a matter for women" and demands fair compensation from Western Oil. When Warri's male community leaders agree to receive and administer a single settlement payment from the company on behalf of the community, instead of accepting the company's offer to distribute individual payments to families who lost loved ones in the blast, Ebiere speaks out against their corruption: "It is high time you start to think of the people other than your selfish, fat pockets." Ebiere organizes a large, peaceful movement against the oil company and is met with the violence of the Nigerian military's Joint Task Force and the police. An innocent protester is shot; the army raids a village, murdering and raping innocent citizens; and Ebiere is eventually arrested, charged, tried, and convicted of a murder she did not commit. At the end of the film, despite the kidnapping plot meant to save her, Ebiere, who has just given birth to a child, is executed by the state.

In both Nollywood movies, the multiple temporalities of petroviolence clash with attempts to represent historical time. The films use narrative conventions that historicize the decades-long fight for resource and environmental justice in the Niger Delta, insisting that what Philip Aghoghovwia describes as "the militarized sociality of energy production and the spectacular violence that flourishes in the Niger Delta" be understood as historical.[79] I submit that these efforts to historicize petroviolence are meant to avoid the representational trap that Aghoghovwia identifies in spectacular images of militancy in the Delta, which "can be read in terms of conventions of representation that depict Africa as crisis-ridden outback of filth, poverty, sickness, violence, insurgents, war, and death."[80] *Black November* and *Blood and Oil* challenge these racist stereotypes of Africa as a timeless abyss of despair by portraying insurgent violence in a context that is open to change. Compressing the oil's decades-long history in the Niger Delta into the length of a feature film presents significant narrative challenges, which each film manages by different means.

Black November examines the history of citizens' calls for resource justice in the Niger Delta through the perspective of gender: the nonviolent activism of women in the film represents the 1990s, while the armed insurgency of male characters reflects a more current time. So within the narrative present, gender difference is meant to stand in for the dominant discourses of two distinct historical periods in the struggle against the exploitation of the Niger Delta. Ebiere's strong defense of nonviolent activism evokes the methods of the widely known Ogoni activist Ken Saro-Wiwa and his Movement for the Survival of the Ogoni People. In addition, the character's death by hanging—which takes place in November, echoing the film's title—alludes to Saro-Wiwa's execution by the military regime of General Sani Abacha on November 10, 1995. Characters in the film also refer to "the military regime" and "the military dictator," placing the fictional story within the historical frame of the Abacha regime, and yet the movie's representation of the male militant's adoption of violence in the fight for control over the Delta's natural resources situates the narrative closer to the present. The women's peaceful marches and protests, organized by Ebiere, are set against the armed resistance of the insurgents, led by Dede (Hakeem Kae-Kazim), a local fisherman who loses his wife in the same blast that kills Ebiere's mother. Ebiere and Dede become lovers. (It is his child she gives birth to in jail before her execution.) And they argue about the use of violence. Ebiere pleads with Dede to give up his arms, but he vows to "fight for [his] land" even until death. The male insurgents give voice to what Adunbi calls the militant activities of "the post-Saro-Wiwa era," when a multiethnic insurgency movement emerged to "shift from protesting against the state and corporations to taking up arms," and they seem to be modeled after members of the Movement for the Emancipation of the Niger Delta (MEND).[81] MEND appeared in Warri, the setting of the film, around 2005 and remained active until a government amnesty in 2009 supported a period of tenuous peace that lasted until 2016 when, according to Watts, a new militant group, the Niger Delta Avengers, appeared on the scene.[82] Tamuno, the kidnapper in *Black November*, might be named after a famous MEND field commander, Tamuno Goodwill, and the militants in the film, like their MEND counterparts, use sabotage, kidnapping, and armed insurrection to curtail the extraction of oil from the Delta.[83]

Wenzel notes that in the Niger Delta, "the conventional discursive technologies of the liberal public sphere have proved irrelevant, even fatally counterproductive, tools for achieving political recognition from the petro-state."[84] In *Black November*, the two white American women reporters, Kristy Maine, the LA producer, and Kate Summers, the reporter on location in Nigeria, stand in for an entire Western media apparatus and ultimately demonstrate Wenzel's point: the liberal public sphere is ineffectual in preventing the violence of the petrostate. The reporters express the idea that telling the story of the Delta will rally the support of a global citizenry and expose the corrupt Nigerian regime, pressuring it to change. Both Maine and Summers hope that, at the very least, bringing attention to Ebiere's captivity might save her life. In the end, however, Ebiere's execution seems to expose the irrelevance of the political pedagogy of the media. The film relies on the emotive cues of melodrama, dramatic music, and tearful close-ups to emphasize the pain felt by Maine and Summers when they learn that Ebiere has been hanged, despite the kidnapping plot and their on-air international advocacy. This might seem like a curious statement from a Nollywood movie that seeks to raise awareness about the exploitation of the Delta in an effort to mobilize audiences. But audiences are meant to understand that media advocacy for Delta communities will be more effective in a post-Abacha Nigeria, the time of the film's release. Audiences in the twenty-first century, once made aware of the petroviolence that has scorched the Delta for decades, are asked to finally act.

Like *Black November*, *Blood and Oil* moves between a Niger Delta community roiled by ecological and insurgent violence and the activities of the overseas corporate headquarters of a fictional multinational oil company, this time Foreshaw Exploration in Houston, Texas. As in *Black November*, an oil executive is kidnapped by Delta militants; cars are set on fire and gun fights break out, although rendered less spectacularly than in *Black November*. In *Blood and Oil*, the leader of the armed resistance is Gunpowder. Formerly a geologist for an oil company, Gunpowder organizes an elaborate, transnational kidnapping scheme that involves the Nigerian assistant of an oil executive in Houston, video connections linking Texas and Oloibiri (a small community in the Niger Delta); and concealed cameras in the homes and offices of the Foreshaw executives. The Nigerians successfully kidnap the wife and daughter of Foreshaw's chairman Robert Powell as well as the family of another company employee and leverage their hostages' release against the company's surrender of its drilling leases. Both films also feature greedy and duplicitous Nigerian businessmen who facilitate the exploitation of Delta communities. These vile men are handsomely rewarded for negotiating on behalf of the oil companies that bribe politicians and village elders and pay off local communities to silence their complaints. The portrayal of Cyril, the general manager of Foreshaw Exploration in Nigeria, references the corrupt Big Man of many

Nollywood movies. An immoral and excessive consumer, he surrounds himself with gorgeous women, smokes huge cigars, and hosts extravagant parties. He assures Powell that if the company has any problems with the villagers: "There is nothing money cannot do."

While Nigerian characters who work for oil companies in the Nollywood Delta dramas have few redeeming qualities, the American oil executives, both of whom are taken hostage by militants, experience personal transformation as a result of what they learn about petroviolence. These rather benign and forgiving representations of the redeemed CEOs function rhetorically to promote various modes of transnational collaboration in the fight for energy justice. Like the journalists in *Black November*, directors Amata and Graham attempt to rally international condemnation of the exploitation of the Delta through White American characters who, because of what they learn and experience, recognize their personal complicity in oil-based violence and accept responsibility for the damage caused by their companies. In *Blood and Oil*, Robert Powell plays a crucial role in the narrative. An idealized figure, he is generous to his Nigerian employees and committed to creating a different kind of oil company. When he receives a packet of disturbing photos of poverty and environmental destruction in Otuabake, the village in Bayelsa state where his company has acquired oil leases, he decides to travel to the village to see the conditions for himself. He is a person with diabetes who must inject himself with insulin regularly, a feature of his character intended to evoke viewers' sympathy, especially when he is kidnapped and becomes ill because he cannot access the medicine he needs. The plot of *Blood and Oil* concludes with the recuse of the kidnapped employees and their families in Texas, and a bloody if poorly executed shootout between Gunpowder's gang and the military in Nigeria. The final sequence of intertitles explains: "There have been over 2100 oil spills in the Niger Delta. There is still no potable water or fishing." In the final scene, main character Timipre Dogra (Olu Jacobs) meets Powell before he leaves Nigeria, and Powell apologizes: "I should have known more than I did." This statement puts into words the remorse expressed on the face of Tom Hudson, CEO of Western Oil, seen in close-up at the end of *Black November*.

Perhaps the most significant difference between the films is that *Blood and Oil* more explicitly situates the current state of the Niger Delta within the long history of oil exploration in the region. The film opens in the Niger Delta community of Oloibiri, which the intertitles explain was the site of the first commercial oil field in Nigeria, a joint venture between Royal Dutch/

Shell Group and British Petroleum in 1956. A short funeral scene, shot in black and white, fades into the present, captured in color. The film uses black and white to indicate a transition to the past, and from this point forward, black-and-white segments represent the memories of the film's central character, Timipre, an elderly man who, in the late 1950s and 1960s, participated in negotiations between the community of Oloibiri and Lesh Oil, the company that discovered oil there. By focusing parts of the narrative through Timipre's perspective, the movie references the history of the early years of oil development in Nigeria and raises questions about the responsibilities of Timipre's generation. Timipre is traumatized by what has happened to his community and deeply troubled by shame and guilt. Throughout the film, he experiences intense flashbacks that connect him to a history of petroviolence, starting with meetings between executives of Lesh Oil and community leaders when he was a young man. Other flashbacks show the death of his wife, whom, we are told, was poisoned by oil toxicity in the water and air. Timipre's character collapses the past into the present, displacing a more difficult—and commercially risky—critique of recent and ongoing violence and exploitation in the region. The film erases the ongoing role of the Nigerian military and, hence, the Nigerian petrostate from what has been its purpose since the 1970s: "to manage the spoils of oil, rather than to represent and effect the will of the citizens."[85] Unlike in *Black November*, where violent action sequences include soldiers who protect oil installations and terrorize villagers and activists, *Blood and Oil* imagines an almost heroic military presence in the Delta. A military officer escorts Powell from the airport and bravely protects him from the armed insurgents who attack the car and kidnap him, sacrificing his life in attempting to help Powell escape into the bush. And, in the end, it is the military that saves Powell and Timipre from Gunpowder and the armed insurgents.

The friendship that develops between Timipre and Powell, like the friendship between Ebiere and American reporter Kate Summers, signifies, on a personal level, the transnational politics the film attempts to advance. Timipre at first rejects Powell's plea for help to escape the kidnappers. He tells his grandson Boname that Powell's "greed brought him grief." He finally relents when Boname asks him to reflect on the Bible he "reads daily." This retort is intended to redefine what Timipre insists is a political issue as a moral one. But Timipre's politics have not wavered. Later in the film, while Timipre leads Powell along the river to a safe hiding place, he lectures him, and the viewer, on the violence perpetuated by transnational oil companies drilling for crude in the Delta. Powell refuses to cede the point. He tells Timipre: "I didn't come here to steal from you. I came here so that my company could learn how to treat your community with respect. . . . Are your people completely innocent? It takes two people to screw, or get screwed." The movement of the characters and action of the plot slow down during this exchange, giving way to the larger "message" the film struggles to impart. This message, which ties the exploitation perpetuated by international oil corporations to Nigerian corruption, echoes a claim stated by Tom Hudson in *Black November*: that the Nigerian state as well as individual Nigerian citizens are complicit in the crimes committed against the Delta and those who live there. Timipre and Powell work together to bring an end to the kidnappers' plot and Foreshaw's plan to extract oil from the Niger Delta, a final statement about the possibility that moral and politically motivated Americans and Nigerians might advance energy justice for the impoverished and vulnerable communities who do not have access to public resources.

My readings of *Arlit, Deuxième Paris*, *Black November*, and *Blood and Oil* have centered on time. But it might also be noted that these films imagine and enact what Rob Nixon calls a "transnational ethics of place" in African extraction zones.[86] Mora-Kpai's documentary supports activist Almoustapha Alhacen, who appears in the film, in raising awareness about uranium mining and slow violence in Arlit, Niger. It tracks the destruction and death wrought by the global uranium economy at one of its extraction sites, a small town built and sustained by transnational energy networks and the African migrant workers who come in search of opportunity. Mora-Kpai's lingering shots of arid and wind-blown landscapes littered with radioactive debris function similarly to the establishing shots in both Nollywood features. They place us in environments made lethal by mining and drilling. The Nollywood coproductions argue for the urgency of a political response to petroviolence and, to that end, seek transnational viewers who, like the American characters in both films, experience an emotional connection to the people and landscapes of the Niger Delta. Following in the tradition of Ken Saro-Wiwa and Wangari Maathai, the producers of *Black November* and *Blood and Oil* seek to inform audiences and mobilize international action on behalf of disenfranchised communities. Their films are cinematic versions of the "transnational meldings" Nixon describes, using the conventions of the action-thriller genre to rally support for the local communities.[87]

Like the concept of the Anthropocene, Nixon's notion of slow violence, which has provided an opening for the analyses in this chapter, asks that we "think on the two vastly different scales of time that earth history and world history respectively involve."[88] Indeed, slow violence as an idea might be thought of as a conceptual bridge between the incomprehensible vastness of earth, or planetary, history and the comparatively minuscule span of human, or world, history. Nixon deals in human temporalities in his study of literary representations of the forms of slow violence that seep imperceptibly across generations. Yet his attention to the "temporal overspill" of ecological violence paves the way for the vast time scales of the planetary and, furthermore, models a method of reading that locates traces of earth history in literary and cinematic renderings of crude spills and nuclear fallout.[89] Focused on energy, this chapter has focused on time as made manifest in art and genre films by African filmmakers. In these films, the materiality of uranium and carbon-based fuels can be interpreted as conduits between the political and ecological violence lived by those trapped in energy's extraction zones and the "unhuman temporalities"[90] of the planetary.

NOTES

1. Nixon, *Slow Violence*, 2.
2. Nixon, *Slow Violence*, 2.
3. Beck, *Risk Society*, 35, 43.
4. Beck, *Risk Society*, 23.
5. Beck, *Risk Society*, 33.
6. Beck, *Risk Society*, 23.
7. Nixon, *Slow Violence*, 6, 8.
8. Yoshimoto, "Nuclear Disasters," 170.
9. *Blood and Oil* appears as *Oloibiri* on Netflix.
10. Nixon, *Slow Violence*, 16.
11. Williams and Chrisman, "Teshome H. Gabriel Towards a Critical Theory of Third World Films," 353.
12. De Luca and Barradas, *Slow Cinema*, 3.
13. Lim, "Temporal Aesthetics of Drifting," 91.
14. See, for example, Charles Piot's *Nostalgia for the Future* as well as *African Futures*, edited by Brian Goldstone and Juan Obarrio, and Jane Guyer, *Legacies, Logics, Logistics*.
15. De Villiers, Jacques, "Approaching the Uncertain Turn in African Video-Movies," 45.
16. Petty, "Sacred Places and *Arlit*," 75.
17. Barad, "No Small Matter," G109.
18. Larsen and Mamosso, "Aid with Blinkers," 62.

19. Hecht, *Being Nuclear*, 10.

20. At the time this documentary was made, French nuclear group AREVA owned and operated two mines in Arlit: Somair, an open-pit facility, and Cominak, an underground mine.

21. Sangare and Maisonnave, "Mining and Petroleum Boom and Public Spending Policies in Niger," 580.

22. Sangare and Maisonnave, "Mining and Petroleum Boom and Public Spending Policies in Niger," 581.

23. Wengraf, *Extracting Profit*, 139.

24. Wengraf, *Extracting Profit*, 139.

25. Conde and Kallis, "The Global Uranium Rush and Its Africa Frontier," 601.

26. Conde and Kallis, "The Global Uranium Rush and Its Africa Frontier," 596.

27. Winde et al., "Uranium from Africa," 761.

28. Beck, *Risk Society*.

29. Beck, *Risk Society*, 41.

30. Winde, et al., "Uranium from Africa," 765.

31. Beck, *Risk Society*, 64.

32. The activist is Almoustapha Alhacen. Although he is not identified in the film, his name and the names of all those interviewed appear in the film's credits. The names, however, are not listed in order of appearance, and so in most cases, it is impossible to know which name corresponds to which interviewee. I found information on Alhacen while doing research for this book, and so I was able to confirm his appearance in the documentary.

33. Hecht, *Being Nuclear*, 115.

34. Hecht, *Being Nuclear*, 109.

35. Hecht, *Being Nuclear*, 23.

36. Hecht, *Being Nuclear*, 105–9.

37. Hecht, *Being Nuclear*, 117.

38. Mbembe, "Necropolitics," 33.

39. Mbembe, "Necropolitics," 34.

40. Lorey, *State of Insecurity*, 65.

41. Hage, "Waiting out Crisis," 97.

42. Hage, "Waiting out Crisis," 97.

43. Lorey, *State of Insecurity*, 66.

44. Nixon, *Slow Violence*, 151.

45. Nixon, *Slow Violence*, 151.

46. Nixon, *Slow Violence*, 155.

47. Amadou tells Mora-Kpai that all the trucks parked in his yard "carry illegal immigrants Via Janet or Tamanrasset in Algeria. They carry thirty to thirty-five people." Another young man identifies himself as a driver and explains that he "broke down eighty kilometers from here" and had to walk back. He tells

Mora-Kpai that on his last run, he carried twenty-five passengers, each of whom paid him fifteen euros.

48. Quayson, *Oxford Street, Accra*, 202.
49. Quayson, *Oxford Street, Accra*, 199.
50. Jeffrey quoted in Masquelier, "Teatime," 486.
51. Masquelier, "Teatime," 486.
52. Gorfinkel, "Weariness, Waiting," 313.
53. Gorfinkel, "Weariness, Waiting," 314.
54. In an exchange over email, Mora-Kpai told me that these interviews were extremely difficult because the women were stubbornly reticent.
55. Hecht, *Being Nuclear*, 40.
56. Hecht, *Being Nuclear*, 42.
57. Beck, *World Risk Society*, 64.
58. Buell, *From Apocalypse to Way of Life*, 205.
59. Buell, *From Apocalypse to Way of Life*, 205.
60. Nixon, *Slow Violence*, 211.
61. Buell, *From Apocalypse to Way of Life*, 205, 208.
62. Haynes, *Nollywood*, 286.
63. Haynes, *Nollywood*, 288.
64. Szeman, "Crude Aesthetics," 424.
65. Kaposy, "Petroleum's Longue Durée," 390.
66. Mitchell, *Carbon Democracy*, 15.
67. Pendakis, "Being and Oil," 387.
68. Kaposy, "Petroleum's Longue Durée," 390.
69. Kaposy, "Petroleum's Longue Durée," 390.
70. Here I borrow again from Gabrielle Hecht (2018), who argues that scalar concepts, such as Anthropocene, are at once descriptive and performative. Such terms make claims implicitly.
71. Hecht, "Interscalar Vehicles for an African Anthropocene," 112.
72. Watts, "Frontiers: Authority, Precarity, and Insurgency at the Edge of the State."
73. Ugochuku notes that a United Nations Development Programme report found that between 1976 and 2001, over 6,817 oil spills dumped more than three million barrels of oil in the region. Nnimmo Bassey, director of Environmental Rights Action, Nigeria, argues that "the number of oil spills and the regularity of their occurrence make nonsense of any claims to acceptable standards by any of the corporations operating in the Niger Delta," 81.
74. Bassey, *To Cook a Continent*, 122.
75. Adunbi, *Oil Wealth and Insurgency*, 2–3.
76. Ugochukwu, "Nollywood and the Niger Delta," 130.
77. Appel, Mason, and Watts, *Subterranean Estates*.

78. Wenzel, *The Disposition of Nature*, 104.
79. Aghoghovwia, "Nigeria," 239.
80. Aghoghovwia, "Nigeria," 241.
81. Adunbi, *Oil Wealth and Insurgency*, 193.
82. Watts, "Frontiers: Authority, Precarity, and Insurgency at the Edge of the State," 478.
83. Watts, "Frontiers: Authority, Precarity, and Insurgency at the Edge of the State," 483.
84. Wenzel, *The Disposition of Nature*, 104.
85. Wenzel, *The Disposition of Nature*, 104.
86. Nixon, *Slow Violence*, 245.
87. Nixon, *Slow Violence*, 235.
88. Chakrabarty, *The Climate of History*, 156.
89. Nixon, *Slow Violence*, 8.
90. Chakrabarty, *The Climate of History*, 58.

TWO

Oil Pipelines and Debt Relations

INTRODUCTION

OIL HAS BEEN FUNDAMENTAL TO postcolonial debt relations since the oil shocks of the 1970s, when diminished global oil supplies resulted in exorbitant pricing for all manner of goods and services and plunged many African nations into economic collapse. The economic stress caused by the 1973 oil crisis in the postcolonial world was meant to be alleviated by loans from the World Bank and other international financial institutions. According to Sophia A. McClennen, the cycle of debt initiated with these loans, whatever the intention, functioned "to lock states into a dependent role on the capitalist market."[1] Given this history, it is not surprising that African films, from Djibril Diop Mambéty's *Hyenas* (1992) to Abderrahmane Sissako's *Bamako* (2006), have agitated against resource extraction and the ongoing history of sovereign indebtedness it causes. In recent years, the films of Chadian director Mahamat-Saleh Haroun have expanded cinema's exploration of African indebtedness, exposing the interplay of sovereign and subjective debt as experienced in Chad, a landlocked country whose oil reserves resulted in new debt, partly incurred to support the three-billion-dollar Chad-Cameroon Petroleum Development and Pipeline Project (CCPDPP). Set during the same time as the immense extraction project, Haroun's films center on African men who struggle to manage individual debts and everyday precarity, conditions produced by the sovereign indebtedness of postcolonial states in what Timothy Mitchell calls "the postwar petroleum order."[2] This chapter develops the historical and political context in which critics have situated African films to include oil wells and pipelines, asking if African cinematic investigations of debt relations might also help us imagine an energopolitics that advances energy justice on a planetary scale.

OIL AND DEBT

My examination of the connections between oil and debt begins with the 1970s oil crisis. In October 1973, a coalition of Arab states instituted an oil embargo to pressure the US government to support a resolution to end the Arab-Israeli War and stop sending military aid to Israel.[3] When the United States rejected the proposal, the price of oil went up. This sudden increase in oil revenues greatly impacted producer states that had been trading oil in US dollars since the post–World War II Bretton Woods agreement. Mahmoud A. El-Gamal and Amy Myers Jaffe explain that oil exporters had a limited capacity to absorb this tremendous trade surplus and so participated in what they refer to as a "massive petrodollar recycling scheme" in which exporter states invested heavily in "dollar-dominated assets."[4] For decades, those investments have kept interest rates in the United States low, strengthened the dollar, and shored up economic growth.

In the 1970s, petrodollar recycling also supported huge investments in military aid to the Middle East. Mitchell documents the benefits of weapons sales to Middle East countries with relatively small populations and widespread poverty. The flood of petrodollars created an imbalance that purchases of ordinary goods could not offset quickly enough. Weapons, however, "could be purchased to be stored rather than used," and therefore weapons sales were not limited by "any practical need or capacity to consume."[5] More relevant to Africa and other postcolonial regions, petrodollars from exporter states channeled into US banks supported "a disastrous series of loans to governments in the global South," which were struggling to cope with the economic fallout of steep and sudden oil price hikes.[6] Jonathan Baker's article in the 1977 *Journal of Modern African Studies* asserts: "No event since World War II has had such an impact on global economic and political relationships as the quadrupling of the international price of crude oil at the end of 1973 and beginning of 1974."[7] Baker lists the cascade of effects that contributed to deepening indebtedness brought on by the oil price hikes: "African countries face large balance-of-payments deficits, not only because of the increased cost of oil, but also as a result of the concomitant rise in the price of manufactured goods imported from the developed countries. These deficits can only be covered by foreign borrowing, and this in turn aggravates the already acute debt problem."[8] In addition, the rising costs of petroleum-based agricultural inputs, like fertilizer, worsened the economic hardships that continued throughout the 1970s and 1980s. To manage the costs of essential imports, African governments had no choice but to borrow.

Scholars and activists have criticized the international financial institutions that attached structural-adjustment economic reforms to petrodollar loans. Across Africa, state-owned assets were privatized; governments adopted liberal economic and trade policies, which resulted in devalued local currencies and high inflation; state services were slashed, and funding for social and educational development retracted. Less remarked on, however, is the crucial role of oil, and oil politics, in the history of postcolonial sovereign debt. It is widely agreed that the impetus for these loans, which were sometimes presented as aid programs, was the recycling of petrodollars, and that in the 1970s and 1980s, this series of loans caused the exponential rise in sovereign debt in the developing world, the impacts of which continue to burden African states today. As Eric Toussaint and Damien Millet note: "From 1968 to 1973 (five years) [the World Bank] granted more loans than from 1945–1968 (twenty-three years)."[9] External debt in developing countries "reached seventy billion in 1978, and $540 billion in 1980. It rose eightfold in ten years."[10] When we talk about sovereign debt in African contexts, we are also talking about oil politics.

In *The Making of the Indebted Man*, Maurizio Lazzarato explains the mechanisms by which the foundations of the debt economy—the structures and institutions that constitute these relations of power—interact with subjectivizing processes, the governmentalities by means of which power reproduces the debt relation and its morality in all social spheres. According to Lazzarato: "Debt creation, that is, the creation and development of the power relation between creditors and debtors, has been conceived and programmed as the strategic heart of neoliberal politics."[11] Debt, he argues, has become the overarching mechanism of political and subjective control. In an earlier publication, I criticized Lazzarato's Eurocentric analysis of debt. All of the instances of debt he theorizes—and the sense of urgency he brings to the issue of indebtedness—stem from the economic decline and austerity measures that followed the 2008 subprime crisis in North America and Europe.[12] Lazzarato completely ignores Africa and the structural adjustment programs that decades earlier had normalized the austerity and economic insecurity only recently experienced in the West. This omission is particularly egregious given that sovereign debt has been ongoing since the colonial period and, after the 1970s, at accelerated rates. It is in the global South, Jean Comaroff and John Comaroff remind us, "that the practical workings of neoliberalism have been tried and tested; in them that the outer bounds of its financial operations have been explored—thence to be reimported to various Euro-American locales."[13] Indeed, debt-creditor relations involving international financial institutions in the global North and former colonies in the global South have been integral to the achievement of the current hegemony of the neoliberal debt economy.

McClennen raises another challenge to Lazzarato's theory of *homo debitor*. She sees the debt-creditor relationship as a feature of a world system in which some states act as creditors and others as debtors: "The marked difference lies in an economy where citizens have consumer debt and one where citizens bear the brunt of austerity measures so that the state can pay its debts."[14] She insists that we analyze debt across and between states not only within them, as is Lazzarato's focus. Interconnected and distinct, the indebted subject and the indebted state represent two models of the debtor-creditor connection. The difference between them is most clear when we consider credit. McClennen writes: "Often the citizen of an indebted state is framed as a credit-bearing subject precisely the moment when she is expected to make due on a claim, paying her share. But this is only on the back end of the deal, for she was never offered the chance to assume her own private debts, even though she will be required privately to shoulder them."[15] As stated, oil money, put in Western banks or converted into dollar instruments, generated billions of petrodollar loans that strengthened the power and importance of the World Bank and locked postcolonial states into the global economy as sovereign debtors. The people living in these indebted states, denied the advantages of personal credit, nonetheless experience debt—the debt taken on by their governments—in all facets of their everyday lives.

SOVEREIGN DEBT IN THE TIME OF OIL

The first films analyzed in this chapter establish clear connections between these two models of the creditor-debt relationship. The opening scenes of Djibril Diop Mambéty's *Hyenas* join private and public forms of indebtedness acted out by residents of Colobane, Senegal. The first scene introduces the impoverished shop owner Dramaan Drameh by highlighting his generosity and the warm relationships he cultivates with his customers. Dramaan serves the women who come to buy rice and other provisions with affection. He asks about their families and gives their children gifts of candy. He invites a man at the bar, Lat Kura, to have a drink with him and, when a group of male patrons arrive and insist that he serve them, Dramaan opens a bottle to share. This episode, as Burlin Barr notes, "acknowledges need and dependence as a commonplace public act."[16] Some of the men who come to drink wear rice sacks instead of clothes. The shop is run down and without electricity; a fan sits motionless in the corner, and soft drinks remain stacked in crates, next to a worn-out refrigerator. Out of shared need, Dramaan's gifts create bonds of friendship. It is Khoudia Lo, Dramaan's wife, who transforms her husband's gift giving into economic arrangements, threatening the conviviality among the men. (Women as sexual conquests also create affective connections between men in this episode: Dramaan shows affection for Lat Kura when he teases him about impregnating a woman called Penda Gueye.) Khoudia Lo's entrance and stern glare convert Dramaan's offerings into debts owed. Dramaan nervously asks the men: "What do you want to do? Ruin my marriage?" And he insists that they pay for the wine he initially offered for free. Khodia Lo's words nullify Dramaan's invitation to socializing when she asks Lat Kura how much he paid for his drink, and he puts down his glass and leaves. The ease with which gifts transform into debt under the authority of Dramaan's wife, whom we later learn Dramaan married for wealth, elucidates David Graeber's argument that "debt is just the perversion of a promise" revoked in the face of punishment.[17] The scene that immediately follows establishes indebtedness as not only common among individuals but also as a feature of public life in Colobane. The furniture in the city hall is "seized" by debt collectors who refuse to negotiate with the mayor's irate assistant.

This display of sovereign indebtedness, stressed by the repossession of public property, emphasizes the dire conditions that cause the town to accept an offer from Ramatou, an allegorical and historical figure through whom the personal and public modes of indebtedness overlap. Debt appears as the central feature of private and public life. Ramatou returns to Colobane to collect on her individual debts as a subject denied justice, and she promises to forgive the public debts of Colobane if its citizens satisfy her desire for personal vengeance. Ramatou is "as rich as the World Bank" and, like the bank, promises to lift the town out of poverty if it meets her conditions. To receive "millions and millions" of francs, she explains, the town must murder the shopkeeper who impregnated her, corrupted the justice system, and forced her to leave Colobane many years ago. Anticipating Ramatou's investment in their town, citizens begin to consume greedily on credit. The film chronicles their indulgence in amusements and conveniences, the energy-hungry pleasures of modern life that depend on the ability to pay for electricity and gasoline. Women buy refrigerators, large fans, and air conditioners; the mayor orders an electric typewriter; people line up to ride a roller coaster, and Dramaan takes a drive in his friend Mory's new car. If the absence of electricity and electrical appliances in the opening scenes signaled shared poverty, energy expenditure now further entrenches the town's debt relations. In a particularly haunting scene, Dramaan visits a church to ask the priest for sanctuary, only to find the priest installing a large, ornate chandelier. Here, electricity represents the shiny allure of excessive consumption, which finally leads to Dramaan's murder. In the meeting at the church, at the very moment the chandler is illuminated, Mambéty cuts to a close-up of Dramaan's face, registering horror at the realization that his life has become a debt instrument.

The teacher and doctor of Colobane plead with Ramatou on the town's behalf. This scene articulates the link between African oil and sovereign debt. Although oil is only briefly mentioned late in the film, it highlights the ongoing oil politics that have perpetuated postcolonial indebtedness despite all contrary claims of oil's promise to bring about widespread national development and provide a path out of debt. This link explicitly ties African oil to African debt. The two men ask to speak about Dramaan's "case" and assure Ramatou that they "have not come to beg, but to talk business." The teacher explains that Colobane has "oil in the soil of the valley of Xaar Yalla" and asks her to extend "credit" to the town so its people might exploit their natural resources and restart the factories. The problem with this plan, Ramatou responds, is that she owns the oil and all the town's riches. She cannot buy what is already hers. She continues: "I'm the one offering a deal. I'm stating my conditions. The world has made me a whore and I'll turn the world into a whorehouse." The citizens' borrowing and Ramatou's vengeful purchase of the town and its industries signal entry into what Barr calls "a system of commodification in which social connections are recast or erased."[18] In this system, all gifts become debts to be paid, and the social bonds portrayed in the opening scenes are destroyed. Ramatou insists that to free themselves from debt, the citizens of Colobane "must cover [their] hands with blood."

The film's reference to African oil introduces a more recent version of a postcolonial credit-debt relationship in which oil extracted from Africa generates new debt. The teacher and doctor voice a common development narrative, one that promotes investment in hydrocarbon extraction to ease sovereign debt burdens and stimulate economic growth. Oil extraction in Africa has a long history; however, in the twentieth century, African oil exploration and production have intensified rapidly, driven by increased energy demands from India, China, and Brazil, among other countries, as well as by expanding middle-class consumption across Africa.[19] Lee Wengraf identifies the current period of neocolonial exploitation as a "new scramble" for African natural resources, while Celeste Hicks details the political and economic context of "Africa's new oil." In a host of African countries, including Ethiopia, Uganda, Tanzania, and Niger, transnational oil companies backed by the World Bank have negotiated hydrocarbon exploration and drilling agreements with African governments eager to attract investment and generate revenue from oil. Hicks reports that since 1990, twenty-five billion dollars has been directed toward exploration and production in Africa, and "proven oil reserves have grown by nearly 120 percent in the past thirty years"—up to 124 billion barrels in 2012.[20] Advanced technologies for finding and exploiting deep-sea crude have enhanced methods of extracting crude onshore; oil companies have tapped reserves off the coasts of Ghana, Liberia, Sierra Leone, Côte d'Ivoire, South Africa, Mauritania, and Senegal. According to Wengraf, in 2009, the United States "imported more oil from Africa than from the Middle East, for the first time."[21] Released in 1992, at the dawn of Africa's oil boom, *Hyenas* sheds light on the moral and economic costs of oil's potential and the resulting expenditure and debt.

Abderrahmane Sissako's *Bamako*, released more than a decade after Mambéty's film, advocates for African subjects whose economic precarity comes in large part from sovereign debt. The characters depicted "[have] never had access to an individual, entrepreneurial credit-driven identity, because they have been collectively supporting an indebted state."[22] The film, more explicitly than any other African film, holds the World Bank and the International Monetary Fund accountable for the indebtedness of African states. A trial is staged in the courtyard of a residential compound in Bamako, the capital city of Mali, forcing the bank to respond to charges brought by African society. Many critics have commented on Sissako's wordplay, which juxtaposes the legal proceeding (court) and the domestic space (courtyard) where it unfolds. Minor scenes with people who live or work in the compound continually interrupt the court proceedings; key among these competing storylines is the breakup of Melé and Chaka's family and Chaka's subsequent suicide. Olivier Tchouaffe refers to these episodes as "small story worlds" that are embedded within an "observational tableaux."[23] Kate Ince describes the film's "plural" narrative as enacting "an aesthetic of disparity or of interruption, one by which the viewer's attention and engagement are continually displaced and referred between the global issues in which the trial deals and the pressing local difficulties of everyday life in Mali's capital city."[24] At the same time, the disparate domestic scenes reveal the lived effects of sovereign debt; they bring to life the creditor-debtor relationship examined through the trial as they are endured intimately and ordinarily by postcolonial subjects living in Africa.

The fantastical core of the narrative—a trial in which African society brings charges against the World Bank—is rendered in a hyperrealist style. The actual location of the setting, the use of nonprofessional actors who play themselves, and the various performances throughout the narrative, including the testimonies of those called as witnesses, create what James Williams describes as "a live, theatrical space of fiction and documentary-style scenes."[25] I am interested in two dimensions of the live space of the film: the self-referential, or performative, moments in the film and the mise-en-scéne, both of which offer access to what Lúcia Nagib calls "the mesh of the real." In an analysis of the films of Raúl Ruiz, Nagib uses the term "intermedial passage" to describe the "self-reflexive procedures" that integrate art and media into the narratives of Ruiz's films.[26] Nagib explains that these passages punch "holes in the narrative mesh through which the spectator can catch a glimpse of the incompleteness and incoherence of real life."[27] In *Bamako*, the many live oral performances continually interrupt and delay the imaginary trial and serve as passages to unscripted reality. These intermedial moments include the untranslated recitation of an elderly man, a griot figure, who performs his testimony at the front of the court; a wedding singer who commands the attention of the entire courtroom when she enters the scene; even the loosely scripted final statements given by the prosecution lawyers. In each case, Sissako aligns the viewpoints of the lawyers and judge—the juridical representatives to whom characters address their remarks—to the camera's perspective, the eye of the film's audience, and by doing so, he essentially doubles the performers. Spectators experience these characters as actors addressing the court in the film and as real people speaking directly to the camera about immediate and urgent political issues.

Beyond his placement and performances of human figures, Sissako's framing and a flattened depth of field position incidental and ordinary objects as traces of "undisguised, uncontrollable living reality."[28] The depiction of Nagib's "ethical realism" involves creating a real and vibrant ecology in the multiplicity of living and nonliving things that connect the production's location to the setting of the fictional story: the trash strewn on the streets that Chaka walks at dawn; the wobbly and battered fan at the front of the court; the clothesline that crosses the space of the yard; the shared faucet and plastic buckets used to collect water for washing and bathing; the cheap chairs rented for court observers and witnesses (the name of the actual neighborhood, Hamdouli, is painted on the chair backs); and the flies that continually buzz about. The insects, in particular, strike me as crucial to Sissako's "realist mode of production."[29] Their living presence in almost every scene signals the overlap of the profilmic event and a vital material world as represented. As de Luca notes about animals in another context, the flies in *Bamako* provide "the dynamic and embodied evidence of an intractable reality surplus within the filmic image."[30] They connect the fictional story of the trial to the materiality of its production. Taken together, these various elements of the setting evidence the film's dedicated attention to the real, which goes beyond linking the global politics of the trial and the hardships experienced at the local level, as argued by Ince. Sissako's beautifully executed sensory realism brings to life the abstract pronouncements spotlighted in the trial and gives physical presence to sovereign debt as experienced by African citizens in their everyday interactions with flies, trash, plastic buckets, and broken fans. These nonhuman elements act on and with human agents throughout the film, producing a phenomenological record of life under the petrostate's indebtedness.

PIPELINE PROMISES

I turn next to Chad, its emergent oil economy, and two films that thematize debt at different registers: Danya Abt's documentary *Quel Souvenir* (2009) and Haroun's feature film *Daratt* (2008). Abt's vitally important documentary, produced in collaboration with the Cameroonian nonprofit organization Relufa, deserves much more attention than it has received.[31] Following the route of the Chad-Cameroon oil pipeline, a major crude transport infrastructure that runs from Kribi on the Cameroon coast to the Doba Basin in Chad, the film builds a case against the CCPDPP, the international effort responsible for the pipeline. The film holds the World Bank and the oil consortium with which it collaborated accountable for egregiously misrepresenting the benefits the project would bring and refusing to compensate communities for the ecological and economic damage it left behind. It is not merely that rural communities did not benefit directly from the construction of the pipeline, but that the CCPDPP continues to deplete resources and destroy opportunities to farm and work.

The plot of the award-winning feature film *Daratt* is straightforward. The film makes no reference to oil or the pipeline project; rather, it describes relationships that evolve from obligation and debt, especially debts assumed by individuals with no support from a state strengthened by its fossil fuel endowments. I insist that we read this debt in relation to the recent history of crude in Chad, especially because Chad's oil economy is not addressed explicitly in the film but has been, nonetheless, fundamental to the sociopolitical history of the civil war and its aftermath. In *Daratt*, the young protagonist Atim is sent on a quest by his grandfather to find his father's killer. Atim's father was murdered in the civil war before Atim's birth, and now he must avenge his death. This search for individual moral reimbursement, demanded because the state fails to bring war criminals to trial, structures the film's narrative and provides another opportunity to reflect on the intimate, subjectivizing processes activated by debt relations. Unlike the films already discussed, *Daratt* uses male bodies to represent affective and labor relations set in motion by the indebted state's failure to confront war crimes. Energy, in this configuration, is embodied as affective potential and the physical exertion required when bodies do manual labor.

Since achieving independence from French colonial rule in 1960, Chad has experienced prolonged periods of political instability and armed rebellion under a series of autocratic rulers, including the current president, Idriss Déby. A former army general, Déby led a coup in 1990 that overthrew the military dictatorship of Hissene Habré. Déby's government steered Chad away from exporting cotton, the country's colonial cash crop, toward oil capitalism. The discovery of oil fields in the south of the country supported major investments in the CCPDPP, a six-billion-dollar megaproject involving Chad and Cameroon, the World Bank, and a consortium of multinational oil companies led by ExxonMobil. Between 2000 and 2006, the CCPDPP developed three hundred wells in southern Chad at Komé, Miandoum, and Bolobo. It also built more than six hundred miles of underground pipeline to transport oil from Chad, across Cameroon, and to the coast, where off-loading storage vessels would load the oil to ship to refineries in the global North.[32] The project is expected to produce one billion barrels of oil over a thirty-year period.

According to anthropologist Lori Leonard, author of *Life in the Time of Oil: A Pipeline and Poverty in Chad*, the project was praised as a model for "a new generation of efforts" to promote development by creating policies to guarantee that oil wealth would support good governance and promote poverty reduction.[33] The World Bank's involvement was meant to guarantee the oil companies' massive investments and ensure that oil revenues would be directed toward national development. The bank determined that the best approach to meeting these objectives "involved integrating Chad into global markets through the sale of Chadian oil, reforming governance, and building institutional capacity in Chad to manage the emerging oil economy."[34] Key to this objective was Law 001, which was passed by the National Assembly in 1998 and required that oil revenues be held in an escrow account in London and disbursed by a third party. It also mandated that 10 percent of oil revenues be deposited into a "Future Generations Fund" and that most of the remaining revenue be dedicated to five priorities, which included education, health, and poverty reduction. The project also implemented strategies to mitigate environmental risks and compensate communities for losses incurred as a result of the project, and it showcased the bank's reformed development strategy by promoting "private sector-led, trickle-down economic growth."[35]

For Chad, extracting and shipping fossil fuels intensified neocolonial relations and expanded its incorporation into the debt economy. Debt relations are always asymmetrical. Because oil extraction is a capital-intensive enterprise, impoverished countries like Chad are often lured into exploitative economic agreements disguised as opportunities for economic growth and national development. These agreements involve extracting, transporting, and transforming a raw natural resource into wealth. The natural resource of the rentier state—in Chad's case, oil—is said to guarantee payment of the debt taken on to extract the resource and support future wealth generation. Research that tracks debt and economic growth in developing oil-exporter states challenges this narrative. *Drilling into Debt*, a comprehensive study by Oil Change International, the Jubilee USA Network, the Institute for Public Policy Research, Milieudefensie, and Amazon Watch collected data from over two hundred countries from 1970 to 2002. It found "a strong and positive relationship between oil export dependence and debt burdens."[36] Revenues generated from oil exports improve countries' abilities to service their debts, which improves the standing of debtor countries with international creditors. However, this also tends to increase their total indebtedness. Irfan Nooruddin explains that oil exporters successfully "leverage their oil wealth to generate huge influxes of foreign loans" that, over time and in a highly volatile oil marketplace, "resul[t] in a massive transfer of resources from poor to rich countries."[37] Loan payments, with interest accrued, represent a steady flow of wealth outward. The unpredictability of oil revenues and the fact that developing countries must pay their debts in foreign currencies compound these already substantial burdens. Chad could only finance its participation in the project and purchase its minority holdings through loans from the World Bank. After the bank pulled its support from the project, Chad turned toward China and accrued additional debt, even as oil revenues began to flow into government accounts. Oil wealth has not improved the quality of life for many of those living in the oil zone or in urban areas but instead has threatened livelihoods sustained by fishing and farming and erected barriers to opportunity. Critics of the Déby regime allege that petroleum contributes in direct ways to its suppression of opposition and consolidation of power.

Under Déby, ongoing civil unrest and armed resistance by rebel groups that had been active since the 1990s were met with unyielding repression and military aggression. Fighting in western Sudan spread into Chad in 2003, escalating an already dire situation, until 2005, when Sudan finally recalled its ambassador from Chad and launched a "proxy war by sponsoring the various new groupings of Chadian rebels."[38] To fund his on-going military campaigns against the rebels, Déby needed oil money, and Law 001 hindered his regime's efforts to buy military arms and equipment. Moreover, as Celeste Hicks reports, "the rigidity of the spending priorities enshrined in Law 001 soon came to be viewed by many in the Chadian government as external interference in a sovereign state's business."[39] In 2005, after Déby amended the constitution to end presidential term limits, rebel groups escalated their efforts to overthrow his government. That same year, President Déby announced that he planned to amend Law 001 to allow his government greater flexibility and autonomy, especially concerning the use of oil revenues for "security spending."[40] The World Bank regarded this move as a violation of the project's terms and withdrew its support. Despite speculation that Chad would abolish the entire law, according to Hicks, "there has been no further attempt to amend it and revenues from the Consortium are still being transferred to and monitored in the London escrow account."[41] The government of Chad cleared its debt with the bank in 2008.[42] But before making this payment, Chad had increased its dependence on Chinese loans considerably. Chad negotiated the construction of a refinery in Djérmaya, about thirty miles north of N'Djaména, with the China National Petroleum Corporation International Chad (CNPCIC).[43] In exchange for the rights to crude extracted from the Bonger Basin, the CNPCIC committed to the development of roads. In subsequent years, Chad also borrowed from the Exim Bank of China to pay for "the construction of a railway connection with Cameroon and a new million-passenger airport for N'Djaména."[44]

Produced in the aftermath of the pipeline's construction, the scope of the documentary *Quel Souvenir* excludes China's entry into Chad's oil economy and deals exclusively with the unrealized promises made by Exxon (referred to as *Esso* in the film) and the World Bank.[45] Starting at the Port of Kribi on the Cameroonian coast, the film documents the pipeline's impact on cities and small villages in the oil zone. The filmmakers remain off screen to highlight the testimonies of their Chadian and Cameroonian interlocutors, who periodically address questions from the filmmakers or make direct remarks to the camera. The documentary uses a conventional format: establishing shots and intertitles situate talking head–style interviews along the pipeline's route. The form is simple but powerful. Cameroonians and Chadians narrate their experiences of oil and call their governments, Esso, and the World Bank to account. Meanwhile, their modest dwellings, an empty guesthouse overgrown with weeds, unpaved streets, and areas with no electricity showcase the austerity and neglect that have yet to be dealt with. In Cameroon, Abiosse Julot, a representative of Kribi's artisanal fisher community, complains that the security personnel who police the perimeter of the offshore installation have restricted fishing near the platform. The movement patterns of the fish have been disturbed, and the already-meager fish stocks seem further depleted. Oil, he says, has done nothing positive for the fisher folks. He asks: "What can the little villager do when everything is already signed and done?" Eko Roosevelt, a teacher and musician who is also the chief of the village Lobi, in Cameroon, explains that people welcomed the CCPDPP; they regarded it as "a beacon of hope" since "where there's oil there's wealth." The musician is surprised when he sits at his keyboard and finds that he has electricity to play it. This unsolicited reaction demonstrates to viewers the regularity of power outages. At the end of this segment, the camera captures the oil platform, illuminated by a tall methane flare, to emphasize the irony that the continuous supply of methane that feeds the toxic flame could be captured and used to generate electricity.

Moving north to the villages of Ndtoua, Nanga Eboko, and Ebaka, people describe the economic boom set in motion by the arrival of workers subcontracted to build the pipeline. The influx of workers grew quickly as men and women from surrounding villages also came to the oil zone to find work. Nzougo Gervais, a farmer, shows the film crew the hostel his brother built to accommodate workers and the prostitutes they hired. Dilapidated and empty, the structure stands as a remnant of the fleeting opportunities the construction of the oil pipeline offered local people. The filmmakers interview a young woman in the waiting area of a local clinic, where she has come to receive treatment for HIV. She tells them that she worked as a waiter in a restaurant at a worker's camp and, like several other young women in the area, contracted the virus during the boom period when the sudden and short-lived burst of economic opportunity created by the infusion of oil money and workers into small towns disrupted community routines and norms. She remembers: "It was like Sodom and Gomorrah; it must be poverty that makes people do things like that," referring to the sex-work industry that emerged near the workers' camp. At a village clinic, nurse Bilock Edang Lisette explains that during the oil boom, she considered leaving her salaried job for a better-paying position sweeping floors for the construction companies. In the town of Belel, the management headquarters of the Cameroon Oil Transportation Company (COTCO), Chief Aboo Mohamadou escorts the film crew to a small shop with a narrow and long fluorescent bulb attached to the ceiling. He tells the filmmakers that COTCO built an electrification infrastructure and provided electricity to the community, without charge, during the two years of the pipeline's construction. When the company left, it cut off the electricity, which, as the camera shows us, ran on power lines that border the main road. The shop owner, who also appears in the scene, adds that the electricity was like "a gift" that was given and then suddenly withdrawn.

A gift implies something offered without condition, something that builds social connections, something that would only be taken away at the risk of undoing those ties. The oil consortium, however, had no interest in building long-lasting social bonds. As Leonard's research demonstrates, the group actually achieved the opposite by enforcing "a relational ethic of detachment" that limited its engagement with and obligations to people in the oil zone to more efficiently extract resources.[46] In this segment of the documentary, people describe the temporary and tenuous forms of economic benefit engendered by the consortium's extractive interactions. Benefit, not development. Development connotes a particular temporality. Linear and teleological, development suggests a future better than the present. It looks ahead and anticipates the fulfillment of a promise. Communities through which the pipeline passes, as represented in Abt's film, benefited only from short-term eruptions of capital and commercial activity, both of which were the incidental by-products of investments meant to expedite the pipeline's completion. Interviewees recall experiencing the ephemeral effects of an extractive boom that in some cases caused long-term harm.

One of the central claims of David Graeber's *Debt* is that the systems of equivalence and calculation on which creditor-debtor connections depend destroy the social bonds strengthened through mutual obligations and the exchange of gifts. In example after example from hundreds of anthropological and historical studies, he documents the various processes of decontextualization and detachment that were put in place to authorize and normalize the credit-debt duality, which he considers a twisted relationship that is held in place as a dominant social and political formation only with the threat of violence. Leonard's ethnography presents a twentieth-century study that extends Graeber's thesis. Her research examines the discursive mechanisms the oil consortium deployed to transform "human relations into mathematics."[47] Supported by the World Bank's endorsement, an extensive administrative apparatus produced a debt discourse that delineated compensation formulas and eligibility criteria, with the aim of rationalizing obligations to living and nonliving things in the oil zone. The Compensation and Resettlement Plan was at the base of this discussion. Designed to govern the expropriation of land and allocation of compensation, it adhered to the World Bank's "standard on involuntary resettlement," which states that "borrowers are responsible for implementing resettlement programs that restore or improve the living standards of those who are displaced by development projects."[48] According to the plan, the consortium of oil companies "was responsible for providing displaced farmers with the replacement costs of lost assets, minus the land itself." Compensation was given in single cash payments, which were intended "to cover lost income, amortized over a number of years, from trees that were cleared, as well as the cost of replacing sheds, beehives, and other structures."[49] Abt's documentary demonstrates the plan's inadequacy and calls on the consortium and the World Bank to fulfill their obligations to those who live and work near the pipeline and production zones. Speakers from Cameroon and Chad essentially redefine the project's inadequate compensation as debt or, in Graeber's words, "an exchange that has not been brought to completion."[50] They use Abt's camera to expose Esso's violations of their compensation agreements and to demand energy justice.

Several scholars have described the geography of oil extraction in Africa as "encapsulated" or "enclaved."[51] The enclave refers to the physical barriers that separate oil facilities and infrastructures from the surrounding areas where crude is pumped. The term describes a kind of detachment that "materializes in heavily fortified production sites, in workers' camps cut off from the outside world, in extremely high-salaried experts supplied with goods and foodstuffs from overseas, in military or private security forces that become alarmed by the slightest curious gaze, and by sophisticated equipment and machinery."[52] Leonard makes the crucial point that in Chad, the pipeline and its installations were not separated and enclosed but instead "were scattered around the oil field region and were part of the everyday geography of resident's lives."[53] Abt's documentary emphasizes this embeddedness visually: as she interviews people near their homes, she frames her shot to include nearby drilling platforms. In Maikeri, for instance, we visit a tiny school, the benches and chalkboard neatly arranged outside a small dwelling, and the camera brings into visibility an oil platform and a row of trailer homes and trucks, behind a high chain-link fence, a few hundred feet from the school. The composition contrasts the poverty in which the villagers live and the well-funded oil company facilities that encroach on their land. The proximity of drilling installations to the homes and farms of residents in the production zone frustrated efforts typically deployed to wall the infrastructure of oil from the surrounding environment as did swelling needs to expropriate additional land because wells were producing far less oil than had been projected. A report commissioned by Exxon states that by 2006, twelve thousand people had been negatively impacted by land acquisitions or other aspects of the project. Of those surveyed, 60 percent had lost more than 20 percent of their land, and about half had to give up more than 50 percent.[54] Abt documents precisely what Leonard has described. Her crew talks with Richard Tolouma, chief of Maikeri, who explains that the consortium's land appropriations, which increased after 2004, have brought famine to the village because farmers and families simply do not have enough land to cultivate food crops. He recounts the discovery of a pipeline leak on his land that he immediately reported to the company. He holds up a black backpack that he says he received from the company to thank him for bringing the spill to its attention. He remarks that the spill released crude over a sizable area of his land, but for this, he was offered no compensation. The bag, he notes, is completely useless to him. He confirms that villagers have lost a great deal of cultivatable land and that the land they do farm fails to produce the yields it did before the pipeline. He worries that the consortium is trying to drive them from their homes.

Leonard's analysis seems to suggest that the Compensation and Resettlement Plan offset the proximity of oil production to local communities by minimizing interactions with farmers and limiting the consortium's obligations

Fig. 2.1 Proximity of Esso oil installation to a small school in Maikeri, Chad. From *Quel Souvenir*. 2009. © Dayna Abt.

and attachments.[55] The plan sought to decontextualize responsibilities to local communities with paperwork, charts, formulas, and equivalences. In *Quel Souvenir*, Nana Ibrahima of Djertou, Chad, thumbs through an illustrated pamphlet and compensation booklet distributed during the pipeline construction period. He laughs derisively as he reads one entry: "'Furnished with 30 tables with benches with two seats plus a table with a drawer and a chair. Six million.' But that is not the quality here." He is not complaining that the compensation is too low but that it reveals ignorance about the local context. He continues: "If you have to compensate us, we are the ones who understand our problems." The film cuts to a shot of several bags of cement piled in the corner of a village classroom. Ibrahim notes that the cement will likely deteriorate before it is used. He adds: "We should be compensated with money."

Finally, *Quel Souvenir* exposes how violence and threats of violence are used to suppress all forms of citizen protest and complaints against the CCPDPP. There are many examples. Activists, politicians, laborers, and farmers in Chad and Cameroon testify to arrest, physical assault, and other acts

Fig. 2.2 Nana Ibrahim, in Djertou, Chad, looks through the Compensation and Resettlement Booklet. From *Quel Souvenir.* 2009. © Dayna Abt.

of intimidation. Their narratives recount troubling encounters with security personal, police officers, and the legal system that systemically worked on behalf of the oil consortium and the state while violating the rights of citizens. Although the content of these interviews is troubling, their form, sketched out in advance and conducted with professional attention to light and sound design, invites a less intense, less anxious, affective response from the viewer than the unscripted intrusions of the oil consortium's security apparatus that occur while the documentary crew is in Chad. While driving between the villages that dot the oil production areas, the crew and their translator, Nadji Nelambaye, encounter Esso's security force. This segment, shot from inside the car and through the window, shows the viewer the electricity pylons and facilities erected by the consortium between communities and close to the road, demonstrating how oil is interlaced with rural life in Chad's areas of production. Unexpectedly, and in English, someone says, "Camera down." The switch to English is out of sync with the rest of the documentary, in which speakers use French or, if they speak a local language, their responses are translated into French, and it alerts viewers to an interruption of the production setup. The camera wobbles, and the screen suddenly goes black. We hear the sound of wheels on the road before the camera starts filming again. Only Nelambaye's hand on the seat is visible, indicating that the camera operator is hiding the camera below the car window. The translator explains that video or sound recording and photography are prohibited in the oil zone, and the fear of arrest or harassment has forced activists like him to gather evidence secretly. In a scene that follows, a large black SUV, an Esso security vehicle, rolls silently into the camera's frame while the filmmakers interview Keiro M'ramarde about the oil spill mentioned earlier. The sudden appearance of the Esso vehicle unsettles the men in front of the camera, who stop speaking and glance nervously behind them at the Esso employee who leans out his window. After several seconds, the vehicle moves out of the frame. The inclusion of these unscripted acts of intimidation "break the boundaries with the phenomenological world at the point of the film's production," as described by Nagib in another context.[56] Nagib uses the concept of "ethical realism" to describe films that reveal an "ethical commitment to the truth of the unpredictable event."[57] These are films that cultivate an openness to unplanned intrusions and other excesses of the film's production. I suggest that *Quel Souvenir* goes beyond exhibiting a commitment to the uncertainty and messiness of reality; the filmmakers, including the Cameroonians and Chadians who agree to appear before the camera, expose themselves to physical danger during the film's production; theirs is a political commitment that involves being vulnerable to violence. By filming these scenes, Abt enables viewers to directly witness the immoral and illegal acts of intimidation perpetuated by the oil consortium against some of the most marginalized citizens of Chad and Cameroon. She brings to light the very real violence that threatens the health, land, and livelihoods of the disenfranchised citizens whose lives and land down their nation's debt.

DEBT REFUSED: DARATT

Residents of the small, impoverished villages in the oil field region and urban residents of Chad experience oil in different ways. The lives and livelihoods of Abt's interlocuters and Leonard's research subjects are interwoven with the materiality of oil and the oil pipeline, and both Abt and Leonard argue that oil has done very little to improve life in the production zone and instead has harmed local environments and severely limited opportunities to farm and fish. A debt is still owed to those forced to adapt to the CCPDP. Urban residents, as shown in Haroun's films, which I discuss in the final section of this chapter, observe oil development in the form of paved roads, increased traffic, new public buildings, and an expanding electricity infrastructure, but few people reap any direct benefit. At the core of many of Haroun's films are men of precarious economic and social standing who labor strenuously in the formal and informal economies and yet must take on debt to survive. These male characters represent the impoverished city dwellers whose embodied energy subsidizes the indebted petrostate.

Haroun's films, to their credit, do not romanticize the personal or community-based credit-debt networks used to help the people overlooked by the indebted state. Individual debt in some cases strengthens social relationships, but it also exposes human bodies to violence and risk. In *Un Homme Qui Crie* (2010), Adam trades his son's life to pay a monetary debt to support the war effort. In the short film *Expectations* (2010), Moussa experiences a cognitive break under pressure from his father and the entire community to make the dangerous journey across the desert to find passage to Europe so he can pay his father's debts, which were incurred on his behalf to finance an earlier attempt to migrate to Europe. In *Grigris* (2013), analyzed in detail in the next chapter, a father's deteriorating health and escalating hospital bills drive the protagonist to steal and sell a truckload of gasoline from the smuggler for whom he drives jerry cans of gas across the border. Unable to pay his debt to his patron and in danger of being killed, he must flee the city with his girlfriend, Mimi. In his most recent film, *Lingui: The Sacred Bonds* (2021), Haroun's protagonist Amina pays off a debt to a neighbor, Brahim, who asks her to marry him. This monetary debt owed to a man who proposes marriage in a similarly transactional way contrasts starkly with the vulnerabilities and obligations shared by women. (At the end of the film, we learn that Brahim raped and impregnated Amina's daughter.) The film celebrates female relationships of reciprocity and care. The female doctor who helps Amina's daughter abort her unwanted pregnancy tells Amina: "You're my sister now. Sisters don't pay." *Daratt*, which I discuss next, indexes events that occur after Déby's violent ouster of Habré and the announcement of the new government's amnesty for all war crimes committed during the period of fighting and civil unrest. The film's production and release, however, take place over a decade after the 1990 coup, after Chad enters the petroleum economy. *Daratt* works within both of these historical moments. Its story of revenge can be analyzed as a narrative about postconflict reconciliation, as most critics have done, and as a cinematic meditation on debt and repayment in the context of oil development, which is my analysis.

In *Daratt*, debt is not monetary but moral and intensely subjective; at the same time, the film's setting reveals how sovereign debt is borne by citizens. *Daratt* begins in a small village in Chad, an impoverished and desolate place where black plastic bags dance across the dry landscape and along the narrow, dusty roads that curve between the mud walls of dwellings. To borrow a descriptive phrase from Kristin D. Phillips's energy ethnography of rural Singida in central Tanzania, the area is "on the carbon periphery, betwixt and between national infrastructures."[58] In this Chadian village, homes are detached from the national electrical grid. No cables or connections are visible, and radios tuned into national broadcasts—which I regard as a loose connection to a national communications infrastructure—run on batteries.

In the first scenes of *Daratt*, the family relationships are portrayed as a field of debt relations in which a debt owed constructs a memory, an interiority, a conscience, and a future for Atim, whose entire sense of self has been shaped by the death of his father. This is a debt he is born into and must cancel with equal compensation. As the voice-over explains, Atim's name means "orphan." This obligation of repayment, like a name, is assigned, not selected; it is a call to an identity that Atim takes on as he is solicited to enact revenge on behalf of someone else, his grandfather. This calling forth is expressed beautifully in the film's opening when Atim's grandfather emerges from a small dwelling and calls loudly for his grandson. The elderly man feels for the ground in front of him with a long cane. His dark glasses and slow, careful gait tell us that he is blind. The camera carries the call through the village. We hear it echo across long shots of streets populated with pedestrians and over an extreme long shot of the desert town. Finally, the camera cuts to Atim, who hears his grandfather and begins to run. We don't know where he has been, so we learn nothing of his life outside and before the call. As a character, his presence on-screen presents itself as an answer to his grandfather's demand: "Where are you?"

The grandfather has summoned Atim because the Chadian National Commission of Truth and Justice is about to announce its findings. Atim and his grandfather sit on opposite sides of their small radio, and when a general amnesty for crimes committed during the civil war is announced, cries and gunshots of protest erupt. Atim looks toward the sounds of gunfire, then stands and walks in the direction of the commotion. The film then cuts to what Eugenie Brinkema might call a grief tableau, a cinematic display intended to render the sensation of loss.[59] In the unpaved street, Atim finds hundreds of discarded shoes, plastic, broken, and mismatched. This long shot composes the scene in a stagelike way, setting up the spatial arrangement as a performance. The frame is cut in two by the horizontal line created where a wall, which resembles the back of a stage, meets the dry and dusty road. To the right of the frame, the standing and split trunk of a tree marks the border of the stage. Atim picks up a single sandal, looks at it, and lets it fall. He walks farther away from the camera and deeper into the frame and then picks up another shoe. This time, he runs his hand over the shoe slowly and turns his head, looking at the field of old shoes around him. He tosses the sandal to the side and walks out of the frame (off the stage). But the camera remains here, holding this moment, suspending narrative time for a few breaths. This tableau, now absent a human figure, looks like a photograph except for the fluttering of a tattered plastic bag among the discarded shoes. The shot is unattributed; that is, it is not aligned with a character's perspective, nor is it explained by film's the narrative. We don't know where the shoes came from. Did they drop from the feet of angry Chadians who fled when they heard the news of the amnesty? Were they thrown in protest? Did they fall from the feet of protesters running from soldiers sent to disperse them? No explanation is offered. Instead, the image remains singular to represent the sensations that attend the nation-state's failure to address war crimes and support victims' calls for justice. Later in the film, a radio commentator remarks: "As long as impunity reigns in this country, there'll be no peace. The blood our families shed must be paid back."

In *The Forms of the Affects*, Brinkema investigates theories that link grief to light and visibility (in Augustine, Freud, and Barthes) and concludes that grief, because it is "the affect most tightly linked to the loss of being, poses a unique set of problems for any system of representation predicated on presencing." This is similar to the cinema, which, she suggests, struggles to create a "visual vocabulary for the in-visible absent."[60] In film, loss—visual absence—impacts the subject at the level of narrative and challenges film form's "endlessly recuperative ability to make absent things present."[61] She outlines the conventions used by narrative films to compensate for missing bodies, to fill the empty spaces left by the material absence of human beings. The first convention denies the loss of the loved one; her presence returns as "an embodied ghost."[62] The second strategy uses the environment to frame the loss. Brinkema explains that "absence is made present visually to the film by displaying the materiality under or behind any being, replacing the substance of a body with the substance of the environment in which that body once existed."[63] Finally, the figure who mourns might stand in for the missing body, staring at her own face in the mirror, for example.

Haroun's tableau resists or significantly modifies these conventional compensatory gestures. Objects in the environment make absence present: the unpaired old shoes evoke the ghostlike traces of the people who abandoned them, and their material presence is used to signify absence. It is not the absence of Atim's dead father that the scene materializes. (The father never appears in the film; his is an incommensurable loss.) We cannot simply assume that the tableau references Atim's personal loss. Instead, it creates a deindividualized and political affective vitality, a charged atmosphere of feeling yet to be channeled into grief, pain, or anger. The image exemplifies Deleuze's "any-space-whatever." He writes in *Cinema 1*: "Any-space-whatever is not an abstract universal, in all times, in all places. It is a perfectly singular space, which has merely lost its homogeneity, that is, the principle of its metric relations or the connection of its own parts, so that the linkages can be made in an infinite number of ways. It is a space of virtual conjunction, grasped as pure locus of the possible."[64] The image reminds us of the lives lost to war, but if we see it as a "locus of the possible," it might also symbolize a visual representation of what affect theorists call the "readiness potential" or the "reserve of energy" incited and shared between bodies, and bodies and things.[65] One could argue that this scene of suspension signifies, in the words of Nigel Thrift, the "little space of time" between action and performance.[66] Thrift uses the term *half-second delay* to describe "the period of bodily anticipation" before nonconscious affect is organized into conscious thought or conscious movement. Using energy analytics, this scene portrays the emotional connection between human bodies and nonliving objects (shoes). It represents emotions as an unformed source of energy, a vital intensity yet to be acted on or named.

The tableau shot immediately precedes Atim's grandfather's demand for compensation. It is intended to contextualize what follows and align our sympathies with Atim and all those denied justice by the state. In the next scene, we see Atim and his grandfather sitting close together in their house. In silence, the grandfather unrolls a square bundle that looks like it might be a Quran. With the intense concentration of performing a ritual, he unwraps a handgun, holds it in both hands, and says to Atim, "This belonged to your father." The act of passing the gun to his grandson enlists his involvement in undertaking the grandfather's "mission" of finding and killing Nassara, his father's killer. Atim does not say a word, but he takes the gun, signaling that he has entered into what Lazzarato calls "a promise of payment."[67] From this point, repayment becomes the "ethico-political labor" that acts on Atim's subjectivity and impacts his future. Lazzarato argues that debt "neutralizes time"; it "harnesses and exercises the power of destruction/creation, the power of choice and decision."[68] For Atim, the debt of his father's murder objectifies and possesses his past. It has become the defining event of his young life and his future. The promise solicited by Atim's grandfather modulates and directs the affective energy expressed in the previous scene. The next day, wearing an old camouflage jacket and carrying the gun, Atim walks through the empty desert to a bus stop on the side of the road and boards a van, already filled with passengers, to the city in search of Nassara.

As Atim travels from the village and into the capital of N'Djaména, he leaves behind a space of energy deprivation to experience the many energy systems and flows of the city. Cars, taxis, motorbikes, and minibuses move on paved roads, and electricity cables drape between poles. Atim buys a cell phone, an electronic device that must be charged, and his first job is to steal light bulbs. The fact that Atim and his new friend Moussa sell the stolen light bulbs to local electronics dealers suggests that many people in the city have access to electricity and use electric lights. Soon, Atim finds Nassara, his father's killer, and starts to work as Nassara's apprentice baker. He learns to operate the few simple machines in the bakery, which also run on electricity. At one point, the power cuts when Atim and Nassara are baking. Without light, the men cannot work, and Nassara exclaims: "May God curse the electric company. Nothing but trouble." Nassara and his wife do not own a generator or automobile, and their radio runs on batteries, but the couple can offer Atim a modest livelihood and electricity's basic affordances.

In her thoughtful review of *Daratt*, Dayna Oscherwitz suggests that the film juxtaposes the two types of labor Atim performs in the city. She writes: "Nassara's bakery, a space where Atim learns to produce something communal that is beyond his own limited sphere, becomes emblematic of an economy of production in which value is added to society. It contrasts with the circular economy of the marketplace in which Atim resells stolen light bulbs and ballasts, the economy of the zero-sum game."[69] The film suggests that Atim's transformation from a petty thief to baker of bread is a kind of personal evolution. The scenes in the bakery aestheticize the materiality of the labor the men perform, and the shared experience of baking bread and the affective atmosphere it generates clearly contribute to the disturbance of Atim's resolve to harm Nassara. But the contrast between Atim's work with Moussa and his work with Nassara obscures the different types of labor that exist in the urban landscape as presented in *Daratt*. The two soldiers who beat Atim for urinating on a wall are paid functionaries of the Chadian war economy. They perform their work, however questionable, when they punish Atim for violating an ordinance prohibiting public urination. In several scenes, itinerant traders, drivers for hire, and mechanics appear on the streets of N'djaména. At one point, Atim leaves his bread stall to help an orange seller balance an enormous load of fruit in a basket that she carries on her head. Next to Nassara's bakery, men slice and roast strips of meat, and at two points in the film, a mobile boulangerie selling "brioche de Paris" parks outside Nassara's compound to lure customers away from his small, run-down bakery where he sells his baguettes from a kiosk made of tin. When Nassara confronts his competitor, the man tells him that he can sell his bread wherever he wants and that he should complain to the WTO. This is a direct reference to the World Trade Organization, one of the international financial organizations charged with policing the economic liberalization policies imposed on African economies since the late 1970s. Nassara's rage implies that competition from the upmarket and mobile bakery threatens his livelihood. These multiple and seemingly incidental representations of work visualize the flourishing of the informal economy, which in Africa provides an entry for ordinary people into an obscenely uneven global system of exchange. They also highlight the human body as a primary source of energy production in low-carbon environments. Bodies fueled by food do much of the work that is portrayed in this film.

The general precariousness of employment in Chad informs Haroun's representation of the physical work Nassara teaches Atim to perform. Nostalgia for what in postcolonial Africa remains an unrealized ideal of productive labor as a basis for masculine identity and social affiliation shapes the scenes of Nassara and Atim at work in the bakery. The self-conscious cinematic artistry of these scenes, which center on the two men's flour-dusted bodies, displays loving attention—precisely what Nassara tells Atim he must bring to the baking of bread. (Nassara explains to Atim that "without love, the bread is not good.") The camera directs our eyes to the choreography of their movements as they slice and weigh the dough and operate the machinery they use to mix and knead the bread. Few words are spoken between Nassara and Atim. Their precise and practiced movements synchronize with the churn and hum of the machines. The camera pans or cuts between close-ups of Atim's and Nassara's faces, as Nassara watches the boy's work or as each is set in total concentration. After Atim tastes the bread from the first batch he has made without Nassara, he leaps with joy, smiles, and raises his hands in the air, displaying a rare and exaggerated expression of happiness. The work of making food, the source of human vitality, becomes pleasurable for Atim, while the men's shared and embodied labor engenders the possibility for relations of cooperation and care to emerge.

Phillips, quoted previously, has conducted pioneering ethnographic research in energy humanities that theorizes the embodied energy expenditures of women who live in rural communities with limited or no connectivity to energy infrastructures. She outlines several insights brought forward by attention to the human body in the anthropological investigation of energy. Embodied energy, she explains, "highlights the interdependency, even the co-constitution of people and nature" and centers "energy as a relational configuration, and of the human body as intermediary—even technology—of energy production."[70] In other words, the human body generates energy from its ability to metabolize the stores of energy in food, which grows from the sun's energy and the soil's nutrients. Ideally, waste returns those nutrients to the soil to continue the cycle. Moreover, Phillips continues, acknowledging human energy spotlights human labor and its crucial contributions to conventional energy narratives that privilege "a fossil-fuel and growth-driven energy regime."[71] Disregarding human energy expenditures in research on energy poverty in particular, Phillips notes, "erases the embodied energy and energy syncretism that drives so much of life in rural parts of the continent, where human muscle power is the dominant energy source."[72] Haroun's film goes beyond simply cataloging or depicting these insights. It focuses our attention on the energies produced by and exchanged among human bodies as well as between human bodies and nonliving things. As I have written elsewhere, his body of work, at least in part, elaborates on a cinematic grammar of the male body and its affective and physical energies.[73] Haroun's focus on male bodies in urban environments might even be said to complement Phillips' work on the embodied labor of women in rural locations, stressing that physical labor remains a dominant energy form for impoverished African urban dwellers.

If the film suggests, as Oscherwitz argues, a comparison between Moussa and Nassara, perhaps it juxtaposes their relations with Atim. Moussa's friendship is given without expectation of repayment. Even after Atim refuses to work for Moussa, Moussa phones him and they agree to meet. Nassara's relations, however, reiterate an ethics of recompense. The charity Nassara offers the boys who appear at his gate to beg for pieces of bread as well as his religious devotion seem intended to pay for the terrible things he admits to Atim that he has done. Nassara's actions are put in circulation to be exchanged for forgiveness. Atim, in fact, angrily tells Nassara that going to the mosque "won't redeem him." The plot implies that Nassara's desire to adopt Atim is another attempt to make up for past crimes. This same logic of repayment dominates his interactions with Atim. When Nassara overhears Atim and his young wife Aïcha making fun of him, he angrily beats Aïcha. Atim hears Aïcha's screams and punishes Nassara by deliberately failing to add yeast to the batch of bread he is preparing. At this point in the film, one hurtful action begets another.

Finally, it is Atim's recognition of Nassara's losses that disrupts this cycle of revenge and violence. Atim's many encounters with Nassara's wounded and aging body intensify the connections forged by the men's combined efforts in the baking of bread and shift Atim's emotional energy toward a future not defined by vengeance. The film highlights Atim's response to Nassara's physical vulnerability and implies that empathy provokes Atim's eventual recognition of Nassara as what Butler calls "a grievable life." For Haroun and Butler, recognizing our and others' physical vulnerability opens up the possibility of an ethics rooted in "the fundamental sociality of embodied life."[74] As Butler states, "The body implies mortality, vulnerability, agency: the skin and the flesh expose us to the gaze of others, but also to touch, and to violence, and bodies put at risk of becoming the agency and instrument of these as well."[75] Butler is describing the body's susceptibility to affective contagion, its unintended openness to the bodies of others and to the environments and objects through which bodies interact. Recognition of the shared experience of corporeality presents, Butler asserts, an opportunity to analyze and ultimately undo relationships of domination and violence. In the film, it is this emotionally charged process that transforms Atim.

The first shift in Atim's relationship with Nassara can be glimpsed during their second meeting, when Atim returns to the bakery with his gun, prepared to kill. Atim watches Nassara's daily distribution of bread to the children who come for alms. Seeing Atim watching him at a distance, Nassara walks directly toward Atim and stands very close to him. Haroun sets this confrontation as a two-shot close-up of the men's faces to depict the intense emotional energy of the interaction. Nassara looks into Atim's eyes, his face animated by a penetrating glare of suspicion. Atim initially refuses to meet Nassara's gaze. Defiant, he looks down. When Nassara puts an artificial larynx to his throat to ask Atim what he wants, Atim's expression changes. He looks up and into Nassara's eyes. He lifts his head slightly and, after a moment of hesitation, responds to Nassara's question with "not charity," referring to Nassara's handouts to the boys. The hesitation that follows the gaze performs a few seconds of affective potential. Ali Barkai, the actor who plays Atim, attempts to dramatize a body charged with emotion. He consciously uses his body to give the impression that a nonconscious (or preconscious) sensation is moving through him. We are meant to see that Atim has been thrown off by Nassara's injury, which he had not noticed until Nassara placed the mechanical larynx to his throat. (Later, Aïcha tells Atim that Nassara was injured during the war when someone tried to cut his throat.) We know that the gun is in Atim's pocket because an earlier close-up captured his shaky hand fumbling with the weapon. At this point, Atim might have responded to Nassara's question with "your life" and then shot his father's killer. But he does not. Again, there is a delay, a sudden tone of emotion passed between the two men, what Massumi calls "a suspensive interval."[76] In this scene, Haroun stages "the transition from immediately-thinking-feeling-lived to reflectively thought." He aims to highlight the shift from affective potential as "bracingly experienced" and "nonconscious" to "a possibility" that can be consciously imagined and ruminated on.[77] It is a moment bristling with energy.

In subsequent scenes in the bakery, Atim sees Nassara first cut his finger and then injure his back. On both occasions, the film emphasizes Nassara's pain and then, again, draws our attention to Atim's reaction. Atim sees Nassara hurt himself and watches him flinch or writhe in agony; he stops working, seemingly arrested by the experience. He pauses for a few seconds before turning away from Nassara and resuming his work. Atim's reaction indicates that he has been unsettled by the sight of Nassara's injured body. Atim's still, taut body shows Haroun's attempt to depict through film the store of vitality that is affect. These instances of affective exchange between Atim and his father's killer intensify after Aïcha loses her and Nassara's baby. The couple's grief undoes Atim's desire for revenge. The suffering and loss of the other, seen, felt, and finally acknowledged, release Atim from his debt and recalibrate the affective potential away from hate and toward empathy.

At the conclusion of *Daratt*, there is no confession, no forgiveness, and no redemption. Believing that Atim will take him to his father so that Nassara can request permission to adopt him, Nassara follows Atim to the desert where Atim's grandfather waits to witness the execution of the man who murdered his son. But Atim does not carry out his grandfather's demand, nor does he consent to becoming Nassara's son. As Harrow notes, "The commandment to take revenge turns against itself as Atim refuses to be the son, the grandson, or the adopted son of the three fathers who tried to claim him."[78] The grandfather reveals Atim's true identity to Nassara, and Nassara obeys his order to lie on the ground and prepare to be executed. Atim points the gun into the air and shoots away from Nassara, allowing his grandfather to believe that he has avenged his father's death. These acts of refusal—of refusing to forgive Nassara and become his adopted son and also of refusing to murder him—are not performed for the grandfather, whose blindness prevents him from seeing that Atim does not do as he is told. Nor are they for Nassara, to whom Atim does not speak, and because Nassara cannot speak, he cannot narrate closure. The refusals, therefore, remain as unspoken possibilities that do not transform into proclamations or lessons. Instead, Atim's rejection of these fathers suggests a possible future outside credit-debt relationships. If David Graeber is right, the creditor-debtor conflict eliminates relationships of care and the social bonds that such relationships create through its violent imposition of equivalence. At the end of Haroun's film, Atim walks away from the debt forced on him and the violence demanded of him to clear that debt. Instead, he affirms human bonds of dependence and support. He reaches for his grandfather's arm and guides the blind man away from Nassara in an act of care and expression of love.

CONCLUSION

In this chapter, I have suggested that we look to African cinema to explore the various connections between debt and energy in postcolonial contexts. Mambéty and Sissako allude to the historical role of petrodollars in producing and perpetuating the sovereign indebtedness of African states, the burdens of which are imposed on ordinary citizens whose precarious and austere livelihoods, in effect, service public debt. Danya Abt's documentary, analyzed beside Lori Leonard's book, reveals the true costs of the CCPDP by taking account of the extractive debt owed to communities forced to assume the ecological burdens of the project. At the end of *Quel Souvenir*, activist Samuel Nguiffo refers to communities of farmers and fishers in Chad and Cameroon whose livelihoods have been threatened by the pipeline. He says that these most "impoverished communities" have had to "subsidize the oil that benefits the wealthiest states and the consumers in the wealthiest states." *Quel Souvenir* actualizes the unacknowledged and unpaid debts to the citizens of states enriched by petroleum, people who were guaranteed the minimum benefits of modernity, such as schools, roads, clean water, and electricity. Abt amplifies African demands that the Chad and Cameroon governments, the oil companies, and the World Bank make good on their promise of fair compensation. Finally, I have looked to Haroun's films as a debt archive and interpreted *Daratt* as a reflection on sovereign and subjective modes of indebtedness as experienced in a newly oil-rich national context. Although *Daratt* does not address the CCPDP, I show the significance of an energy analytics in relation to debt in two ways. First, I look outside the narrative frame to situate energy—in this case, petroleum infrastructures that are buried beneath the ground, lodged offshore, or threaded through remote regions of Chad—as crucial to the history and politics portrayed in film. Second, I analyze Haroun's cinematic language of embodied energy as expended in physical labor or stored as affective potential. Haroun's *Daratt*, I have argued, creates, on screen, the intimate biopolitical atmospheres experienced by citizens of an indebted petrostate.

In the last decade, the climate crisis and its intensifying impacts have brought climate-debt discourse into the mainstream. The Sixth Assessment Report of the Intergovernmental Panel on Climate Change, released in 2022, emphasizes climate justice in its recommendations related to decarbonization, mitigation, and sustainable development by outlining solutions to global warming that acknowledge "common but differentiated responsibilities" among countries of the global North and South for emitting into the atmosphere and benefiting from unsustainable levels of carbon."[79] The idea of "common but differentiated responsibilities" is not new. Naomi Klein reminds us that it was codified in the 1992 United Nations Framework Convention on Climate Change.[80] In 2010, the World People's Conference on Climate Change and the Rights of Mother Earth went further and called on developed countries to "recognize and honor their climate debt in all of its dimensions as the basis for a just, effective, and scientific solution to climate change" and followed with a detailed set of demands and recommendations. To conclude, I want to underscore that energy debt and energy justice are central to tepid and radical appeals for climate justice as well as those that fall between. As Klein explains, the global South is owed a debt for "the fact that wealthy countries had used up most of the atmospheric capacity for safely absorbing CO_2 before developing countries had a chance to industrialize."[81] African cinema demonstrates that petromodernity remains out of reach for most in the developing world, even though more and more crude extracted from Africa supplies ever-larger global demands. Perhaps equally important, these films depict the interwoven systems of debt and energy created by petromodernity. The films studied in this chapter qualify climate debt discourse by uncovering the violence perpetuated by debt equivalence and emphasizing the mutual obligations of care and support that point toward a just and sustainable planetary politics of the future.

NOTES

1. McClennen, "Rights to Debt," 19.
2. Mitchell, *Carbon Democracy*.
3. Mitchell, *Carbon Democracy*, 183–184; El-Gamal and Jaffe, *Oil, Dollars, Debt, and Crises*, 122.
4. El-Gamal and Jaffe, *Oil, Dollars, Debt, and Crises*, 9.
5. Mitchell, *Carbon Democracy*, 156.
6. Mitchell, *Carbon Democracy*, 214.
7. Baker, "Oil and African Development," 194.
8. Baker, "Oil and African Development," 194.
9. Toussaint and Millet, *Debt, the IMF, and the World Bank*, 52.
10. Toussaint and Millet, *Debt, the IMF, and the World Bank*, 62.
11. Lazzarato, *The Making of the Indebted Man*, 25.
12. Garritano, "Living Precariously in the African Postcolony."
13. Comaroff and Comaroff, *Theory from the South*, 122.
14. McClennen, "Rights to Debt," 14.
15. McClennen, "Rights to Debt," 15.
16. Barr, "Iconographies of Hunger," 74.
17. Graeber, *Debt*, 391.
18. Barr, "Iconographies of Hunger," 75.
19. Wengraf, *Extracting Profit*, 133. Wengraf notes that Exxon produced kerosene from sites in Africa over a century ago, and Britain purchased its first concession to Nigerian oil in 1889.
20. Hicks, *Africa's New Oil*, 4.
21. Wengraf, *Extracting Profit*, 137.
22. McClennen, "Rights to Debt," 14.
23. Tchouaffe, *The Poetics of Radical Hope*, 70.
24. Ince, "Ethics, Universality and Vulnerability," 171.
25. Williams, "Neoliberal Violence," 296.
26. Nagib, *Realist Cinema as World Cinema*, 155.
27. Nagib, *Realist Cinema as World Cinema*, 155.
28. Nagib, *Realist Cinema as World Cinema*, 160.
29. Nagib, *Realist Cinema as World Cinema*, 24.
30. de Luca quoted in Nagib, *Realist Cinema as World Cinema*, 162.

31. REFLUFA, or the Network for the Fight Against Hunger in Cameroon, was established in 2001 to combat the structures that support economic, social, and environmental injustice on a national level.

32. Horta, "Public-Private Partnership and Institutional Capture," 204.

33. Leonard, *Life in the Time of Oil*, 4. Leonard conducted research on the pipeline project in Miandoum canton and several villages near the Miandoum oil field between 2000 and 2014.

34. Leonard, *Life in the Time of Oil*, 5.

35. Horta, "Public-Private Partnership and Institutional Capture," 206.

36. Kretzmann and Nooruddin, "Exec Summary," *Drilling into Debt*, 4.

37. Nooruddin, "The Political Economy of National Debt Burdens," 162, 177.

38. Hicks, *Africa's New Oil*, 26.

39. Hicks, *Africa's New Oil*, 27.

40. Arbogast, "Project Financing," 2.

41. Hicks, *Africa's New Oil*, 47.

42. *Chad Prepays World Bank Pipeline Debt*. However, after this repayment, Chad still had an outstanding debt with the International Finance Corporation, a subsidiary of the World Bank, from which Chad took a 200 million loan to cover its stake in the project.

43. Hicks, *Africa's New Oil*, 54.

44. Hicks, *Africa's New Oil*, 55.

45. My analysis of Abt's documentary draws from two versions of her ongoing project. The first was produced in 2009 and made available to me as a DVD in 2019. The second, much shorter edit of *Quel Souvenir* was prepared as part of a talk she planned to give at my campus in 2020. Unfortunately, her visit had to be canceled due to precautions taken at the onset of the COVID-19 pandemic.

46. Leonard, *Life in the Time of Oil*, 44.

47. Graeber, *Debt*, 16.

48. Leonard, *Life in the Time of Oil*, 44.

49. Leonard, *Life in the Time of Oil*, 69.

50. Graeber, *Debt*, 121.

51. Ferguson, *Global Shadows*, 2005; Appel, *The Licit Life of Capitalism*, 2012; Schareika, "Creative Encounters," 2017.

52. Schareika, "Creative Encounters," 42.

53. Leonard, *Life in the Time of Oil*, 44.

54. Report quoted in Leonard, *Life in the Time of Oil*, 59.

55. Leonard, *Life in the Time of Oil*, 44.

56. Nagib, *Realist Cinema as World Cinema*, 175.

57. Nagib, *Realist Cinema as World Cinema*, 178.

58. Phillips, "Prelude to a Grid," 72.

59. Brinkema, *The Forms of the Affects*, 94.

60. Brinkema, *The Forms of the Affects*, 94.
61. Brinkema, *The Forms of the Affects*, 94.
62. Brinkema, *The Forms of the Affects*, 95.
63. Brinkema, *The Forms of the Affects*, 95.
64. Deleuze, *Cinema 1*, 10.
65. Massumi, *The Power at the End of the Economy*, 44, 70.
66. Thrift, *Non-Representational Theory*, 61.
67. Lazzarato, *Making of the Indebted Man*, 39.
68. Lazzarato, *Making of the Indebted Man*, 42, 49.
69. Oscherwitz, "Review of Mahamat-Saleh Haroun's *Dry Season*," 238.
70. Phillips, "Prelude to a Grid," 75.
71. Phillips, "Prelude to a Grid," 75.
72. Phillips, "Prelude to a Grid," 76.
73. Garritano, "Living Precariously in the African Postcolony."
74. Butler, *Precarious Life*, 28.
75. Butler, *Precarious Life*, 26.
76. Massumi, *The Power at the End of the Economy*, 88.
77. Massumi, *The Power at the End of the Economy*, 75.
78. Harrow, *Trash*, 229.
79. IPCC Sixth Assessment Report, 1–50.
80. Klein, *This Changes Everything*, 410.
81. Klein, *This Changes Everything*, 409.

THREE

Energy Infrastructures and Petronoir Sensibilities in African Cinema

IN THE PREVIOUS CHAPTER, I discussed the role of oil in generating and structuring debt relations in the African postcolony, and I argued for the importance of considering oil in generalizations about the effects of structural adjustment policies on everyday life and on the cultural forms that explore the experiential dimensions of this ordinary *adjusting*, especially in African films about neocolonial indebtedness and normalized economic precarity. This chapter continues to focus on oil, but here I examine the infrastructures through which oil and other sources and forms of energy circulate. Except for the first, *Faat Kiné* (2001), the films discussed in this chapter—*Up at Night* (2019), *Viva Riva!* (2011), and *Grigris* (2013)—deal with patchwork, failed, or underdeveloped energy infrastructures, but they also explore the new labor and social relationships that emerge in response to energy shortage. In other words, these films, by criticizing infrastructural breakdown and failure, make infrastructural demands and, at the same time, testify to the creativity of Africans living with broken and underdeveloped energy infrastructures. The petronoir films *Viva Riva!* and *Grigris*, in particular, might be celebrated as forms of art ingeniously responding to and enabled by infrastructural failure. In these features, African filmmakers repurpose genre to create global films that portray the unequal development generated by oil extraction in Africa.

In the opening section of this chapter, I interpret *Faat Kiné* and *Up at Night* as articulating two iterations of what Stephen Collier calls "infrastructural modernity."[1] In his brilliant book on post-Soviet urban infrastructures, Collier references the work of Paul Edwards to stress the widely accepted belief that infrastructures produce and are produced by modernization. He also contends that infrastructures should be understood as "sociotechnical systems" that both express and support "many forms of infrastructural modernity."[2] The concept of infrastructure as a sociotechnical apparatus derives partly from Foucault's writings about biopolitics. Collier uses *sociotechnical* to refer to systems and mechanisms linked to various iterations of modernity. These biopolitical systems are not purely material, he insists, but are connected to the affective and social dimensions of modernizing projects, like urban development or social welfare, which support particular forms of modernity.[3] In the context of Soviet cities and a "socialist biopolitics," Collier investigates infrastructure "as a political technology."[4] In other words, he demonstrates that particular infrastructures do particular kinds of political work. I make a similar claim about the films I discuss next. These films also use infrastructure to support and project certain kinds of modernity; they deploy, or represent, infrastructures of energy (electricity and gasoline) to give expression to sociotechnical claims about modern citizenship. Considered together, *Faat Kiné* and *Up at Night* invite consideration of a similar infrastructural ideal of universal access to the energies required for citizen-subjects to be modern. However, the films position infrastructure as a component of two different forms of modernity; following Collier's definition of these forms, I suggest that the first form, as seen in *Faat Kiné*, opens infrastructure to "liberalization and marketization." The other, in *Up at Night*, is oriented toward "the equalization of infrastructure provision across national populations" and calls on the state for its guarantee."[5]

Unlike many African films that address or portray energy and its infrastructures, Sembène Ousmane's *Faat Kiné*, a film about the manager of a Total petrol station, Faat Kiné Diop, portrays an African city in which infrastructure works. The flow of energy sources—in this case, gasoline—is unobstructed and plentiful. A striking counterpoint to the petronoir films discussed later in this chapter, *Faat Kiné* depicts a Senegalese "petroutopia," a term borrowed from Stephanie LeMenager, who uses it to describe the "U.S. landscape of highways, low-density suburbs, strip malls, fast food and gasoline service islands, and shopping centers ringed by parking lots or parking towers."[6] In Sembène's film, Dakar is not nearly as urbanized or commercialized as the US landscape LeMenager describes, but it is nonetheless presented as a city in which oil infrastructures generate movement, prosperity, power, and freedom. Not only is petroleum the source of the good life for the film's protagonist; its availability and easy circulation, supported by a well-developed delivery infrastructure, guarantee the movement of people and capital across the city. Cars travel the busy streets of Dakar in an orderly fashion; they do not stall or get stuck in traffic. At some points, people block others' movement by double parking or crossing in front of a car, but any hindrance to mobility is not caused by scarcity of gasoline or a failed infrastructure.

Early in the film, Sembène includes a scene in which we watch gasoline and diesel being delivered to Kiné's Total station in a large tanker truck in the light of day, on time and without incident. (There is no need for black-market petrol in Kiné's Dakar, it seems.) We see Kiné, wearing a white lab coat and holding a laboratory beaker, authoritatively test and verify the quality of the gasoline and diesel before permitting their release into her station's underground tanks. This brief scene, which is completely unnecessary to the plot, shows that Kiné is the boss and is as strong, intelligent, and capable as any man. It also makes an implicit claim about the regulation of gasoline and its infrastructures. As the manager of the Total station and an entrepreneurial subject, Kiné ensures the legitimacy and safety of her product. Similarly, her uniformed and professional employees serve the vehicles that come and go from her station, handing out receipts and restroom keys to paying customers. Kiné's Total gas station, as shown in this scene and throughout the film, demonstrates that a privately owned commercial enterprise operated efficiently, legally, and profitably facilitates and protects the infrastructural modernity promised by oil.

A sexually liberated and economically independent woman, Kiné represents, in the words of Lindsey Green-Simms, "a new type of feminist automobility."[7] She is the hero of the film, a modern woman whose oil-powered economic prosperity affords her freedom of movement through urban space as well as the freedom to dismiss the men who have mistreated her and create a future of her own making. Following Matthew Huber's analysis of oil in the production of the competing individuated subject, we might describe Kiné as an entrepreneurial subject made by petroleum products. For Kiné, petrol acts as "the condition of possibility of an individuated freedom to control space at three critical scales of lived experience—mobility, the home, and the body itself."[8] The film's portrayal of a petroleum-based infrastructural ideal acts as a techno-political machine that enables the creation of a liberal, autonomous subjective agent on which the narrative is built. Perfectly functioning roads, stoplights, oil pipelines, and gasoline pumps as well as a formalized and functioning banking system (even if it loans money at an interest rate too high for Kiné to accept) undergird the self-sufficient and mobile subjectivity modeled by Kiné. Her freedom of movement, lifestyle, sexual freedom, and outspokenness depend on the wealth she derives from Total oil, which flows from the massive infrastructural apparatus that moves crude, gas, and capital around the world.

Because cars so obviously represent Kiné's independence and the film idealizes movement as an expression of modernity, the appearance of two male characters whose disabilities limit their mobility is noteworthy. When Kiné's feminist automobility confronts these characters, who assume minor roles in the film, the purpose seems to be to provide narrative opportunities for Kiné to articulate an ethics of personal responsibility that disavows the structural and economic advantages that sustain her autonomy. The men's bodies, in other words, signify a biopolitical relationship between citizens and the state. The men cannot use their legs, so they rely on the strength of their arms for mobility. Pathé pushes himself on a small cart, and the other man rides a hand-powered bicycle. Early in the film, Pathé is scolded by Kiné when he tells her that his wheelchair—which, she reminds him, she bought for him—was stolen by a couple he allowed to stay with him. The English subtitles render Kiné's response as follows: "Pathé, we felt sorry for you because you are poor. We saved to buy you a wheelchair. You can't find anything better to do than to have a live-in girlfriend? See, I think it's God who is punishing you." Kiné's response to Pathé's need (and his generosity) reveals that the gift of the wheelchair was part of an unspoken contractual arrangement in which he was expected to derive utility from her charity. Kiné's lecture addresses him as an agentive subject, not a human being deserving of support or care, and is meant to shape him into a self-reliant and autonomous citizen. Later in the film, when Kiné hails another man with a disability, riding an arm-powered bike through the streets of Dakar, a man whom she mistakes for Pathé, the film reiterates this lesson in entrepreneurial subjectivity. Kiné offers the man a few bills, which he refuses. He indicates the sign attached to the back of his bike, which explains that he is a messenger for hire and therefore not in need of charity. The exchange is meant to represent a person with a disability as strong, smart, and independent. It highlights and empowers those who have been marginalized by colonialism and capitalism, as is common in Sembène's work. But the scene also promotes an ideal of self-reliance that discourages consideration of social support for those in need and a politics motivated by an obligation of care (and not by entrepreneurial drive). In both scenes, the portrayal of disabled men emphasizes that movement is essential to life and that one bears personal responsibility for making his way.

Faat Kiné's depiction of operative oil infrastructures and the liberating potential of petroleum is unusual. (Indeed, the film's portrayal of capitalism as a force for feminist liberation makes the film an outlier in Sembène's oeuvre.) Failing energy infrastructures and African people's ability to maneuver around and within them are emergent themes across types and genres of African film in recent years. For example, Nelson Makengo's video-art installation *Up at Night* (2019), unlike *Faat Kiné*, makes claims about the state's obligations to build and maintain energy infrastructures. It juxtaposes sound and image to criticize the state's failure to provide the form of modernity that links citizenship to access to a reliable supply of electricity. Shot at night during a power outage, *Up at Night* captures the nighttime sensorium of Kinshasa's unlit streets. The Democratic Republic of the Congo (DRC) is among the world's least electrified nations; power outages like the one documented in the video typically occur as a result of load-shedding, a system of distributing a supply of electricity insufficient to meet demand, that involves deliberately cutting the power supply in certain areas of the city, at certain times, to provide electricity to other neighborhoods or sectors. For over 90 percent of its electricity, DRC relies on hydropower generated from the Inga Dam site on the Inga Rapids of the Congo River, an ambitious multiphase project. More than half of the country's external debt has been allocated for financing the dam project. Since Inga Dam 1 and Inga Dam 2 became operational in 1972 and 1982, respectively, electricity production has been significantly below capacity, impeded by low water levels, political instability, lack of investment, and a poorly maintained and rarely updated infrastructure.[9] Makengo produced his video between December and January 2019, following the democratic elections in DRC. The elections had led to a peaceful transfer of power from President Joseph Kabila, who stepped down after eighteen years, to the newly elected opposition candidate Felix-Antoine Tshisekedi Tshilombo, who promised to prioritize the completion of Inga Dam 3, which had been stalled for many years. The video explores Kinshasa through energy failure and raises critical questions about energy availability and national development.

The short film might best be described as a collection of dimly lit scenes of urban nightlife taking shape around power outages and electrical disconnection. It records and participates in the unexpected forms of sociality that Filip De Boeck has described as "new spheres of social interaction and new coping strategies," which emerge in the shadows and gaps of DRC's failed energy infrastructure.[10] The camera engages interlocutors and observes groups of people as they listen to a radio broadcast or collectively work to secure sources of light. From a distance, it also surveys Kinshasa's unevenly illuminated neighborhoods and streets. Makengo presents the entire installation as a three-way split-screen montage, sometimes replicating a single shot three times, and less frequently showing different angles or views of an object or space in one frame. The repetition of a single image tends to intensify its emotional charge; for example, several close-ups of an elderly woman in the opening and closing scenes heighten the urgency of her appeal. She looks into the camera and explains: "The whole neighborhood is always in the dark. We don't go out at night anymore because of the lack of electricity.... We suffer a lot." She describes her efforts to obtain the cable her neighborhood needs to connect to the electricity grid, and in the closing shot, she appears with a thick and heavy cable wrapped around her shoulders as she describes the benefits promised by connectivity. "We're going to celebrate all these holidays in the light. Our freezers will work again. Our children and grandchildren will be able to watch TV again. We have endured the darkness for too long." The repetition of the single close-up here visually emphasizes the woman's testimony. In another scene, three different shots capture a group of young people placing batteries in flashlights, which they light and string along a cord, perhaps preparing to display them for sale. In this instance, the split screen presents three perspectives of the same place and time and contributes to a sense of redundancy, the feeling that throughout the city, similar activities are repeated as people carry out routine practices to light up an unelectrified night.

The video uses juxtaposition to comment on the failures of postcolonial modernity. Chiaroscuro lighting contrasts the darkness created by the absence of light with the glare of an artificial light source. Makengo creates this striking difference by illuminating his lens with small LED lights similar to those used by the people in the film. This style of lighting transforms darkness into a condition that is lived with and through. It is not just a backdrop against which lighted action takes place; darkness limned by light has presence and form. Another mode of juxtaposition holds audio and image in tension across the three-way montage. Scenes chronicling the banality of a city-wide blackout contradict and disrupt the diegetic and extradiegetic radio broadcasts that narrate official reports of infrastructural development. For example, in the scene described previously, an out-of-frame radio plays while the group puts batteries into the hundreds of flashlights stored in shopping bags (one of which features a picture of President Barack Obama) stacked at their feet. The broadcaster announces that "the extraordinary potential of our country is soaring" and praises the "high-quality cement" produced in DRC, which can build the "homes, roads and infrastructure" the Congolese need. In another segment, a small child sits in shadow, looking directly into the camera with a radio to her ear. An extradiegetic voiceover promises that the Inga Dam 3 will generate an abundance of electricity for Congolese industry and regional consumers.

A final scene of juxtaposition includes two takes, one a close-up of a somber young man, which then cuts to a second shot of the man's hands holding a small transistor radio. In the recording that plays over this montage, President Joseph Kabila lists his administration's accomplishments: "Congo has come a long way . . . access to improved basic services and unprecedented progress in democratization and the rule of law." These divergences of sound and image reveal the massive gap between the official discourse and the reality of a modernity continually deferred. The radio, which provides audio in several episodes of the installation, not only enables this tension between sound and image but also functions as a trope. A common media device that is an essential source of news and information during load-shedding events or in areas with no electricity, the battery-operated transistor radio connotes the success and failure of modern technologies of connectivity. Brian Larkin notes that radio, a colonial technology, was intended to bring colonial subjects into modernity, to connect them across distances of various scales, "inserting them in overlapping, sometimes competing, circuits of political identity."[11] In postcolonial African cities where technological breakdown and disconnection contribute to the rhythms of life, the small battery-powered radio marks both the success and the failures of modernity. Larkin writes: "Media still do the work of representing modernity, circulating information, generating new consumption practices, mediating urban space, and organizing new modes of leisure for individuals and groups. Yet at the same time they signify a lack."[12] In the video, the lack is not linked to radio technology, which functions for the men and women captured by Makengo's camera. Instead, reliance on the radio during a blackout signals lack as related to technologies of electrical production and delivery.

Regarding infrastructure in Nigeria, Larkin describes the autonomous generator as "bear[ing] witness to the collapse of the integrated infrastructuralist idea and reconfiguration of the state's ambition to provide developmental progress."[13] Makenga's short film likewise portrays fragments of night as experienced by those who are disconnected from the nation's electricity network, a situation that necessitates reliance on petroleum-powered generators. A scene shown three times during the twenty-minute installation features a single-shot, thrice repeated across one frame, of gasoline being poured from a blue jerrican and into a yellow generator. (The person pouring the petrol is out of frame.) The scene ends when a small hand, perhaps the hand of a child, places and tightens a cap on the generator's tank. In the first of the three instances, the montage cuts to a tripled long shot of the patchwork illumination of an urban neighborhood at night. The soundscape amplifies the loud hum of a generator, suggesting with editing and sound that a failed electrical infrastructure is the source of the uneven distribution of light made visible in the frame. Like the American films noir studied by Patrick Keating, *Up at Night* "use[s] artificial light to comment on modernity—in particular, that aspect of modernity concerned with the spread of industrialization into everyday life as manifested in the diffusion of electrical technologies into public and private space."[14] But in this installation, patches of bright light in a dark cityscape make visible the limited diffusion of electricity.

AFRICAN PETRONOIR CINEMA

Up at Night renders noir as a material experience, while the feature films *Viva Riva!* and *Grigris* adopt the generic conventions of films noir to imagine African criminal networks that exploit gasoline shortages and stoppages. In these films, set in Kinshasa and N'Djaména, respectively, the smuggling of petroleum across national borders moves narratives forward and leads to extreme violence and ruthless immorality. Protagonist Riva returns to his family home in Kinshasa from Angola with a truck of stolen gasoline in Djo Tunda Wa Munga's *Viva Riva!* Cesar, the Angolan crime boss who owns the gas, chases Riva to Kinshasa, where he and his gang search the city for Riva, murdering anyone who interferes. Mahamat-Saleh Haroun's film *Grigris* follows the dancer Souleymane, also known as Grigris, who steals barrels of smuggled gasoline from his boss Moussa in part because his stepfather is sick, and Grigris needs money to pay for his care and medicine. Both films retool the narrative and formal conventions of noir films to challenge the false promise of petroleum-based prosperity for countries in the global South. At the same time, they narrate and, as cinematic forms, exemplify the modes of creativity and labor that flourish in the ruins of infrastructural modernity.

These films are about energy infrastructures, but, of course, they are produced within and shaped by evolving media infrastructures. Since the 1990s, major structural changes have radically extended and diversified the African cinema and media landscapes.[15] I have discussed some of these changes, particularly relating to African auteur directors, in the introduction to this book. More crucial to the hybrid, transnational films analyzed here are the availability of new production technologies and an exponential increase in channels and platforms of distribution. This has led to various forms of commercial and independent filmmaking in Africa and throughout the diaspora. These new systems and infrastructures of finance, production, and distribution have also given African filmmakers new ways of collaborating on an international scale. Additionally, the global expansion of film festivals, described by many critics as global "festivalization," has provided African filmmakers with unprecedented opportunities to share and promote their work and to access global cinema and media networks. Boukary Sawadogo, referencing the writing of Jedlowski, uses the term *transnationalization* to describe the wide range of these recent changes, which have created the conditions necessary for the emergence of new types and forms of African media and film as well as ever-growing numbers of productions.[16] In the twenty-first century, the boundary around the objects of study defined by the phrase *African cinema* has become much less solid; it is bigger, messier, more dynamic, and more flexible than it seemed when African cinema, for the most part, meant serious, francophone films by African filmmakers and when film distributor California Newsreel was responsible for preserving the canon of African cinema.

Djo Tunda Wa Munga's thriller *Viva Riva!* is one of several recent African urban crime films and dark thrillers. This group of films, which includes titles such as *Confusion Na Wa* (Nigeria, 2013), *Burn It Up Djassa* (Ivory Coast, 2012), *Nairobi Half-Life* (Kenya, 2012), *Death for Sale* (Morocco, 2012) and *Zero* (Morocco, 2012), represents some of the most exciting and novel forms of filmmaking from African filmmakers today. Suzanne Gauch's observation that Moroccan films noir "have taken a globally popular genre with multiple origins, and wide-ranging and varied features, and have at once highlighted its provincial origins and refashioned it into a uniquely global Moroccan genre" might be expanded to include this group of films, adjusting the national context in each case.[17] These African films noir challenge the socialist-realist approach to reading African cinema, which, as Gauch notes, "neglects the importance of genre, style, and aesthetics" and freezes African film as a reflection of "local, forever exotic, realities."[18] Wa Munga addresses the question of genre directly, explaining that he wanted to make a film that was widely accessible and therefore drew on elements of film noir—"the femme fatale, the money, the villains"—to achieve this goal.[19] With support from Canal Plus in France, *Viva Riva!* traveled through festival networks as a high-brow African film, despite being influenced by Hollywood gangster and noir themes in its narrative, style, and sensibility. As Pier Paolo Frassinelli wrote, Wa Munga "impos[es]" the history and geography of Kinshasa on a genre associated with "Western mass cultural production and commercial cinema and fiction."[20] I agree that Wa Munga extends the boundaries of genre, but not only because he sets his film in Kinshasa. In turning noir toward petrocapitalism in the African postcolony, he expands the genre to explore the technopolitical dimensions of energy infrastructures as expressions of modernity.

Petroleum smuggling flourishes in DRC, Chad, and other African countries due to several interconnected factors, primary among which is that Africa lacks refining capacity to meet the growing demand for gasoline and diesel, particularly in urban areas experiencing increases in population and car ownership.[21] In some parts of Africa, bad roads and political instability also contribute to chronic fuel shortages and high prices at the pump. Global pricing dynamics and economies of scale further disadvantage African downstream petroleum markets. Gasoline and diesel, where available, are expensive: shipping crude and petroleum products to African countries in relatively small quantities is costly, and small African markets do not benefit from effective competition.[22]

The opening montage of *Viva Riva!* establishes the lack of fuel as the event that precipitates the story's progression. In the highly stylized opening montage, a fast-paced series of shots detached from character or point of view sets up the scenario into which Riva and his stolen cargo of gasoline enter. Wa Munga begins with an establishing shot above a city street overrun with crowds of people walking, not driving. The camera then cuts and fades rapidly through a series of images of hands counting money, of petrol being poured or siphoned from plastic containers into cars, and of stalled and parked vehicles. This epilogue-like montage concludes with a subjective long take of a sign that reads "Plus de Carburant" (No Fuel Left). The shot then passes a line of cars waiting at a gas pump, their owners shouting in frustration, and finally slides into the dark gasoline tank of a parked car. The opening associates gasoline with thwarted mobility, corruption, scarcity, and delay, and yet, quick cutting and a fast-moving camera create a sensation of flow that contrasts with the scenes of immobility. This sense of movement anticipates Riva's return and the gasoline hustle he orchestrates.

Fig. 3.1 Petroleum for sale on the roadside near Damango, Northern Region, Ghana. 2023. Photo by author. © Carmela Garritano.

Henrik Gustafsson makes a compelling case for understanding film noir as an expression of motion, energy, and affect, instead of relying only on formalist or narrative-based methods rooted in generic features. Although Gustafsson only discusses American and European films produced in the twentieth century, his analysis of the "erratic mobility of noir" resonates with *Viva Riva!*[23] Opening in motion, the film continues to portray energy and movement. In Gustafsson's words, it seems "impelled by a certain thrust steering toward the edges of the world, rupturing its borders."[24] The feature film begins with Riva at the bow of a swiftly moving wooden barge loaded with barrels of stolen gasoline. The boat is paddled quietly downriver by a group of men that transports smuggled fuel from Angola to Congo across the Congo River. From there, black-market petrol rolls easily into a city crowded with stalled vehicles that wait for gasoline. Gauch describes the young male protagonists of the Moroccan noir films she analyzes as "urban, largely uneducated yet street-smart" who get ahead by "twist[ing] in their favor the intertwined, local, transnational, and global networks of power and economic status."[25] This describes Riva, too, and more broadly applies to the figure of the petrol smuggler, an emergent character-type prevalent in the films discussed here.[26] Riva is a playboy and hustler who accumulates social and economic capital by navigating between transnational and local oil infrastructures. He is always in motion, an example of what Karen Bouwer in her analysis of the film calls "lively mobility."[27] Riva's appearance in Kinshasa causes trouble for his friend J.M. by putting him in motion, too, luring J.M. from his wife, children, and home and pulling him into crime and immorality. Riva liberates his love interest Nora from her entrapment in Azor's big house, and the gangsters follow Riva from Angola to a barn on the outskirts of Kinshasa, where the plot ends in violence and fire. Riva's good looks, generosity, and swagger pull others, including the audience, into his orbit. However, he is at once attractive and reprehensible; his appetite for women and power goes too far, perpetuating exploitative sex and violence.

In *Viva Riva!*, power outages occur regularly, but at no point do they halt the action or foil plans. (The electricity fails during Riva's first night in Kinshasa, in fact, but the partying continues.) The Kinshasa residents, as represented in the film, have clearly developed ways to manage the failure of nationwide electrification. Irregular electrification, an important part of the setting, like crumbling buildings and cratered streets, serves as evidence of the deterioration of public infrastructures and the erosion of modernity. *Viva Riva!* visualizes ugliness in excess, using an oversaturated color scheme to direct attention to Kinshasa's landscape. In scene after scene, we are made to confront infrastructural breakdown, a kind of hyperugliness deliberately emphasized. On the drive from the river where the gasoline is loaded onto a rundown cargo truck and transported into the city, the camera speeds past lines of dilapidated shacks, an auto yard littered with car parts, and piles of burning garbage smoldering in an open lot. The reunion between Riva and J.M. at the entry to J.M.'s house once again highlights disrepair. The frame remains wide to bring the litter, sludge, broken pavement, and crumbling walls into visibility. In another scene, the overcrowded and rusted train Cesar disembarks pulls into a derelict station on the only track not covered in weeds and trash. Later in the film, when Madame Commandante leads the gangsters to the stolen gas held in a warehouse on the city's outskirts, the camera follows her sandaled feet, in bright white socks, as she weaves through concrete rocks, mud puddles, and garbage. And as if the extremely ugly setting were not enough, the Angolan gangsters make numerous comments on the filth of

Kinshasa and the corruption of the Congolese. Following the Commandante, Cesar sarcastically says: "Kinshasa the beauty. Kinshasa the garbage.... Your country is the worst shit pile I have ever seen."

In this artfully colorized film, the vibrant ugly replaces the wet darkness of noir to re-create something of Kinshasa's sensorium. And like the metaphorical function of darkness in films noir, the many images of infrastructural decay and breakdown in *Viva Riva!* exceed their function as markers of setting and indicate immorality and corruption. Cesar and his men brutalize their enemies; the film portrays their attacks as excessively and sadistically violent. Decay eats away at state and other formal institutions charged with the protection of the public good. Agents of the state (police, military officers, and border patrol authorities) as well as members of the Catholic church engage in illegal and immoral activities for self-enrichment. When Cesar arrives in the city, his taxi takes him to the army barracks where Madame Commandante stays, and the camera captures a large sign that reads "La Discipline Est La Mere des Armees" (Discipline is the mother of the army), a motto rendered ironic by the entire plot of the film. No relationship, including friendship and love, is safe from filth and corruption. Friends turn against each other, and sex is voyeuristic, sordid, and graphic, a point best exemplified by Riva's first encounter with Nora. He follows her from the dance floor and secretly watches her urinate. Like the trash-strewn streets of the city, everything and everyone in Kinshasa is dirty.

PIPELINE PROMISES AND GASOLINE SMUGGLERS IN GRIGRIS

Frequently described as the largest private investment in sub-Saharan Africa, the Chad-Cameroon Petroleum Development and Pipeline Project implemented groundbreaking strategies to mitigate financial and environmental risks, compensate communities for losses incurred as a result of the project, and direct oil revenue toward poverty alleviation and development. According to anthropologist Lori Leonard, author of *Life in the Time of Oil: A Pipeline and Poverty in Chad*, the project was praised as a model for "a new generation of efforts" to promote development by creating policies to guarantee that oil wealth would support good governance and promote poverty reduction.[28] It initially involved a consortium of transnational oil companies, led by Exxon-Mobil, the World Bank, and the governments of Chad and Cameroon. The plan included the development of three oil fields in southern Chad at Komé, Miandoum, and Bolobo and the construction of more than six hundred miles of underground pipeline through which crude extracted in Chad would be transported through Cameroon to oil tankers off the coastal town of Kribi. The project cost more than four billion dollars and has been projected to produce one billion barrels of oil over a thirty year period.

In part, the World Bank's involvement in the project was meant to ease concerns about the ability of the Chadian government, under President Déby, to manage oil revenues for national development given the country's history of civil unrest and the Déby regime's corruption and disregard for human rights. For the World Bank, the best approach to achieving this "involved integrating Chad into global markets through the sale of Chadian oil, reforming governance, and building institutional capacity in Chad to manage the emerging oil economy."[29] Key to this objective was Law 001, which was passed by the National Assembly in 1998 and required that revenues from oil be held in an escrow account in London and disbursed by a third party. It also mandated that 10 percent of oil revenues be deposited into a "Future Generations Fund" and that most of the remaining revenue be dedicated to five areas of concerns, which included education, health, and poverty reduction.

As Haroun's films remind us, civil unrest and armed resistance by rebel groups since the late 1990s were met with unyielding repression and military aggression by the government. Fighting in western Sudan spilled into Chad in 2003, escalating an already dire situation, until 2005 when Sudan recalled its ambassador from Chad and launched a "proxy war by sponsoring the various new groupings of Chadian rebels."[30] To fund his ongoing military campaigns against rebels, Déby needed oil money, and Law 001 hindered his regime's efforts to buy military arms and equipment. Celeste Hicks reports that "the rigidity of the spending priorities enshrined in Law 001 soon came to be viewed by many in the Chadian government as external interference in a sovereign state's business."[31] In 2005, after Déby amended the constitution to end presidential term limits, rebel groups escalated their efforts to topple his government. That same year, President Déby announced that his administration planned to amend Law 001 to allow his government greater flexibility and autonomy, especially concerning the use of oil revenues for "security spending."[32] The World Bank saw this move as a violation of the project's terms and, in 2008, withdrew its support.

After the World Bank pulled out of the project and demanded full repayment of its investment, Chad negotiated the construction of a refinery in Djérmaya, about thirty miles north of N'Djaména, with the China National Petroleum Corporation International Chad (CNPCIC).[33] In exchange for the rights to crude extracted from the Bonger Basin, the CNPCIC promised to develop infrastructure, including roads and, most importantly, an oil refinery. The refinery was meant to "finally give ordinary Chadian citizens a taste of the benefits of their country's oil production through the promise of cheaper fuel and an extra 20 megawatts of electricity generation."[34] However, since the refinery began production in 2011, numerous disputes between Chad and its Chinese partners over pricing have frequently delayed or stopped output.[35] In his book *Untapped: The Scramble for Africa's Oil*, John Ghazvinian emphasizes the ugly irony of this unequal oil development. Ghazvinian visits Chad years after the project's completion and describes purchasing black-market petrol from roadside vendors. He reports that he did not see one gas station during his time traveling the country.[36]

Grigris shows viewers nothing of the pipeline project. It's not referenced in the narrative, nor is oil pipeline infrastructure featured as part of the landscape (as is seen, for example, in the documentary *Quel Souvenir*, discussed in the previous chapter). This is partly because the film is set in and around N'Djaména, which is approximately 270 miles north of the Doba oil fields. Petrocapitalism, however, is central to the film's plot and to the everyday precarity that influences its setting and tone. As Leonard remarks: "In Chad, development dreams have always hinged on oil. For more than a quarter of a century people anticipated oil and talked about it. Oil was something out there on the horizon, a harbinger of hope and the promise of a future that would be different."[37] Examining *Grigris* with a focus on energy highlights the significant gap between the billions of dollars invested in off-shore and inland crude extraction across Africa and the severe underdevelopment of infrastructures to produce and deliver fuel to African consumers. Haroun's film suggests that oil's promise of the good life has been withheld from most, but that in the small spaces of oil infrastructures, people find new ways to make money and secure their futures.

Grigris has much in common with Haroun's *Daratt*, discussed in chapter 2. Its style is slow and contemplative; it is an art film that borrows from film noir (unlike *Via Riva!*, which tends toward a noir thriller). Set in N'Djaména, the story, like Haroun's earlier films, follows a young man who struggles to maintain a secure life for himself and family. The movie also focuses on work and male bodies at work. *Grigris* is set at around the same time as the film's release, but the civil war, a major event in Haroun's earlier films, is not referenced. There is peace in the city, but its residents still experience economic instability. Souleymane and his family live in a modest home in an impoverished part of the city where the streets are unpaved and few dwellings appear to have electricity. Souleymane does not own a cell phone, the family does not have a car, and electricity is used very sparingly. (Souleymane sews with a manual machine and only plugs in lights when he organizes his studio for his girlfriend Mimi's series of portraits.)

The film's first ten minutes introduce Souleymane (Grigris) as a young man with a disability caused by muscular atrophy of one leg, who, nevertheless, works tirelessly to care for his mother and stepfather. He sews in his stepfather's tailoring business and develops photographs there, too. Souleymane accompanies his mother to the river, where the two wash clothes by hand and then struggle to push their cart loaded with laundry across town, delivering clean clothes to customers even as the sun sets. Haroun also emphasizes that Souleymane performs as a dancer for money. Dance is work. Justin Izzo makes a related point, claiming that "Haroun never quite lets viewers forget" that Grigris's performances "are, first and foremost, forms of labor."[38] The film's opening credits play over a scene, staged as a tableau, featuring one of Grigris's performances. Importantly, Haroun interrupts the dance with a series of crowd shots that show how Grigris puts his body and strength on display for the pleasure of the paying audience. The dance itself is a feat of agility and endurance. Grigris manages to overcome and also exploit his disability; the dance is alluring largely because Souleymane dances with and despite his atrophied leg. Mary Ellen Higgins calls Souleymane's dancing "a mix of disability and agility, injury and maneuverability, strenuous bodily labor and aesthetic pleasure."[39] Importantly, the camera continues to follow Souleymane after his show. Shot from behind, he walks with an unusually pronounced limp as he leaves the club. When the nightclub's manager (or owner) approaches Grigris with a small bundle of cash, Grigris's glare expresses his anger at the pittance he has earned. In a later scene, Grigris, desperate to pay for his stepfather Ayoub's medical expenses, appears to audition for work as a dancer in another venue. His performance is evaluated by a man in the empty theater who watches in silence. Souleymane performs in an open space, without crowds or music, which accentuates the intensity and physicality of his routine as well as the demands he makes of his body. His dancing, daring and disjointed, seems powered by jolts of electricity. When Souleymane finishes, the man for whom he dances does not applaud or speak but only casts his gaze downward. In the following scene, Grigris sits alone on a park bench, where he props up and gently rubs his atrophied leg, suggesting that he is in pain and disappointed because, it seems, he was not hired. In every instance, the film reminds us that Souleymane performs only for the promise of payment.

Janet Roitman's research on the emergence of unregulated commercial networks in the Chad Basin provides insight into the economic relationships attached to energy infrastructures as shown in *Grigris*. Roitman details "transformations in the way in which the economy (or more specifically 'the economic') is transcribed in national space" under global processes.[40] She explores frontier markets that flourish "in the peripheries of the infrastructures of state power" and documents the normalization of petro smuggling and other forms of illegal economic activity as legitimate labor in these commercial zones.[41] Roitman's research also shows that these forms of business and labor are widely regarded as legitimate work that provides "a means to participate in prevailing modes of accumulation and prevailing methods of governing the economy."[42] These illegal economic activities are widely accepted partly because they imitate and repeat legal methods of accumulating and governing even while "circumventing government."[43] In the African petronoir films, trading in stolen gasoline raises no alarms and brings no punishment; it seems to be an ordinary way of accumulating wealth and building social relationships. Indeed, the wealth and status of Souleymane's boss Moussa suggest that smuggling is a highly lucrative enterprise. *Grigris*'s sole focus on Souleymane shows that he joins the gang of petroleum smugglers because he needs a job. Moussa and his gangsters refer to what they do as "business," and the number of people who come to Moussa to buy cans and bottles of fuel and the frequency of the petroleum runs signal a high demand for black-market petrol.

The films present two distinct configurations of illegal trade networks for moving and selling petrol. In *Viva Riva!*, as previously explained, state officials actively participate in transnational petrol smuggling, while in *Grigris*, the gangsters move illegal goods with no support from government officials and successfully evade the police. Indeed, the Chadian state is noticeably absent from Haroun's *Grigris*, failing to protect or support citizens. The clinic where Ayoub receives treatment, which we can assume is part of the state health care system, appears to be understaffed and lacking proper equipment. Ayoub must pay to receive treatment, and the only people we see attend to the sick man's needs are family members. Determined to buy the medicines his father needs, Grigris obtains a loan from a wealthy businessman, referred to as Alhaji. It seems that Souleymane has no access to formal economic support, whether loan or charity. The police appear twice during nighttime smuggling operations, but they are unable to apprehend Moussa and his gang of smugglers. In a car chase through the dark streets of N'Djaména, Souleymane and the gang members easily evade the police and secure for Moussa an SUV loaded with jerricans of stolen petrol. When the gangsters assault Souleymane and threaten his life, he ignores Mimi's advice to seek police assistance. Instead, they leave the city, saying goodbye to friends and families, and travel far into the bush to stay with Mimi's friend Fatimé, who lives in a tiny, remote village beyond the reach of the national electrical grid and state radio broadcasts.

Although the country's social and security services as well as its health care infrastructure, as portrayed in the film, have not benefited from oil development, Hicks notes that the city of N'Djaména has been "transformed" by the construction of new and paved roads around the city.[44] Haroun's portrayal of Moussa's smuggling operations also aligns with Roitman's observation that oil wealth "has brought brand-new, four-wheel-drive vehicles, satellite phones and computers and cash" into the country's frontier zones.[45] Souleymane has access to these oil-based forms of mobility and connectivity only after he joins Moussa's business, and his use of them is linked directly to his labor. He drives an SUV with smuggled fuel through the city streets at night, using a mobile phone to communicate with his employer. For Souleymane, Moussa represents not only economic opportunity but also social capital and connection. The film again clarifies Roitman's assertion that these networks provide benefits beyond the economic; they "guarantee forms of protection; and they offer sociability to people who are often marginalized."[46] Moussa offers his protection to Grigris right at the beginning of the film. He warns the manager of the club where Grigris dances not to cheat him: "This is my man.... If you ever try to rip him off, I won't be happy." Moussa betrays this vow of friendship when he insults Mimi, and it is this act that turns Souleymane against him.

In *Carbon Democracy*, Timothy Mitchell documents the transition from coal to oil-based fuel products and the shift in labor relations that followed. Mitchell claims that oil significantly limited workers' opportunities to control the flow of energy and, subsequently, to gain and assert political power. Expanding on Mitchell's points and directing attention toward infrastructure, Darin Barney explains that oil, unlike coal, is "a commodity whose material properties lent themselves to movement via infrastructures (pipelines and tankers) that required less human labor and were more flexible [than those used to transport coal], thereby reducing the impact of disruption and undermining or sabotaging the growing political power of organized workers."[47] The materiality of oil, in particular its flexibility and fluidity, made its transport in massive quantities feasible, while the tanker ship, invented in the nineteenth century, meant that, unlike coal, "oil could be moved cheaply between continents. From the 1920s onwards, about sixty to eighty percent of world oil production was exported. So much oil was moved across oceans that, by 1970, oil accounted for sixty percent of seaborne cargo worldwide."[48] Petrol smuggling, like piracy, evidences the success of highly efficient, transnational infrastructures, which, as Larkin notes, generate "possibilities for their own corruption, placing in motion the potential for other sets of relations to occur."[49] The petronoir films discussed here demonstrate that the same qualities that enable oil's planetary power, its liquidity and lightness, facilitate the redirection of its flow by fuel "pirates," making it a valuable black-market commodity. Oil-derived liquid fuel flows with relative ease and speed from global infrastructural networks into much smaller containers that people can transport furtively on roads and river passages. The films make no reference to the transnational infrastructures—pipelines, ship channels, or roads—that deliver crude products to local agents. We do not know if the gasoline was stolen from an African refinery, drained from a tanker truck, stolen from a barge, or bunkered from a pipeline. Our focus, instead, is drawn to those who capture liquid fuel and forge an illegal channel for its distribution. In petronoir African films, the labor of those who reroute gasoline is "infrastructural," in the sense developed by Degani. The smugglers create new pathways for energy and extend its reach.[50] Contrary to Mitchell, we might argue that the smuggler's sabotage, made possible by oil's materiality, manipulates the movement of oil, not by stoppage, as was the case with coal, but by redirection. Although not explicitly political, like a coal workers' strike, smuggling is still an approach used within and against an energy infrastructure by those with limited or no access to the benefits it delivers.

Both petronoir films also show that smuggling gasoline creates an intimate and dangerous connection between people and fuel.[51] In places with well-developed and maintained energy infrastructures, gasoline and diesel remain hidden from human senses and bodies are protected from exposure to toxicity. In smuggling, the films emphasize, the human body works as a hinge or node that links oil infrastructures. We see men sucking and siphoning gasoline into drums and jerricans, containers that they then haul and unload. (Moussa remarks on how much he loves the smell of petrol.) To underscore this bodily intimacy, *Viva Riva!* and *Grigris* shift the focus from the infrastructural origins of the stolen fuel and instead center their stories around isolated transfer points where men exert their labor power to move containers of black-market fuel along remote river crossings, through clandestine alleys too narrow for automobiles, and into urban markets. *Grigris*, in particular, provides a close look at the male body as a fuel-transport machine, emphasizing the risk involved in smuggling jerricans filled with fuel across a national border. The film follows Grigris, Moussa, and the other men from the very start of their work, which, like Riva's transport route in *Viva Riva!*, begins on a river, a passageway free of the infrastructures associated with legitimate trade, such as checkpoints. In this case, it is the Logone River, the natural border separating Chad and Cameroon.[52] To get the job, Grigris lied to Moussa, assuring him that he can swim and is strong enough to handle the physical demands of the work. But maneuvering large jerricans of petrol across a river from Cameroon to Chad and then through narrow concrete canals in N'Djaména proves too much for Souleymane. He struggles in the deep water and has to be rescued, and when the police arrive, he threatens the gang's escape because he cannot run as fast as the other men. At the end of the scene, Moussa angrily tells him: "This is not a job for you. You're fired." Throughout the duration of the sequence, Haroun brings the camera close to the men's straining and glistening bodies as they swim beside, pull, carry, and load gasoline-filled containers. The men, the jerricans of fuel, and the ropes work as a loose configuration of bodies and things, each connected to another and reliant on human and nonhuman flow and energy to move. Grigris's weakness disrupts the arrangement.

Dramatic violence ignites in the tense climaxes of both petronoir films. After a protracted scene of murder and torture at the warehouse where Riva has hidden Cesar's fuel, Madame Commandante launches a projectile grenade into the gasoline-filled barrels stacked in the back of the truck where the gasoline is stored. The ignited petrol explodes instantly, a visual spectacle that stresses the destructive potential of oil. Although it is men who perpetuate sadistic and brutal acts of violence in *Viva Riva!*—often in dark and isolated indoor areas like the inside of the warehouse—it is the women who are responsible for the violent murder that concludes *Grigris*. In the bright light of the sun, the women of the village where Souleymane and Mimi have taken shelter gather in an open field to kill the gangster who has been sent by Moussa to murder Souleymane for stealing his fuel. The women surround the gangster and beat him to death with clubs and sticks. They take no pleasure in the act, nor do they achieve any kind of cathartic release. Haroun's camera tracks across the women's faces from below to accentuate their flat affect, while the soundtrack amplifies the horrible rhythm of the women's weapons striking the gangster's body. A match is struck to light the fire that burns the dead gangster and his car, and the women vow to take the secret of their crime to the grave. The women's solidarity and allegiance to their guests contrast with the self-serving and transactional nature of the male social relationships centered around Moussa. Moussa supports and protects Souleymane as long as his work benefits Moussa's business enterprise. Souleymane mistakes Moussa for a friend, so when Moussa demands that Souleymane end his relationship with Mimi, Souleymane feels betrayed and so betrays Moussa by stealing and selling his gasoline. These continuous betrayals and acts of retribution by men stop only when the village women collectively decide to defend the young couple who have come to stay with them, jeopardizing their own well-being to help the strangers.

Finally, neither film offers much hope for the children whose presence signals the ethical obligations the present owes to the future. Anton, the street hustler whom Riva befriends, pretends to drive away from the scene of the murders and explosion with a bag of cash, but he is playing a game of make-believe. The pleasure he derives from this imaginative play affirms the gender difference that supports a masculine fantasy of wealth and unrestricted mobility. This is the same fantasy that seems to have motivated Riva's return to his hometown, his attempt to make good by his parents, and his seduction of the femme fatale, Nora. It is a fantasy expressed in fast cars and stacks of cash. Perhaps *Grigris*, unlike *Viva Riva!*, allows for the possibility of a less energy-intensive, less economized, and instrumentalized future. The ending of the film might imply that the village offers Mimi's unborn baby the love of community as well as peace and safety. However, the villagers are impoverished and marginalized, and their community is organized by gender differences, just like the petrol-smuggling gangs it opposes. (The women tend to home while the men harvest the farms.) At the end, Mimi and Souleymane are alive and well, but the somber mood of the final scene hints at an uncertain future.

This chapter has drawn on energy humanities scholarship to analyze energy infrastructure as portrayed in three feature films—*Faat Kiné*, *Viva Riva!*, and *Grigris*—and one video-art installation, *Up at Night*. In *Faat Kiné*, I explored infrastructural modernity and the entrepreneurial subjects it creates. I suggest that Sembène's film provides a striking counterpoint to the other films, which in various ways are sharply critical of modernity's infrastructural failures as related to energy. *Up at Night* captures the experiential aspects of power outages, a defining feature of Kinshasa's nightlife, and gives expression to people's desire for a more effective infrastructure. *Viva Riva!* and *Grigris* retool the narrative and formal conventions of film noir to challenge the false promise of petroleum-based prosperity for countries in the global South. These petronoir films disconnect oil wealth from shared or widespread prosperity and tie it to illegal and violent activities that hinder development.

Clearly, the films studied in this chapter do not aim to uncover environmental violence or propose a politics or an ethics for the Anthropocene. These films do not criticize extraction economies or the world's dependence on fossil fuels. So what is their role in relation to global warming and energy justice? These four films portray what Jennifer Wenzel, following James Ferguson, describes as "Africans' just desires for inclusion and a better life."[53] The films make us aware of what we know but take for granted: that modern ways of life depend on access to affordable energy and fuel. In *Up at Night*, an elderly woman wants electricity to power her refrigerator and television. She and her neighbors wish for streetlights so they feel safe at night. The figure of the petrol smuggler in *Viva Riva!* and *Grigris* not only converts infrastructural failure into economic opportunity; he also embodies a masculine longing for status and mobility. In *Faat Kiné*, Kiné's strength is derived from the flow of fuel through oil infrastructures. Her wealth undergirds her independence, and the film celebrates her, at least in part, because she has fought her way into the male realm of gasoline and automobiles. Put another way, these films creatively narrate "developmentalist structures of feeling on which petromodernity is grounded," but, crucially, from the perspective of those denied modernity's promise of human flourishing.[54]

In the final chapter of *The Climate of History in a Planetary Age*, Dipesh Chakrabarty asks us "to work toward a planet that no longer belongs to the human-dominant order that European empires, postcolonial and modernizing nationalisms, and capitalist and consumerist globalization created over the last five hundred years."[55] His book puts human-centered philosophy and theory in conversation with posthumanism and earth systems science to make room for the discussion of political and humanist ideas that involve the planetary and the nonhuman in order to address the climate crisis in a meaningful way. Like Wenzel, Chakrabarty argues that our efforts to generate this "new politics" must come to terms with "the desire to be modern that anticolonial ideologies of the twentieth century expressed" and that have been "stoked by a global-imperial and expanding universe of travel, exposure, and cosmopolitan conversations that were in turn made possible by the extensive use of energy extracted from fossil fuel."[56] Chakrabarty traces the origins of this "third-world desire for energy-intensive, mostly fossil-fuel driven modernization" to developing-world intellectuals such as Senghor and Nkrumah, men of the generation of African nationalists whose portraits adorn the walls of Faat Kiné's home.[57] Twenty-first-century African petronoir films demonstrate the intensity still attached to this endlessly deferred achievement of modernity. Drawing out the ideological and affective aspects of energy infrastructures, these African films craft story worlds out of infrastructural longing as it is experienced by people who continue to lack the basic benefits of modern life. More crucially, the films generate a series of ethical and political issues fundamental to our advocacy for the planet and for those in the global South whose lack of infrastructural modernity has subsidized the energy-intensive consumption normalized in the global North. African cinema reminds us that our efforts to address climate crisis and break free from fossil fuels cannot disregard the modest and justified energy longings given expression in African cinema.

NOTES

1. Collier, *Post-Soviet Social*, 206.
2. Collier, *Post-Soviet Social*, 205.
3. Collier, *Post-Soviet Social*, 205.
4. Collier, *Post-Soviet Social*, 20, 205.
5. Collier, *Post-Soviet Social*, 206. Collier refers to Stephan Graham and Simon Marvin's 2002 book *Splintering Modernism* to describe these two moments of infrastructural modernity.
6. LeMenager, *Living Oil*, 74.
7. Green-Simms, *Postcolonial Automobility*, 185.
8. Huber, *Lifeblood*, 73.
9. See Gnassou, "Addressing Renewable Energy Conundrum" and *Country Energy Report*. Scholarly sources consulted include Oyewo et al., "Repercussion of Large Scale Hydro Dam Deployment"; McDonald, *Electric Capitalism*.
10. De Boeck, "'Divining' the City," 50.
11. Larkin, *Signal and Noise*, 49.
12. Larkin, *Signal and Noise*, 63.
13. Larkin, *Signal and Noise*, 244.
14. Keating, "Film Noir and the Culture of Electric Light," 60.
15. Adejunmobi, "Evolving Nollywood Templates"; Farahman, "Disentangling the International Festival Circuit"; Garritano, "Introduction: Nollywood."
16. Sawadogo, *West African Screen Media*, 15.

17. Gauch, "Darker Vision," 339.
18. Gauch, "Darker Vision," 339.
19. Stephen Saito, "Djo Munga Celebrates *Viva Riva!*" *IFC*, June 7, 2011.
20. Frassinelli, "Heading South," 297.
21. The statement is supported by many of the sources I consulted for this chapter. See, for example, Ghazvinian, *Untapped*; Hicks, *Africa's New Oil*; Leonard, *Life in the Time of Oil*; and Gary and Reisch, "Chad's Oil," 15.
22. Matthews, "Opportunities and Challenges," 83.
23. Gustafsson, "A Wet Emptiness," 60.
24. Gustafsson, "A Wet Emptiness," 50.
25. Gauch, "Darker Vision," 340.
26. The 2021 documentary *Zinder* by Aicha Macky, set in an impoverished urban neighborhood in Niger, features several characters who work as petrol smugglers. Among them is a transgender woman, Ramatou, who, like Faat Kiné, succeeds in a hypermasculine economic sphere and whose power comes from her ability to navigate transnational petrol networks.
27. Bouwer, "Life in Cinematic Urban Africa," 71.
28. Leonard, *Life in the Time of Oil*, 4.
29. Leonard, *Life in the Time of Oil*, 5.
30. Hicks, *Africa's New Oil*, 26.
31. Hicks, *Africa's New Oil*, 27.
32. Arbogast, "Project Financing," 2.
33. Hicks, *Africa's New Oil*, 84. Hicks notes that in 2006, the CNPCIC purchased the rights to oil fields near Mimosa and Ronier from Canadian company EnCana. In exchange, the CNPCIC promised to build a refinery and to undertake a huge infrastructure project that involved building roads, an airport, and a railroad link between Chad and Sudan.
34. Hicks, *Africa's New Oil*, 84.
35. See "Chad: Fuel Shortages in N'Djaména"; Hansen, "Petrol, Price Protests."
36. Ghazvinian, *Untapped*, 260. Ghazvinian writes about Africa as a journalist, and his account of the recent scramble for African oil frequently relies on tired stereotypes of Africa as a depleted wasteland, but for all of the book's problems, the chapter on the Chad-Cameroon Petroleum Development and Pipeline Project offers information and analysis helpful to understanding Chad's fuel scarcity as an ordinary feature of life.
37. Leonard, *Life in the Time of Oil*, 3. See also Onishi and Banerjee, "The Perils of Plenty," 4.
38. Izzo, "Cinematic Economies of the Hypercontemporary," 30.
39. Higgins, "At the Intersection of Trauma, Precarity, and African Cinema," 95.
40. Roitman, *Fiscal Disobedience*, 151.
41. Roitman, *Fiscal Disobedience*, 198.

42. Roitman, "Ethics of Illegality," 249.
43. Roitman, "Ethics of Illegality," 264.
44. Hicks, *Africa's New Oil*, 87.
45. Roitman, "Ethics of Illegality," 248.
46. Roitman, "Ethics of Illegality," 256.
47. Mitchell, *Carbon Democracy*, 215.
48. Mitchell, *Carbon Democracy*, 37.
49. Larkin, *Signal and Noise*, 221.
50. Degani, *The City Electric*, 155–156.
51. In fact, jerricans were designed to transport small quantities of fuel into war zones where big tankers could not safely travel. They are also made to float.
52. See Alesso Iocchi's "Informality, Regulation and Predation: Governing Déby's Chad," *Politique Africaine* 154 (2019): 179–197. Iocchi describes the trade zone between Chad and Cameroon and explains that fuel is among the manufactured goods brought into Chad from Cameroon.
53. Wenzel, *The Disposition of Nature*, 83.
54. Amatya and Dawson, "Literature in an Age of Extraction," 7.
55. Chakrabarty, *The Climate of History in a Planetary Age*, 203.
56. Chakrabarty, *The Climate of History in a Planetary Age*, 113.
57. Chakrabarty, *The Climate of History in a Planetary Age*, 106.

FOUR

Electrifying Movies in Northern Ghana

IN RAMESH JAI'S FOUR-MINUTE FILM *Life!* (2017), Kweku carries the burdens of his family's expectations when he leaves his village and migrates to Ghana's capital city, Accra. In his fast-paced film, Jai, a graduate of the National Film and Television Institute in Ghana, interweaves shots of Kweku's struggles to find work in the city with close-up shots of his loved ones addressing him and the camera about his obligations to send money. The language and tone of these direct addresses become gradually more aggressive as Kweku searches unsuccessfully for office work and then performs a series of physically demanding jobs for which he receives very little pay. He cleans toilets, clears gutters clogged with plastic waste, and washes cars. Eventually, his mother, father, and fiancée tell him not to return home. Kweku does not speak throughout the film, but his increasingly forlorn expression makes it clear that he is distraught and hopeless. After a visit to an online suicide chat room, Kweku pulls apart the hot and neutral wires of an electrical cord in his courtyard; he touches one to the other to create a spark and then proceeds to fill a large bucket with water. He holds the wires and steps into the bucket, and just as he is about to plunge the wires into the water and electrocute himself, the light bulb behind him flickers, the lights go out, the screen darkens, and a loud, communal groan is heard. Kweku looks up at the camera. Power outage.

Jai made the short film in the last year of the 2014–2017 *dumsor*, or "electricity crisis," in Ghana, one of the worst in the country's history. *Dumsor*, which in English means "on-off," is the popular expression Ghanaians use to describe prolonged periods of load-shedding and electricity rationing, which are typically brought on by low water levels in the Akosombo Dam reservoir. Hydropower provides most of the electrical power in Ghana, and since the 1980s, periods of rationing have been intermittent, but numerous. The 2014–2017 dumsor, however, was perhaps the longest single period of load-shedding in recent memory, following similar but shorter events in 2002, 2005–2006, and 2007–2008. Jai's film exemplifies a creative, if improbable, storyline inspired by electricity; in this case, the frustration with the national grid's failure to provide a steady and reliable flow of electricity to consumers. Self-inflicted electrocution seems like a strange and gruesomely painful way to commit suicide, but Jai sacrifices realism to riff on an experience common to Ghanaians at the time of his film's production. The short film's dark humor captures the widespread irritation and frustration experienced by people living in areas affected by load-shedding. In a Facebook chat, Jai told me: "Dumsor has been a way of life in Ghana. Ironically, it also gave [Kweku] a second lease of life."[1]

The energy story portrayed in *Life!* is quite common to Africans and Africanists alike. Scholars who write about energy infrastructures and electrification in Africa tend to focus on breakdown and failure because, in many places, those are the most pronounced features of the energy landscape. Despite many power shortages, Ghana is actually an African energy success story. In this chapter, I take an unconventional path and discuss a local screen media formation made possible by access to the national grid. I assert that Ghana allows us to not only investigate the cultural products that respond to a lack of reliable electricity but also to consider the local cultural expressions that develop when an energy infrastructure works, most of the time. To that end, this chapter describes the development of a cluster of video production and distribution in and around the northern city of Tamale in relation to electricity. I am interested in the kinds of artistic production that develop around energy and analyzing African screen media that expands the pioneering ethnographic and archival research of Jonathan Haynes, Onookome Okome, Brian Larkin, Moradewun Adejunmobi, Alessandro Jedlowski, Abdalla Uba Adamu, Carmen McCain, Katrien Pype, Claudia Böhme, and Matthias Krings, all of whom have explored small local movie and media centers and networks in Ghana, Nigeria, Kenya, Uganda, and Tanzania. Their research demonstrates the value of detailed attention to the methods of production and distribution and the individual creative and business agents that support and shape Nollywood and other commercial cinemas in Africa. Following these works, I show that our understanding of African film and media production is enriched when we pay attention to the electricity that inspires the imagination and supports the material properties of creativity. Video technologies powered by electrical charge and flow have been foundational to small local-language industries throughout Africa, including Nollywood. In Tamale, producers rely on digital video technologies to create movies that affirm Dagbamba cultural identity; in these video films, computer-generated and enhanced sounds, movement, and images give physical presence to the key elements of Dagbon origin narratives and drum histories. They make the mythic real to the senses and alive in the present. Here I consider electricity and electronics in relation to film production and distribution and then try to plug electricity back into the movie texts by focusing on the electrified imaginary created in a representative example of a "back to the source" movie from Tamale.

ELECTRICITY AND MOVIES IN TAMALE

Since Ghanaian independence from British colonial rule, electrification has been a state-funded effort, driven by development goals that included rapid industrialization and the improvement of citizens' lives. The Akosombo Dam and hydroelectric power plant, a major modernization project inaugurated in 1966 by Kwame Nkrumah, the first president of Ghana, harnessed the energetic potential of the Volta River to, initially, provide electricity to an aluminum processing plant and, over time, bring power to businesses and homes throughout the country. Rural electrification did not become a national priority, however, until 1968, when the Electricity Corporation of Ghana allocated funds to establish small generating plants, some of which were fueled with diesel, in western and northern areas of the country, including in the small city of Yendi in the Northern Region.[2] Extension of the national grid to rural areas throughout the north progressed slowly. In 1972, only about 10 percent of Ghanaian citizens had electrical power, and most of them lived in the southern part of the country.[3] It was not until 1987 that head of state Jerry John Rawlings, with support from the International Monetary Fund and the World Bank, launched the National Electrification Program, which aimed to extend electrification to the entire country by 2020.[4] To expedite the electrification of rural areas, the Self-Help Electrification Programme (SHEP) built on urban infrastructure to connect rural communities within twenty kilometers of a transmission line to the national grid.[5] By 2005, SHEP had brought electricity to almost four thousand towns and small villages, and the rural access rate jumped to a remarkable 54 percent.[6] In the Northern Region, the number of households with electricity increased by 58.91 percent from 2000 to 2010.[7] NEDCo., the government unit responsible for distributing electricity throughout the central and northern areas of the country, reported that its customer population had "grown at an average rate of about 13 percent plus per annum from less than 20,000 in 1987 to 888,023 by March, 2019."[8] Problems with power generation have impeded the extension of the electrical grid. Most electricity in Ghana is generated by three hydroelectric dams: the Akosombo Dam; the Kpong Dam, built in 1982; and the Bui Dam, completed in 2013. In addition, a string of oil-powered and geothermal generators as well as three solar plants supplement hydropower production.[9] Chronic and long-lasting power shortages and rationing, as experienced during the 2014–2017 dumsor, have been blamed on low water levels. However, some scholars believe that governments have invested massive resources on expanding the grid while paying too little attention to maintaining the generation, transmission, and distribution systems needed to meet the growing demand.

In contrast to the developmental origins of the national electrification effort, the gradual liberalization and privatization of Ghanaian media institutions in the 1990s led to the expansion and diversification of the networks and systems of production and distribution that support movie-making in the country today.[10] Accra is at the center of English-language movie production in Ghana (this segment of the industry is sometimes referred to as Ghallywood), but several local-language film production hubs have emerged in Kumasi, Ho, and, Tamale. Unlike the earliest English-language producers, most of whom were involved in the sale and distribution of video and other electronic technologies, the first generation of movie producers in Tamale, including Rasheed Bawa and Hamidu Fusheini, founded or participated in Dagbani drama groups. Bawa's first movie, which at the time was referred to as a "drama," was a videotaped play performed by his troupe. Several producers were also involved in Dagbani-language radio and television programs sponsored and distributed by the Ghana Broadcasting Corporation.[11] At the start, then, Dagbani-language movie producers were loosely connected to state-funded efforts to communicate to local audiences in their first language and to preserve Dagbamba culture, and production was based in and around Tamale. Wunpini Fatimata Mohammed's brief history of Dagbani movies lists the titles *ŋuni Taali* (*Whose Fault?*), released in 1989, and *Ya Nmaha* (*Nowhere Cool*), released in 1990, as being among the first movies made in Tamale. They both explore "themes on family, relationships, and household issues" and

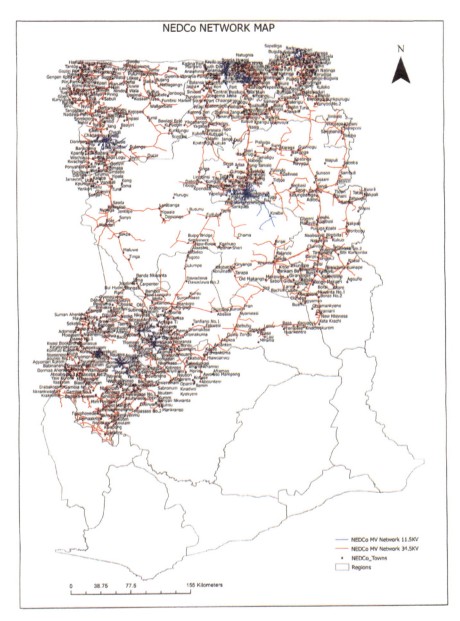

Fig. 4.1 The reach of the electricity grid in the north of Ghana. Courtesy of NedCo. Photo by author.

reflect the influence of Bollywood movies, which were extremely popular with producers, directors, and spectators at the time.[12]

The industry grew throughout the late 1980s and early 1990s, when the movies were a novelty, and, like commercial movies in southern Ghana and Nigeria, features were made and released on video. For most movie patrons in the north, a television and videocassette player were prohibitively expensive, so viewers in Tamale paid a small fee to watch movies in neighborhood video parlors on a large television or projected onto a screen. Producers traveled with their movies and video projectors to villages in the area, creating a culture of local film consumption for rural patrons with limited access to local or global media flows, with the exception of national radio broadcasts. Several factors contributed to a major slowdown in Dagbani-language movie production in the late 1990s. Over time, video equipment became less expensive and easier to find in Tamale, making it possible for amateurs to make and sell movies, which quickly led to an overcrowded and largely unorganized market. As the ownership of televisions and DVD decks became more common, producers began selling individual copies of their movies on video cassettes, which intensified the already dire problems with piracy. New, independent broadcast and satellite stations gradually emerged, giving consumers with access to television more choices than previously available. By the end of the decade, audiences seemed to have lost interest in local films.

All of this changed in the twenty-first century. In the last ten to fifteen years, Tamale producers have seen a remarkable revival in production and exhibition. The most accomplished and successful filmmakers generate revenue from screenings at local venues, like hotels, but it is the sale of individual copies of movies, reproduced on videocassette discs (VCDs) or replicated as higher-quality DVDs, that has sustained this Dagbani-language media production hub. Most people in the Northern Region continue to watch local movies on televisions connected to DVD players, a mode of viewing rendered nearly obsolete by satellite television, expanding mobile phone networks, and higher rates of Internet connectivity at faster speeds in Accra. In fact, the most successful producers of media in Accra, including Kofi Asamoah, Shirley Frimpong-Manso, Kwame Boadi, and Peter Sedufia, continue to release high-end serials and features through a combination of platforms and circuits—television, YouTube, Netflix and other subscription streaming channels, and cinema—but rarely if at all as DVDs or VCDs. Lower-end movie producers—those who make money by producing many movies quickly and releasing them straight to VCD—have struggled to survive in the last few years, and many, including those who were part of the industry's founding generation, have abandoned moviemaking entirely. Some have gone into television, and others work as content providers for corporations and nongovernmental and governmental entities.

Although I have been conducting research in Ghana since 1998, it was not until 2017 that I made my first trip to Tamale to learn more about the small Dagbani-language movie industry there.[13] Moviemaking in and around Tamale, the third-largest city in the country and the capital of the Northern Region, was flourishing. Meanwhile, producers in Accra and Kumasi, the more affluent and larger cities to the south, were struggling to save local movie culture. I attended a public meeting with members of the northern branch of the Film Producers Association of Ghana (FIPAG). We were joined by Socrate Safo, a longtime friend who had been a successful filmmaker in Accra and who was in Tamale in his capacity as the public relations officer of FIPAG to discuss upcoming FIPAG elections. The fifteen Tamale producers who were present—all of whom made movies in Dagbani, the most widely spoken language in the Northern Region—reported to Safo that it was not unusual to sell ten thousand DVDs of a single film and that the most successful movies might exceed sales of eighteen thousand. At this time, producers in Accra, once the largest hub for Ghanaian moviemaking, were very lucky to unload five hundred DVDs of their features.

I wanted to understand the gap between the two cultural formations in the same country. Research conducted in 2017 and subsequent trips in 2019 and 2022 suggested to me that rural electrification in the north had a lot to do with the reemergence of this cluster of straight-to-DVD local-language moviemaking. Many urban and rural areas throughout the north of Ghana have access to electricity, and the government tries to keep electricity affordable for low-income users in northern, rural areas with targeted subsidies. In even the smallest and poorest villages where poles and lines have been installed, most residents are able to connect to the grid, with paid or pirated connections. Indeed, Ghana's state-sponsored electrification initiative has been among the most successful in Africa.[14] It was one of only four African countries in 2011 with an access-to-electricity rate greater than 50 percent.[15] In 2013, that rate reached over 70 percent, far outpacing neighboring countries Nigeria, Cote d'Ivoire, Sierra Leone, and Liberia.[16] Three years later, the number had increased to 82.5 percent.[17] The World Bank estimated in 2020 that 85.9 percent of the population had access to the national grid.[18] Although electrification has been successful in northern Ghana, Internet connectivity remains limited

Fig. 4.2 Domestic electricity connections in Tamale, Ghana. Photo by author. © Carmela Garritano.

and, where available, prohibitively expensive for most. This combination of easy access to electricity but limited Internet connection has supported the revitalization of the market for Dagbani movies, sold exclusively as individual DVDs. The distribution of Dagbani movies in a material form has, in a sense, safeguarded their value in the north even as many consumers in southern Ghana, like media consumers in other parts of the world, find and buy screen media electronically, with Internet download and streaming services.

Dagbani moviemakers in the Northern Region have made films for audiences in their native language that are distributed in an affordable format that, locally, is still used widely. More than that, they have taken advantage of a gap between what I referred to in the third chapter as social state and neoliberal state articulations of infrastructural modernity. Electrification, as I have noted, has been largely provisioned by the state, while connectivity to the Internet, although supported by various state initiatives and policies, has been ceded to the market. Although access to the Internet has expanded rapidly in

Tamale and other northern cities, in impoverished rural areas, connectivity remains limited, fragmented, slow, and prohibitively expensive. Even most city dwellers cannot afford daily visits to a Vodafone Internet hub to buy a one-time Wi-Fi access code or a high-speed domestic or mobile phone plan. Dagbani-language movies are not shown on television, and satellite television, widely used in the Northern Region, offers a wide range of African movies in English and Akan, another Ghanaian language, but not in Dagbani. Local filmmakers, counting on dependable flows of electricity, have managed to maintain a small market for Dagbani movies that circulate as DVDs among growing (digital) distribution networks.

Digital moviemaking, at every level, requires electricity. This is a statement perhaps too obvious to make. Electricity powers equipment, computers, and batteries. Filmmakers use digital cameras, which rely on electrical current to translate and then re-create images and sound into cinematic content. Unlike a film camera in which light interacts with a chemically coated strip of film, the digital-video (DV) camera uses an electrically charged sensor to convert changes in light energy into electrical energy.[19] The camera's rechargeable batteries provide power to the sensor, which transforms the quality and character of the light—for example, its intensity or brightness—into a specific electrical charge. This charge is then read by the camera's firmware and used to create images. As explained by D. N. Rodowick: "Digital video samples light values and encodes them as symbolic notations of color, intensity, position."[20] The DV sensor, in other words, maps the path of electrons motored by light and then rewrites their movement "into a machine-readable notation."[21]

Affordable and easy-to-use digital video cameras and computer-based workstations, powered by reliable and affordable electricity, have contributed significantly to the twenty-first-century revival in Dagbani moviemaking, bringing creativity and new talent into the northern Ghana media landscape. As Brøvig-Hanssen and Danielsen point out, digital video has made a wide array of tools easier to use, much less expensive, and far more efficient.[22] The digital edit is nonlinear and nondestructive; the software's user-friendly interface allows the editor to quickly cut, copy, paste, and swap scenes and shots with a click and drag of the mouse. Perhaps most important, digital software that is designed for general use has allowed aspiring filmmakers with little formal training to make movies independently, eliminating the need for professional editors or directors of photography as well as the aesthetic and financial constraints of hiring outside help. To supplement the visual and sound effects included with postproduction software, digital editors can access online libraries that store hundreds of shareable video and audio files. The quality of the low-budget and unprofessional films that come from these processes varies considerably, but digital technologies are flexible and forgiving, allowing novice crews, writers, editors, and directors to make errors, release mediocre movies, gain experience, and improve with each new project. Since light (and sound) have been converted into code, or information, a digital recording can be manipulated and replicated (copied without losing quality) with no loss of signal. Digital production, enabled by electricity, supports content creation that is far easier and more affordable for nonprofessionals than either celluloid filmmaking or high-quality analogue-video moviemaking.

ELECTRIFIED EFFECTS AND EPIC TALES

Leonard Atawugeh Kubaloe, known as OBL, is the most successful and exciting Tamale-based filmmaker working today. A nurse educator with an MPhil in Public Health Nutrition, OBL balances a full-time teaching position with running his own media production business. He is a self-taught filmmaker and special effects artist. This is not exceptional in Ghana, where untrained moviemakers created a booming independent, commercial movie industry in the 1990s. What sets OBL apart is the amount of time and money he has dedicated to learning how to be a director, editor, and visual effects artist. He has taken on all of these roles in his productions, achieving an incredibly high level of expertise with YouTube videos, online courses and workshops, and software tutorials.[23] In 2009, he established OBL Studios in his family compound house, where he mentors and employs young men and women with an interest in the art of filmmaking and the creation of digital effects. With a salaried teaching position, OBL can afford cameras, computers, microphones, lights, and other equipment, and he maintains a high-speed Internet plan for the studio, which allows his team to download and stream the tools and materials they need. OBL began making movies when he served as director of photography, editor, and visual effects artist on *The Chase* (2011), an English-language Ghanaian horror movie. In 2013, he shot and directed his first Dagbani feature film, *Gonda Sheje*, which was set in the precolonial past, a structure and setting that distinguish his films from others made in Tamale. His second movie, a melodrama called *Biegni* (*Tomorrow*), was released in 2015; two years later, he made *Pieli: The Rise of Montana*, which I discuss in detail in this chapter. At the time this book went to press, he was in the final stages of completing *Gangdu*, another quest movie set in the precolonial Dagbon kingdom.

I argue here that OBL's use of special effects brings the violence and magic embedded in the history of Dagbon to the screen, materializing supernatural strength and occult power for viewers. This strikes me as an entirely "traditional" use of technology intended to affirm cultural identity; computer-generated and enhanced sounds, movement, and images give physical presence to the key elements of Dagbon origin narratives and drum histories. I propose that this use of digital attractions to enhance historical storytelling blurs the distinction between narrative and spectacle. The display of occult violence and power, even when it dominates viewer engagement and seems to break free of the plot, is intended to bring to life the heroic, enchanted acts of violence that historians and anthropologists believe are the most significant plot points in the founding narrative of Dagbon. Kristen Whissel's concept of "effects emblem" is useful here: "stunning (and often computer-generated or digitally enhanced) visual effects that give spectacular expression to the major conceits, themes, anxieties, and desires both of the films in which they appear and of the historical moments in which they were produced and exhibited."[24] Whissel's book, which I build on in this chapter, challenges the widely cited generalization in film studies that cinematic effects represent a kind of affective or sensory attraction distinct from narrative pleasure. She explains that in many Hollywood films, digital effects function like emblems; they often articulate the themes, characters, and plots of films, enhancing narrative instead of interrupting or even overtaking it. In *Piele* and other back-to-the-source movies produced by OBL Studios, visual effects are incorporated into mythic, cultural narratives to revive and reimagine well-known stories of hunters and heroes and to make perceptible the hidden or magical powers they wield. They not only dazzle but *signify* as features of Dagbon oral history.

Piele was intended to be a pilot for an Internet series. OBL wanted to create a one-hour feature that would generate enthusiasm that he could leverage if he were to find a streaming platform interested in supporting future installments of the project. *Piele* was a smash hit in the north; it screened locally for weeks in spaces transformed into cinema theaters, like a hotel conference room or a local cultural center; not surprisingly, it generated most of its revenue on DVD. OBL estimates that at least twenty thousand viewers have paid to watch the feature, and many more have seen pirated versions. *Piele* follows a similar pattern to OBL's other movies set in precolonial Dagbon.[25]

In these back-to-the-source movies, a male character learns that malevolent, supernatural forces threaten him, his family, or his lineage. To defeat these enemies and restore order, he must complete an arduous and dangerous journey that takes him far from home and into the forest (or bush) where he crosses a threshold between the real and supernatural realms to find the solution to the existential dilemma he faces. The young hunter Katari is the hero of *Piele*, and in the opening scene of the film, his father, Suglo, charges Katari with the duty of killing the ghost-warrior Montana, who has returned from the dead to destroy Katari's lineage.

Piele is especially interesting among quest adventure films because it refers explicitly to the precolonial history of the kingdom of Dagbon. Similar films of this genre, like *Gonda Sheje*, build story worlds about brave hunters and fierce warriors and draw on widely known oral morality tales, but they do not reference origin stories. In an action-packed scene from *Piele*, two warriors abduct Katari and drag him through the forest to another village, where Katari's father comes to rescue his son. Suglo warns the three young men that the sons of Dimali cannot hurt each other and instructs them to listen and learn about their shared lineage. The pace of the story slows as the young men form a circle around Suglo, who assumes the role of the oral historian. To dramatize the significance of the oral tradition, the montage cuts between close-up shots of Suglo and flashback sequences that portray the history he recounts. These events began, he says, "a long time ago, after the demise of Tohaje and before the advent of chieftaincy." In the drum history of the Dagbon, Tohaje, or the Red Warrior, is the mythic ancestor from whom the Dagbamba people are believed to have originated. According to the drum history, Tohaje's great-grandson Gbewaa "migrated into the northeast corner of modern Ghana as the founder of a kingdom that Gbewaa's sons later divided into Dagbon, Mamprugu, and Nanun, whose peoples call themselves Dagbamba." The son Sitobu established Dagbon, but it was Sitobu's son Na Nyagse who, in the fifteenth century, conquered the indigenous people of the area and consolidated power into a state. Na Nyagse is credited with establishing the Dagbon kingdom and the institution of chieftaincy, to which Suglo refers.[26]

Dagbamba history is traditionally recited in "drum histories by drummer praise singers at ceremonies of chieftaincy and other formal occasions."[27] Emmanuel Forster Tamakloe, one of the first people to translate and record the history of the Dagbamba, refers to the drummers as "traditionists" who work as "drummers to the kings, and to all the kindred chiefs of Dagbon."[28] MacGaffey describes the drum chant as a form of praise singing that involves the recitation of "epic poetry, together with the complex repertoire of rhythms and dances."[29] It is, MacGaffey notes, the primary art form of the Dagbamba and is closely associated with their history and cultural identity. There is no single, authorized "true" drum history of the origins of Dagbon. Historians have drawn on a shared body of transcribed accounts and drum performances, and it is widely recognized that performance of the drum histories is not a historical recitation but a political act "meant to praise the dynasty and current chief."[30]

Suglo's origin story is fictitious and incorporates no drumming or ceremony. OBL explained that he deliberately avoids referring to actual clans or lineages for fear of being pulled into contemporary political disputes. Despite its simple narration and fictionalized elements, the story Suglo tells to the young hunters includes meaningful aspects of the Dagbon conquest story, which, MacGaffey notes, adopts the "invasion model" of origin narratives. According to this type of oral history, outsiders migrate across foreign territories to conquer the indigenous peoples and establish a kingdom. The story of Montana, like the Dagbon drum history, also involves migration, patriarchal lines of descent, and acts of "competitive violence" among men.[31] In the drum chants, warriors and their enemies deploy "occult maneuvers," and it is believed that the fighter with "superior magic" is victorious.[32] In *Piele*, Suglo tells the young men that six fierce warriors, including one called Montana, moved through the land capturing territory and murdering those who resisted them. "No one knew to which tribe they belonged" or where they had come from. These undefeated, foreign fighters sought to conquer Katari's family, but his great-grandfather Chinto, a *tindana*, or earth priest, refused to cower before the outsiders and challenged them to a battle. He "took the blood of a virgin girl" and mixed it with millet. As he confronted the warriors, he threw the mixture at their feet. They ate it "like birds" and under its spell, are buried alive by Chinto. Only one invader "refused to be held by the grave," a man called Montana, who rose from the ground every twenty-one days to continue his violent destruction. To prevent Montana from resurrecting, the gods required that Chinto sacrifice a virgin girl every twenty-one years. Although the sacrifice has been made as demanded, Suglo explains, Montana has risen again. As if conjured by the mention of his name, Montana enters the village and kills Suglo, the tindana, and the two young hunters. Katari, the remaining son of the house of Dinmali, fends off the invader and remains the only person alive who can kill the ghost warrior and restore peace. The rest of the one-hour film follows Katari's attempt to fulfill this destiny.

In *Piele* and other quest movies, plots rely heavily on convoluted stories characters tell each other, as shown in my description of the opening scene. OBL does not work with a trained or experienced screenwriter, which might explain his reliance on this rather contrived plotting device in which a character recounts to another a series of past events that explains an obstacle demanding action in the present. The plot is then moved forward by the protagonist as he faces and overcomes the obstacle. This plot structure imposes a tiresome narrative rhythm in which fast action enhanced by special effects halts to allow for episodes of extended dialogue, or storytelling. Even if understood as an artistic weakness, this structure nevertheless emphasizes the importance of oral tradition to the precolonial Dagbon state and Dagbamba cultural identity. In the narrative, words have the power to create and stop movement.

The mise en scène of *Piele* combines actual locations and historically accurate costumes with small digital effects to create an atmosphere that is both hyperrealistic and enchanted. In the opening scene, when Montana appears for the first time, OBL has added digitally manufactured mountains to the actual location where the film was shot. This is one of many such hybrid-space composites that merges realistic computer-generated images with plate shots captured on location. The mountains are easily recognizable as digital effects to the trained eye and to those familiar with the terrain of the region, and they transform the real landscape—a flat savanna plain in a remote, rural area—into an otherworldly, strangely magical space. Katari enters the spirit world through a digital embellishment: an arch that appears to be built from stones piled on top of each other that magically stand erect. With the amulets he has received from the tindana before the start of his journey, Katari passes through the gateway, and as he does, the space under the arch fills with fire.

Throughout the film, the absence of electrical poles or generators and the stacks of wood (for fuel) that sit near thatched-roof mud huts convey the idea of time, signaling the premodern era. This unelectrified rural landscape, moreover, enhances the dazzle and shine of the manufactured digital effects, like the radiant gateway. When Katari meets Azima, his first guide in the world of the spirits, she brandishes a long wooden staff at the top of which OBL has added an effect that simulates a bright, flashing white light, which seems to emanate through a tear in the "real" as described in the story. Katari follows the light across an open, flat plain, framed horizontally to emphasize the reach and intensity of Azima's out-of-place and otherworldly beacon.

Fig. 4.3 Katari crossing the threshold. From *Piele*, OBL Studios.

For moviemakers in Tamale, each project is an opportunity to learn new skills with new tools, and *Piele*, OBL's third feature-length release, includes some of his most sophisticated and convincing digital effects. OBL experiments with software that combines live-action and computer-generated images, erases unwanted elements from a scene, and inserts digitally crafted objects and forms. He adds color and intensity to animate the magic contained in enchanted objects, which are typically ordinary things like a stick or gourd. He gives Montana superhuman strength and agility as well as the ability to lift and manipulate inanimate objects, like leaves and weapons, with his gaze. Tall and thick and covered in white clay, Montana cannot speak. Circles painted in red decorate one of his eyes, chest, and back. He wears a red cloth around his waist and leather bands on his forearms. This costume combines historical realism with artful and elaborate design, giving his figure an aura of the supernatural. He looks and moves like a temporal nomad, a humanlike creature who is out of place in the setting of the story. He is what Whissel calls an "analog-digital hybrid"; a human actor whose strength and abilities are enhanced with digital processes.[33] Like the creatures Whissel discusses in detail, he embodies "the very notion of a 'life force' so excessive as to be uncontainable, noncommodifiable, and deadly."[34] Whissel makes a compelling case for understanding the creatures in *Jurassic Park*, *The Mummy*, *King Kong*, and *Splice* as beings that "emblematize fantasies about and anxieties over the increasing technological mediation of life and death and the blurring—or even the disappearance—of the lines that separate the organic and the artificial, the biological and the technological, genetic code and binary code."[35] The cultural work performed by OBL's vital creatures is different from that done by Hollywood's digital monsters. Montana and the other hybrid figures that populate Dagbani-language films affirm the Dagbon cultural identity by bringing to life heroes of the mythic Dagbon past and visualizing their power.

Achille Mbembe, in *On the Postcolony*, describes the cultural context that gives rise to contemporary cartoons and comics published in Cameroonian newspapers. Although I am analyzing a movie from northern Ghana, Mbembe's exploration of the autochthonous orality and the principle of "simultaneous multiplicities" sheds light on the cultural work that a film like *Piele* tries to do.[36] Mbembe claims that in a cultural context where language was not written but expressed through a generalized field of narration—as it was in precolonial Dagbon—the spoken word informs "the very rules governing the production of knowledge and learning." He writes: "To publicly articulate knowledge consisted, to a large extent, in making everything speak—that is, in constantly transforming reality into a sign and, on the other hand, filling with reality things empty and hollow in appearance."[37] In this system of double meaning—the thing and what that thing is made to speak—the "great epistemological—and therefore social—break was... between what was seen (*the visible*) and what was not seen (*the occult*), between what was heard, spoken, and memorized and what was concealed (*the secret*)." Mbembe suggests that this interplay of presence and absence, or of the world and the otherworldly, informs a "general subconscious" that persists in the contemporary period.[38] *Piele* re-presents the doubled reality Mbembe describes; it narrates the entanglements of "the world of the living and the world of the spirits."[39] It also creates that world by revealing the hidden and imperceptible to the senses. OBL offers audiences a cinematic and sensory rendition of drum histories, infusing them with new energy and reviving their power and pleasure.

Digital effects in *Piele* make visible that which is believed to be unseen, and by doing so, they function as a cultural tool that imagines and reiterates a world of simultaneous multiplicities. The film makes deliberate use of effects: only tindanas and hybrids, like Montana and Azima, can conjure, deploy, or pass on occult objects. Katari can only contain Montana's "deadly vitality" with help from these spiritual guides, who share their knowledge of the invisible and offer him magical (vital) objects so that he, a mere hunter, might send Montana back to the grave. The significance of these guides downplays human, individual agency and instead highlights the power of the one aware of and able to translate hidden knowledge. The guide fills things with meaning, as Mbembe states, and the hero relies on occult or magical words, objects, and individuals to do what he is required to do. The tindana warns Katari that in the spirit world, nothing is as it seems and nothing is free. Azima tells Katari to travel to the forest to find what he seeks. There, he encounters another guide, whom he addresses as "elderly one." This hybrid figure, like Montana, wears a red garment around his waist, and his body is adorned with white circles. He agrees to help Katari only when he learns that it is Montana whom Katari must defeat. He leads Katari through the forest and to a tree with a forked trunk. He reaches between the split branches, and his arm seems to disappear into yet another space of digitally created invisibility. The guide then gently pulls his arm back into Katari's sensory field to reveal a gourd filled with liquid orange light, another computer-generated effect. For Katari, this enchanted object, like the others, functions as a hinge between surface and hidden realities. The guide tells Katari that the potion in the gourd can "arrest up to twelve spirits," and he gives it to him only because he wants Montana in exchange. To unleash the power of the potion, the guide recites an incantation that Katari must also use against Montana.

With vital object in hand, Katari tracks back through the forest and to the threshold. Here, the film ends suddenly, at a moment of high tension, after Katari passes through the archway to exit the world of the spirits. On the other side, he finds Montana waiting for him. Empowered with the enchanted object and words, he fends off Montana's attack with the chant and potion. The curse seems to freeze Montana in place, and, abruptly, the film ends as Katari readies himself to strike Montana down.

Up to this point, I have avoided citing Jane Bennett's *Vital Matter* because, among energy and environmental humanists, the book has been used to the point of cliché. However, Bennett's analysis of an electricity grid as an assemblage of human and nonhuman agencies allows me to pivot slightly to propose a metaphorical reading of *Piele*. I want to suggest that computer-generated effects not only materialize magic but also allegorize electricity.

Fig. 4.4 Enchanted gourd pulled from a tree. From *Piele*, OBL Studios.

The film includes effects that mimic the charge carried by an electric current. For instance, when Azima strikes Katari with her staff, the energy appears as a shock of force. It ripples through the air and knocks Katari off his feet. Like electricity, the force is invisible and abstract; only the charge it delivers, its effect, is perceptible. In the flashback where Suglo tells the story about the human sacrifice needed to keep Montana in his grave, a tindana taps the forehead of a young woman who reacts as if she has been electrocuted. Her body glows and shakes before she turns and walks into the river, where we assume she drowns. In these and other examples, occult power travels like a flow of electrons and becomes perceptible as a force only when it makes contact with a human body or nonliving object, like the gourd that fills with light. It is relational and is conducted across bodies and surfaces. The film's digital effects show people, things, words, and magic working as (and in) a group, defined by Bennett as an entity that "owes its agentic capacity to the vitality of the materials that constitute it."[40] Human figures direct action, but always in relation to words and objects infused with "vital materialities."[41] The film uses digital effects to bring into visibility that which is hidden or underground and to represent the kinds of horizontal and intersubjective relationships implicit in the doubled world Mbembe describes.

A note of caution. I am not saying that Dagbani-language movies articulate an indigenous conception of vital materialism that moves us toward what Bennett calls "a new discernment," which might "inspire a greater sense of the extent to which all bodies are kin in the sense of inextricably enmeshed in a dense network of relations."[42] To make such a statement would, it seems to me, ignore much of what we have learned from poststructuralist and postcolonial theory, which warn us against disregarding the discursive and institutional political forces that produce and authorize certain forms of knowledge, even those imagined to be free from the imprint of anthropology or colonial power. Moreover, to understand OBL's movies as representations of traditional stories that can offer a fresh ecological perspective is to diminish the creativity and worldliness of *Piele* and other Dagbani-language movies. OBL's archive includes local and global sources; the drum tradition he draws from is a lively, dynamic, and historical form that has never stalled, and he pays tribute to the form by re-creating it anew.

Additionally, in OBL's movies, I do not find lessons or meanings that speak to anthropocentric climate crisis and its impacts. What I stress here is that Dagbani-language movies, in their modes of production and circulation and in the cinematic worlds they project, say a lot about the advantages that access to electricity provides. I have tried to develop a critical perspective that pays attention to, perhaps even looks for, energy in and around African cinema. As we imagine a more sustainable and just energy future, we might seek inspiration from the creative endeavors of moviemakers who work on the energy margins.

CONCLUSION

In June 2022, I spent a month in Tamale, updating my research and circulating drafts of this chapter. It was my first trip to Ghana since 2019 when the COVID-19 pandemic prevented international travel. Dagbani movie production had been nearly flattened by the economic impacts of the pandemic and its aftereffects, like skyrocketing inflation and huge increases in the cost of fuel, food, and other necessities. Compounding this macroeconomic crisis were two local stressors that had been slowly squeezing producers since before the pandemic. First, the market is oversaturated, and distribution is unstructured. The success of moviemakers like OBL has attracted attention and enticed many aspiring, and mostly untrained, producers to make feature films. Too many producers make more movies than the market can absorb, and without an agreed-on mechanism for controlling and limiting the release of movies on a weekly basis, few producers make any money at all. Producers argue that they must release their movies as soon as possible because whatever small profits they make are needed to finance the next production. Nonetheless, the inability to organize and establish a release schedule might hasten the collapse of the market.

The second major challenge is pen drive piracy. The demand for pirated local movies copied to USB devices, or pen drives, has expanded throughout the Northern Region with the spread of smartphones and satellite television decoders equipped with USB ports that can accommodate small drives loaded with illegally copied movie files. More and more people in urban areas own computers or smartphones that can play movies. And when a customer purchases a dish and decoder and connects them to their set, satellite television is free in the Northern Region, therefore, many people in urban and rural areas own decoders. Movies are easily copied from a disc to a USB device and shared among friends or sold to customers who cannot afford a DVD. OBL has proposed building on pirate networks and distributing films on pen drives, but his plan poses risks and would require capital. He talks with other producers about supporting pen drive distribution, but in a dying market, change involves economic risks that many producers cannot afford to assume.

In the next chapter, I write about art created from energy waste, namely plastic waste. In this chapter, I have described a media structure reliant on polycarbonate plastic DVDs and VCDs and therefore responsible for generating the kinds of nonbiodegradable and toxic trash that are thematized in the works studied in the following chapter. There are no recycling facilities in northern Ghana, and most DVDs and VCDs likely end up burned, buried, or polluting rainwater gutters and lakes. So, if electricity feeds and grows this vibrant cultural industry, it also yields significant toxicity and other dire ecological effects.

I end this chapter by noting that all forms of energy produce material risks and costs, many of which permeate human and nonhuman ecologies and unknown planetary futures. Chapter 5 looks to film and art for responses to the massive and unavoidable problems caused by energy waste. I consider art from Ghana that addresses petroculture's by-products and invites political and ethical responses grounded in the histories and complexities of the materiality of plastic and other forms of oil waste.

NOTES

1. Facebook conversation between author and Jai, January 9, 2024.
2. Miescher, "The Akosombo Dam," 326.
3. Miescher, "The Akosombo Dam," 331.
4. Kemausuor and Ackom, "Toward Universal Electrification in Ghana," 2.
5. Akpandjar and Kitchens, "From Darkness to Light," 32.
6. Abavana quoted in Akpandjar and Kitchens, "From Darkness to Light," 36.
7. Akpandjar and Kitchens, "From Darkness to Light," 38.
8. NEDCo, "About Us," http://www.nedcogh.com/about-us/#.
9. In 2019, solar accounted for only 0.35 percent of electricity generation, according to the Volta River Authority (VRA), the government entity that oversees power production. At the time this book went to press, three solar plants, the Navrongo Solar Plant in Bolgatango, the Lawra Solar Power plant in Lawra, and a floating solar plant at the Bui Dam were operational. In 2022, the VRA announced plans to construct the Kaleo Solar Plant in the Upper West region of Ghana.
10. For a detailed history of colonial, national, and independent film and movie production in Ghana, see my book *African Video Movies*.

11. Mohammed, "Globalisation and Indigenous Cinemas," 6.
12. Mohammed, "Globalisation and Indigenous Cinemas," 6, 10.
13. In this chapter, I use the word *Dagbani* to refer to the language spoken by the Dagbamba people. By doing so, I am following the suggestion of my Dagbani tutor, Abdulai Zakaria Olivier at the University of Developmental Studies in Tamale, as well as adopting the convention found in published, peer-reviewed research, by linguists, on the Dagbani language.
14. This claim is not meant to diminish the violence and suffering inflicted on human and nonhuman ecologies during the construction of dams, the Akosombo in particular. See Tsikata, *Living in the Shadow of the Large Dams* and Miescher, *A Dam for Africa*.
15. Gore, *Electricity in Africa*, 12.
16. Kemausuor and Ackom, "Toward Universal Electrification in Ghana," 2.
17. https://data.worldbank.org/indicator/EG.ELC.ACCS.ZS?locations=GH.
18. https://data.worldbank.org/indicator/EG.ELC.ACCS.ZS?locations=GH.
19. The image sensor used by most digital cameras is a charge-coupled device. Some cameras use complementary metal oxide semiconductor technology instead.
20. Rodowick, *The Virtual Life of Film*, 135.
21. Rodowick, *The Virtual Life of Film*, 114.
22. Brøvig-Hanssen and Danielsen, *Digital Signature*, 13–15.
23. OBL has learned and uses Davinci Resolve Studio, Maya, Houdini FX, Nuke, Adobe ProTools, and Blackmagic Fusion, among other applications. Acquiring expertise in these tools represents hours and hours of work.
24. Whissel, *Spectacular Digital Effects*, 171.
25. These films are the 2013 film *Gonda Sheje* and *Gangdu*, a film still in postproduction at the time this book went to press.
26. MacGaffey, *Chiefs, Priests, and Praise-Singers*, 18; Staniland, *The Lions of Dagbon*, 18–19.
27. MacGaffey, *Chiefs, Priests, and Praise-Singers*, 35.
28. Tamakloe, *A Brief History of the Dagbamba People*, v.
29. MacGaffey, *Chiefs, Priests, and Praise-Singers*, 36.
30. MacGaffey, *Chiefs, Priests, and Praise-Singers*, 36–38.
31. MacGaffey, *Chiefs, Priests, and Praise-Singers*, 82.
32. MacGaffey, *Chiefs, Priests, and Praise-Singers*, 47.
33. Whissel, *Spectacular Digital Effects*, 91.
34. Whissel, *Spectacular Digital Effects*, 93.
35. Whissel, *Spectacular Digital Effects*, 91.
36. Mbembe, *On the Postcolony*, 145.
37. Mbembe, *On the Postcolony*, 144.
38. Mbembe, *On the Postcolony*, 146.

39. Mbembe, *On the Postcolony*, 145.
40. Bennett, *Vibrant Matter*, 34.
41. Bennett, *Vibrant Matter*, 30.
42. Bennett, *Vibrant Matter*, 120, 13.

FIVE

Sustainability, Ecological Thought, and Ghanaian Plastic Waste in Film and Art

CHAPTER 5 SITS AT THE intersection of energy waste and art, at what we might conceptualize as a switching point at which plastic garbage and other forms of trash generated by human energy use are recovered and remade so that they return to the oil-commodity cycle. In the documentary and plastic art installations examined in this chapter, energy is experienced in the waste generated from its commodity forms, politics, regimes of labor, and social life. Taking on energy waste as their material and theme, these trash-based works reckon with human and nonhuman relations in the age of climate catastrophe more explicitly than the African films analyzed in earlier sections of the book. As presented in the feature-length documentary *Welcome to Sodom* (2019) and the installations of Ghanaian artists Serge Attukwei Clottey and Patrick Tagoe-Turkson, plastic waste created from oil energy commands attention in its liveliness and vibrancy and raises crucial questions about plasticity as a condition of life within global South petroculture. The pervasiveness of plastic is planetary in scale; however, the expressive forms discussed here reflect on the deeply historical patterns through which plastic circulates and accumulates.

Petroleum-derived plastic represents an "unprecedented kind of waste."[1] A nonbiodegradable material produced in massive quantities, plastic is persistent; it permeates all dimensions of daily life and accumulates over time, anticipating its futurity by design. It is found in most products, from cosmetics to appliances, and it "has integrated with or even replaced almost all other substances," including wood, rubber, paper, and textiles.[2] It cannot be eliminated from the planet; plastic leaches and breaks apart, but because it does not biodegrade, it collects in the soil, the air, the oceans, and the bodies of animals and humans. Plastic waste is what Elizabeth DeLoughrey theorizes as an "anthropogenic ruin," a substance "no longer permeable to decay and now oddly decoupled from nonhuman nature."[3] Although in one sense, plastic is detached from "nature," in another sense, it demonstrates the futility of trying to separate "nature" from human culture and technology. Plastic infiltrates all spheres of human and nonhuman life. It is "found in household goods and medical products, technological and transport networks, bodily interiors and industrial processes."[4] Some estimates suggest that humans ingest, on average, approximately two thousand minuscule pieces of microplastics, the weight equivalent of a credit card, each week.[5] Arctic scientists have identified plastic in glacial ice, and environmental scientists estimate that since 1950, more than 8.3 billion metric tons of plastic have been produced.[6]

The space-time ubiquity of plastic vividly exemplifies Timothy Morton's description of a hyperobject. Morton explains that hyperobjects are weirdly enormous entities that humans have only recently become attuned to as a result of advances in science and technology, like computer modeling and big data. Immense and vastly distributed across space and time, these entities endure for hundreds of thousands of years: "materials from humble Styrofoam to terrifying plutonium will far outlast current social and biological forms."[7] They are lively and exert their force over us. One example Morton gives is plutonium: "We think of light as neutral or benign. Radiation is poisoned light. We think of 'objects' as passive and inert, as 'over there.' Just by existing, this hyperobject affects living tissue. Radioactive materials are already 'over here,' inside our skin."[8] In all their incomprehensibility, "hyperobjects seem to force something on us, something that affects some core ideas of what it means to exist, what Earth is, what society is."[9] Making sense of this "something" requires new practices of contemplation, reading, feeling, and creating, and Morton turns to contemporary art to demonstrate these emergent modes of thinking, being, and making. I build and expand on the reach of Morton's analysis here, in particular exploring his ideas about hyperobjects and ecological thought. My analysis considers the documentary *Welcome to Sodom*, Clottey's Afrogallonism, and Tagoe-Turkson's flip-flop tapestries as responses to our planetary plastic problem and significant contributions to the contemporary art discourse of waste, which, like Morton's writing, has tended to focus on art made in and around the global North. The creative works discussed in this chapter grapple with plastic and electronic forms of energy waste as hyperobjects, suggesting ways to connect ecological ideas with African environments and economies, extending Anthropocene art discourse by engaging it from locations in Ghana. Situated in the African postcolony, my analysis reframes critical conversations about ecological artist and the political interventions it performs or imagines in response to petroculture.

WELCOME TO SODOM AS SUSTAINABILITY DISCOURSE

I start with the documentary *Welcome to Sodom*, which might be described as a commodity biography.[10] Wenzel uses the term *commodity biography* to describe "narratives that disseminate knowledge about commodities: texts that tell commodity stories—or commodities that tell their own stories—and thereby implicate consumers in the forms of violence that surround them."[11] *Welcome to Sodom* provides information about the commodity of electronic and plastic waste, the toxic remains of the technologies of petrocapitalism that are picked through, picked up and apart, sorted, burned clean (in some instances), bundled, and finally sold by the men, women, and children who work in the scrap-metal yard and waste dump in the Agbogbloshie neighborhood in Accra, Ghana. These trash workers turn waste into raw materials like copper, aluminum, and bags of recyclable plastics and then sell those materials to generate meager incomes. Austrian directors Florian Weigensamer and Christian Krönes spent three months in Agbogbloshie making their documentary, which they describe as an effort "to make users reflect on their desire to always have the latest devices in hand.... We hope this film appeals to a young and critical cinema audience and will bring them to reflect on their own purchasing behavior and sensitize them against the current doctrines of our throwaway culture."[12] Their explanation of intent, published in press materials that come with the DVD or that can be downloaded from the film's website, directs us to watch their documentary for the lessons it offers to individuals about their consumption in relation to sustainability.

Welcome to Sodom gets a lot wrong. The documentary's opening intertitle states: "Agbogbloshie, Accra is the largest electronic waste dump in the world. About six thousand women, men and children live and work here. They call it 'Sodom.'" Here, and throughout the film, the filmmakers conflate an entire urban area in Accra, called Agbogbloshie, with the scrap-metal yard and household waste dump located within the area.[13] The documentary's montage flattens the large heterogeneous neighborhood by mixing and making no distinction among scenes from the waste dump, the scrap-metal yard, and the surrounding slum. The area is not, in fact, called "Sodom" by those who live there. "Sodom and Gomorrah" is the derogatory name used to refer to the slum area in Agbogbloshie, which was originally called *Fadama*, a Hausa word meaning "swampy." This name was given to what was then an extensive swampland by its Hausa-speaking residents who migrated from northern Ghana in the 1960s and 1970s.[14] Today, an estimated 120,000 people live in the residential slum, which is bordered by an industrial zone and abuts the Korle Lagoon. Many residents continue to move there from the poorer and less developed northern regions of Ghana.[15] In addition, the scrapyard is not, as the intertitle states, an electronic waste dump. It is a place where traders bring machinery, computers, air conditioners, and other household electronics to be dismantled and sold, and at less than half a square mile, the yard is not even close to being the largest in the world.

Welcome to Sodom operates according to the assumption that viewers will be motivated to reduce their consumption if exposed to the vast amounts of revolting and toxic waste their consumption generates. It very explicitly adopts what Jacques Rancière calls "the *pedagogical* model of the efficacy of art," which "confer[s] on the artwork the power of the effects that it is supposed to elicit on the behavior of spectators."[16] Shocking images of trash and trash workers are meant to provoke viewers to adopt behaviors that promote environmental sustainability. (The need to shock might account for the filmmakers' loose adherence to facts.) The closing intertitle, like the first, stands in for a voice-over to convey the lesson, or the truth, the documentary is meant to reveal: "Every year about 250,000 tons of sorted out computers, smartphones, air conditions [sic] tanks and other devices from a very electrified and digitized world end up here, shipped to Ghana illegally. Agbogbloshie, Sodom will most probably be the final destination of the computer, the Smartphone you buy today."

This intertitle imposes a lesson on the diegesis, a lesson that presents what Amanda Boetzkes, in her brilliant book *Plastic Capitalism*, describes as a "moral curative" against "apathy toward the condition of the planet."[17] Boetzkes, referring to Rancière, explores the limits of this pedagogical approach to climate warming, which she sees as one version of sustainability discourse. The problem with sustainability discourse, she explains, is that it relies on and reenacts "a bad duality."[18]

> On the one hand, environmentalists have come to focus on sustainable practices, with the particular goal of regulating the output of carbon emissions—and rightly so, given the real threat of global warming.

On the other hand, the global market has implanted an insatiable desire to consume the same nonrenewable resource that creates those emissions, and has taken sustainability as a model of energy management that does nothing to change the constitutive problem of defining wealth through stockpiling and consumption of a depleted energy source.[19]

For Boetzkes, sustainability discourse is inadequate because it proposes moral constraint on consumption as a solution to intensive energy expenditure and its carbon and toxic impacts within a system where consumption is a form of politics, a way of shaping identity, an act of pleasurable transgression, and even an expression of liberty. This closed system, Boetzkes argues, prevents us from asking fundamental questions about alternative systems of value and meaning. Sustainability discourse provides, in Rancière's words, a "model (or counter-model) of behavior" but maintains the "cartography of the sensible and the thinkable" on which petroculture stands. In other words, it affirms the dominant system of values and the structures of feeling that normalize fossil fuels and energy-intensive ways of life.[20]

My reading of *Welcome to Sodom* recalibrates Boetzkes' insights to argue that sustainability discourse not only solidifies the sensory and ideological regimes that contribute to the generation of massive carbon emissions and energy waste but also, in many iterations, relies on and advances colonial regimes of representation. *Welcome to Sodom* allows us to consider what is at stake when the political impact of a work of environmental art, or eco-art, reinforces the dominant "distribution of the common" that renders Africa and African subjects unthinkable, unsayable, or unseeable. By using the images and stories of waste and waste workers in Agbogbloshie to jolt a "Western" audience out of its complacent use of electronics, the documentary greenwashes a colonial narrative. I am not, like Iheka, whose recent book devotes considerable space to Pieter Hugo's photography book *Permanent Error*, which centers on the workers in Agbloboshie, interested in debates about what constitutes "poverty porn," nor in whether eco-criticism can rehabilitate pedagogical art. My reading of *Welcome to Sodom* follows Rancière and Boetzkes to challenge the modality of art that seeks to "reveal" a horrible truth so as to teach and inspire action and, relatedly, I push against Iheka's efforts to amplify the lessons conveyed through images of polluted environments and toxic labor in Africa. Pedagogical art about African ecologies fails because it superimposes a series of oppositions that on the one hand misrepresent and obscure history and, on the other, naturalize hierarchies between culture and nature, agent and victim, and subject and object that are rooted in colonial modernity and remain inadequate to petroculture and our current planetary crisis.

Welcome to Sodom, at ideological and affective registers, addresses a consumer, a "you," whose excessive consumption of electronics causes the suffering of the people who work in Agbogbloshie. These residents are portrayed as objects of the documentary's objective focus and the discourse it participates in. This lesson about the unequal global distribution of petroculture's waste and risk imagines a world divided into two parts: those who consume excessively are wealthy human agents in the global North who willfully cause suffering to passive and helpless African victims in the global South. This binary does succeed in communicating something about the enormous economic imbalance between those who produce the greatest amount of electronic waste and the Agbogbloshie laborers who add value to it, but this is only a very small slice of a much larger, global dynamic.[21] The film tells us nothing about the transnational trade in trash and recyclables, and, perhaps most egregiously, it completely erases local and regional African consumers and producers. Ghana is not closed off from the world of technology and consumption; in fact, some researchers have suggested that most of the waste at the scrap site featured in the documentary is produced within the West Africa region.[22] The documentary's total omission of Africans as agents capable of contributing to or participating in petroculture confirms Sylvia Wynter's point that "the struggle of our times" remains "the struggle against the overrepresentation" of the globally hegemonic "ethnoclass" of Man as human.[23] Sustainability art like *Welcome to Sodom* risks subsuming the humans on whose behalf it aims to advocate into the category of "Human Otherness."[24] Wynter's "Man" is the subject hailed by *Welcome to Sodom*; it is humans in the global North who are held responsible for Agbogbloshie's toxicity and are addressed as capable of answering the documentary's call for action. These humans stand in for—or, to use Wynter's term, are "overrepresented" as—the species whose consumption threatens the planet. The Ghanaians, as portrayed, have no agency in either creating or solving the crisis shown in *Welcome to Sodom*, and since within the logic of its articulation human subjects are defined by their will to act (for good or bad), the documentary seems to discount Ghanaians as fully human.

The filmmakers take the lives of garbage pickers in Agbogbloshie as the raw materials that they set out to save from electronic waste. The montage and soundscape, in particular, are designed to advance this project of moral rescue. Staying in and around Agbogbloshie, the film shifts continually between distance and proximity, between extended landscape shots that emphasize accrual and filth, and intimate interactions with the protagonists whose livelihoods are interwoven with trash. The back-and-forth seems intended to remind viewers again and again that their excessive consumption has created these repulsive mountains of trash from which these impoverished men, women, and children must piece together a precarious livelihood. Close-up and extreme close-up shots of the faces, feet, and hands of the salvage workers call attention to the effort of sorting through trash but seem meant to incite shame or pity instead of appreciation or understanding. For example, the film often centers its gaze on the children who work at the dump, and one of the central narratives is voiced by a young boy who collects metal at the scrapyard. He is, in fact, the first worker we see.[25] The shot captures him dragging a large magnet across the ground, which pulls bits of iron from the dirt. Only his small feet, tattered shoes, and legs are visible initially, leaving us with the impression of poverty and vulnerability, and we hear only the amplified, ambient sound of electromagnetic hum. It isn't until he bends over to push the magnet that his body and face enter the frame. Then, in voiceover, finally, we hear the boy describe his work. His narrative explains that his magnet is "very powerful" and that "everywhere you can find small iron on the ground. It is like money, but nobody owns it." Referring to Lucy Walker's *Waste Land*, a two-year documentary project about Brazilian artist Vik Muniz and his work with garbage pickers at the Jardim Gramacho landfill in Rio de Janeiro, Boetzkes demonstrates that the film "consolidates a circular coordination of art, politics, and waste: it affirms the moral reprehensibility of garbage and wastefulness (particularly the waste of the wealthy), the implicit lowliness of the garbage pickers' lives, and the redemptive capacities of art."[26] *Welcome to Sodom*, likewise, announces itself as a work of higher purpose, a project positioned apart from the polluted and revolting environment it uncovers and from which it intends to save this child and the others who mine its waste.

The documentary's soundscape layers ambient sounds from the scrapyard and waste dump under an extradiegetic narrative track composed of monologues crafted and spoken by the workers selected to be the documentary's central personalities. The monologues, recited in response to questions submitted to the speakers by the filmmakers, were recorded in a makeshift sound studio built on-site. For the most part, the monologues are powerful testimonies to the creativity, intelligence, expertise, and aspirations of the workers. They describe their labor; some also talk about why they live in the area or where they have come from. One or two allude to their wish to return home, to the northern region of Ghana, or to find a way to travel abroad. But hearing the workers speak in voice-over, about themselves but outside the space of the story, creates the impression that the workers' voices have been "upcycled" like materials collected from the dump. Their narratives have been shaped by the filmmakers' prompts and questions, captured in the studio, and edited as part of the postproduction process. The documentary similarly takes the workers and their stories and adds value, remaking them as political art that, in turn, proposes to redeem the waste-generating consumers viewing the film. And like the iron drawn out of the dirt by the young boy's magnet, the stories of these workers must have seemed to the filmmakers as if they were available for the taking.

To salvage copper from computer cords and other electronic cables, waste workers in Agbogbloshie set small controlled fires to burn away plastic casings. This open-air method of burning plastic releases dangerous toxins into the air and soil. The documentary tries to visualize these invisible hazards in spectacular shots of blazing mounds of fire set against pitch-black soil. We see the workers monitor the fire, stir it, wait as it slowly expires, stamp it out, and finally pour water over the smoldering copper to cool the wires for bundling. Fire here signifies destruction and toxicity, and it is rendered in strangely terrifying beauty. One of the workers featured prominently in the documentary is among those who scavenge for copper. In his monologue, he calls himself "a man of the fire" and acknowledges that the work he does can be painful and might turn his insides "black." The alarming yet stunning images of the fire evidence the danger and discomfort he describes. The very end of the film puts on display a series of visually dramatic shots of two young men who work with fire at the dump. They look directly into the camera as they perform a series of daring feats with burning rubbish, and their display is at once stunning and horrifying. I assume that the filmmakers highlight the labor of the men burning plastic to stress their agency and expertise in manipulating fire. Still, the segments render the young men as otherworldly and exotic and stage their Otherness in equal measure to their strength and agility.

In her book *Reclaiming the Discarded: Life and Labor on Rio's Garbage Dump*, anthropologist Kathleen M. Millar describes a transformative experience in her relationship with the Jardim Gramacho trash dump. Initially, she explains, she conceptualized the story of the dump as "a straightforward story of environmental degradation."[27] But over time, and through the experience of conducting research at the dump and working beside her interlocutors, she "began to see the entangled relations of life, labor, and the dump."[28] The materiality of garbage changed as she picked through, sorted, and bundled it. A "generalized feeling of disgust" gradually gave way to an appreciation of the dump as "a rich assemblage of things."[29] Millar's book details the forms of labor and social relations generated by waste and the diversity of experiences and life worlds she finds at and around the dump. The book concludes that no single story of a trash site can capture its multiplicity and productivity. The major limitation of *Welcome to Sodom* is its insistence on affirming and teaching only one story of trash and degradation. What is interesting and somewhat paradoxical about the film, however, is that the meanings and feelings incited by the diegesis put pressure on the sustainability lessons its directors impose. The diegesis at points resists the intertitles that frame it. Viewers enter Agbogbloshie with an impression of its filth and degradation, what Morton describes as "dark-depressing," but over time, that sense of the dump becomes tinged with "dark-uncanny," and even "dark-sweet."[30] The sharpening of attunement to the uncanny and sweet emerges from the viewer's attention, and might easily be overlooked by the distracted or impatient spectator. The more time we, the spectators, spend looking through the camera at the dump and imagining its sensorium, the more time we devote to watching and listening, the more expansive our understanding of its multilayered and messy ecology becomes. As our eyes become more familiar with the landscape, the order and logic of the waste and scrap sites become visible. We recognize how waste has been arranged in the scrapyard, where separate areas have been designated for certain electronic devices. Computer monitors here. Motherboards stacked there. The garbage workers, too, develop over time in front of the camera, and at points, their actions and narratives push against the film's sustainability lesson. Workers haggle over the price of a bag of iron scrap or discuss the potential value of an old computer monitor. Through these exchanges, viewers get a sense of the kinds of expertise trash workers possess and the social connections that emerge through their waste work. The monologue of one of the scrap dealers, who tells us his name is Americo, asks viewers to keep sending their waste to Ghana because he and the others know how to make money from it. In these and other examples, the workers at the dump refuse to be seen as trashy objects in need of redemption.

Morton's exploration of hyperobjects involves a critique of environmentalism that alerts us to another fundamental problem with the sustainability discourse about Africa as exemplified by *Welcome to Sodom*. Morton argues that environmentalism is a way of thinking about the planet and an approach to climate politics that is completely inadequate to the geological and temporal scale of hyperobjects, including plastic. Environmentalism fails in part because it relies on an idealized notion of nature—which Morton spells with a capital N, Nature—produced within and therefore integral to modernity. In Nature, modern humans "saw the reflected, inverted image of their own age... Nature was an ideal image, a self-contained form suspended afar, shimmering and naked behind glass like an expensive painting."[31] This concept of nature as a space outside of human history has functioned to prop up an imaginary, distinct sphere of human culture. Morton notes that there was never really an untouched "natural" space out there, outside modernity, that needed to be preserved or mourned. The natural and the human have never been a duality. Moreover, this reified object called Nature cannot sustain scrutiny because it "collapses into *impermanence* and *history*." In *Ecology without Nature*, Morton explains: "Life-forms are constantly coming and going, mutating and becoming extinct. Biospheres and ecosystems are subject to arising and cessation. Living beings do not form a solid prehistorical, or nonhistorical ground upon which human history plays. But nature is often wheeled out to adjudicate between what is fleeting and what is substantial and permanent. Nature smoothes over uneven history, making its struggles and sufferings illegible."[32]

Morton does not dwell on the racial geography of environmentalism's static conception of Nature, and I want to explore that further. Postcolonial theory has shown that the idea of a nature without history or human imprint in part was a product of what Said calls the "imaginative geographies" of European colonialism.[33] The colonial archive creates and reiterates Nature as "a backdrop for human action," an empty and undeveloped space "in opposition to culture, the city and industry, to technology and human work."[34] This empty and nonhistorical Nature served to smooth over and shore up colonial extractive violence. Amitav Ghosh's *The Nutmeg's Curse* describes the brutality of Dutch "colonial terraforming" in the Banda Islands to control the extraction of and trade in nutmeg.[35] Ghosh connects the colonial exploitation of the Banda Islands—and the displacement, death, and ecological engineering it perpetuated—to European settlement in the Americas. He notes that the colonial drive to terraform in the Americas meant transforming "territories that were perceived to be wastelands into terrain that fitted a European conception of productive land."[36] Land was deemed unproductive, wild, or empty and therefore available for humans' exploitation. Environmentalism that assumes the existence of Nature upends but maintains this colonial opposition. The colonizer's "unproductive" Nature is coded as pristine Nature that now is under threat from human terraforming.

This type of colonial, environmentalist thinking, conveyed in the cliché of an African oral tale, informs the opening segment of *Welcome to Sodom*. Before the film's title and first intertitle appear, the camera crawls slowly across the body of a golden chameleon while a young person's voice narrates a story set "some time ago" when the earth was "a paradise." The storyteller explains that because humans did not respect the land or care for each other, the gods became angry and took everything away except fire. "The people are damned to watch over the fire," the storyteller concludes as the montage cuts to images of smoldering and burning waste. In this fable of degradation and loss, fire evokes horror, danger, and destruction. Orality functions to indicate that the story taps into some form of ancient African authenticity that, like the natural paradise bestowed by the gods, has been lost to human greed and carelessness. This story of loss restates the morality lessons shown in the intertitles and is underscored by the camera's lingering gaze over the trash-covered landscapes of the dump and scrapyard. In the first image of the household waste site, the camera slowly tracks across a wide expanse of the household dump. This establishing shot is meant to create an impression of the space as terrifyingly vast, disordered, abandoned, and toxic. Herds of goats eat from and nest in a field of flattened plastic. Boys and men, alone and in pairs, meander across the garbagescape, dragging large white sacks, while another group tips a small garbage truck to its side and releases a load of trash. The gray sky and air appear hazy-thick and smoky. Slow horizontal scans of the site like this recur throughout the film, creating a sense of distance from the scene as if we are looking at it from an uncontaminated place. It remains detached from human subjectivity and, like the intertitles, provides an objective eye that sees and reveals truth.

Various kinds of discarded plastic—black bags, clear water sachets, soda bottles, shoes, casings, pipes, sheeting, and more—carpet the ground in this and every scene in *Welcome to Sodom*, but there is no commentary on it. Plastic's hypervisibility, paradoxically, renders it unremarked on in a film about toxic waste. A similar play of presence and absence characterizes Iheka's chapter in Hugo's *Permanent Error*. Plastic is clearly visible in the photos of Agbogbloshie, but Iheka never mentions plastic as a topic of ecological concern in his discussion of e-waste recovery and recycling work as "digital labor."[37] I suggest that, in part, the scale and banality of plastic pollution make it impossible to address in pedagogical works of art that aspire to limit individual habits of consumption and disposal. This silence helps us understand plastic as hyperobject. It reveals, perhaps unwittingly, that the problem of plastic waste involves more than disposing of used and potentially toxic materials, more than sanitizing our environment from its pollution.

The most persistent form of plastic waste in Ghana and many other parts of Africa is undoubtedly the water sachet, a small, translucent plastic bag used to package small quantities of clean and safe drinking water. A short segment of the documentary, in fact, focuses on a woman who sells water in sachets in Agbogbloshie. She explains that she works in the area, where clearly there is a need for clean drinking water, so that she can pay her children's school fees. She represents a significant part of the growing business of producing and selling packaged water in the country. Writing about Ghana's failed national water grid, Ian Yeboah refers to the business of producing plastic water sachets and water bottled in plastic as components of a privatized water system.[38] Since the neoliberal Ghanaian state cannot guarantee universal access to a regular supply of safe drinking water, either in the home or at public taps, many people must purchase drinking water from private businesses, whose numbers increase annually to meet a growing population's demands for safe drinking water. In Accra alone, between 2003 and 2008, the number of residents reliant on sachet water increased by more than 439 percent.[39] Water sold in plastic sachets is far cheaper than water sold in bottles. It can be purchased in bulk or individually for a few coins and is sold everywhere, in shops and stores and by itinerant traders on the street.

An individualized plastic product for the distribution of potable water in limited quantities, the water sachet incorporates petroleum-based chemicals into the most ordinary and necessary bodily practice. Drinking water from a small plastic bag creates a close connection between humans and plastic through which petroleum is integrated into routine and life-sustaining activities. Lightweight and vacuumed-sealed, the sachets are designed to be used and immediately disposed of. Therefore, it is not surprising that in Accra, plastic water sachets have become a major source of plastic pollution responsible for clogging gutters and drains, blocking rivers and waterways, and increasing the incidence of malaria and cholera while adding a substantial burden to the 250 tons of plastic waste generated in Ghana daily.[40] Moreover, this product is manufactured in Ghanaian plastic plants that specialize in polythene bags. This form of energy waste is home-grown everywhere. The recalcitrance and prevalence of water sachet show us the diverse and widespread complexity of plastic and how it affects our daily lives. As Boetzkes so eloquently writes: "There is no outside to which plastic can be relegated."[41] Plastic waste, she continues, "is not an incidental consequence of the 'life cycle' of objects; rather it is a disposable substance whose contamination of the environment is a function of its design."[42]

In 2022, I visited Agbogbloshie and traveled to the site of the wasteyard featured in *Welcome to Sodom*. The area where the pickers sort through discarded waste and burn plastic-covered cords and wires to extract copper was significantly less active than it appeared in the film. I visited the dump and surrounding neighborhood with two Ghanaian friends, both of whom live in Accra, and they explained that the entire area had recently been cleared by the city authorities. The women, men, and children camped in and around the dump had been removed by the local police in a campaign to clean up the area, which had been declared illegal and unsafe. It is precisely this kind of violent eviction that might be instigated by a well-intentioned but woefully uninformed environmentalist project like *Welcome to Sodom*.[43] On the day of my visit, the sheer folly of the forced removals was apparent. Men and women had already begun to return to the site and build new camps. Trash pickers were sorting through piles of plastic, and a few young men had started to burn wire on the outer rim of the dump. Their economic precarity was in no way resolved by the evictions, nor did the electronic and plastic waste stop accumulating.

If *Welcome to Sodom* pursues a moral agenda regarding plastic and other forms of pervasive energy waste, the Afrogallonism of Serge Attukwei Clottey and the flip-flop art of Patrick Tagoe-Turkson elicit responses that are more playful, fluid, and collective, aligning with what Morton calls "the ecological thought," the approach to hyperobjects and coexistence that Morton's critical theory advances. Clottey's installations, built from plastic jerricans recovered from waste sites in Accra, and Tagoe-Turkson's colorful tapestries, made from discarded flip-flops salvaged from beaches in Takoradi, decontextualize and reconfigure objects that embody petroleum's integration into everyday life. They bring plastic into the open and transform the mundane into weirdly dazzling artistic forms.

Plastic has not always been a petroleum product. Natural materials, such as tree resin and animal bone, yielded the first plastics. It wasn't until the late 1930s that materials derived from coal, petroleum, and natural gas were used to make plastics.[44] Matthew Huber writes: "Frustration with low yields for certain crudes forced refiners to devise 'cracking' methods for turning what used to be considered 'waste' into more valuable products."[45] In the global North after World War II, life quickly became saturated with plastic. Plastics were incorporated into an entire way of living underscored by "visions of freedom, domesticity, and health."[46] In Ghana, the first plastic processing plant opened in the 1950s, and today, plastics molding has become a major industry. Most plastics enter Ghana as polymeric materials that are heated, compressed, and shaped into plastic products for industrial and household use in Ghanaian plastic plants.[47] Ready-made and imported plastic bags, toys, food and beverage containers, and other finished products account for less than half of Ghana's estimated plastic consumption.[48]

The plastic jerricans Clottey recovers from trash sites in Accra to create his large plastic-waste tapestries are likely produced in Ghana. Clottey coined the term *Afrogallonism* to describe his practice of assembling large and fluid tapestry-like installations from small, hand-cut plastic squares stitched together with copper thread.[49] He is one of several contemporary African artists who makes art with plastic jerricans.[50] This use of the ordinary jerrican points toward an interest in thinking about plastic as a ubiquitous and multifaceted material, the planetary reach of which depends on its ability to be readily situated to its context. On the one hand, the value of plastic comes from its flexibility, disposability, durability, and mobility. Cheap to produce, it is also associated with safety and cleanliness, at least in relation to the storage of water.[51] On the other hand, and as *Welcome to Sodom* demonstrates, plastic resists disposal and harms ecosystems. As waste and recyclable material, it "becomes the material of agglomeration, sedimentation, and perpetual return."[52] Plastic provides the material basis for countless products and technologies, reaching every corner of the planet and far, far into the future. Yet because it is malleable and can be formed into any shape, it is particular to contexts and uses. Plastic products appeal to consumers in specific places and life situations, making them inherently tied to history and context.

The jerrican exemplifies plastic's multiple and conflicting purposes and associations. As discussed in relation to petrol smuggling, it facilitates the transfer of liquid fuel products in small quantities and with human labor. It is essential in places without a developed or well-maintained water infrastructure; many of these places are postcolonial nations subjected to loan conditionalities and mandates to privatize issued by international financial institutions, which preclude major public investments in water infrastructure, and this is the use to which Clottey's work speaks. In Ghana since 1995, various administrations, backed by reports from the World Bank and other loaning institutions, have proposed a variety of private-sector participation schemes "to improve management, operations and performance" of the state-owned water company.[53] In urban areas, private water vendors deliver water to the homes of paying customers or make water available for a fee at stationary pipes or boreholes.[54] Both methods depend on people having their own plastic containers, like jerricans, to receive and store water for their household. In this way, the jerrican functions as one of many plastic "coping mechanisms to fill gaps in water security."[55] Ghanaians often refer to jerricans as "Kufuor gallons," the meaning of which Clottey explains in an interview with Arielle Bier. During the presidency of John Kufuor, "between 2002 and 2005 there was a serious water shortage. Sometimes the water would run only once a week. As children we carried these plastic gallons for kilometers to collect water."[56] His comment affirms that just like the plastic water sachet discussed previously, the jerrican functions as a biopolitical tool that incorporates oil, in the form of plastic, into the activities that sustain life.

In Ghana, flip-flops are known as *chale wote*, a phrase that in Ga, a language spoken widely in and around Accra, means something like "Friend, let's go." Patrick Tagoe-Turkson collects large quantities of plastic flip-flop remnants from the massive amounts of rubbish that wash onto beaches in Takoradi, where he lives, teaches, and creates art. Tagoe-Turkson assumes that most of what he collects comes from outside Ghana, although local rubbish cast into storm gutters drains toward the ocean and can end up banked on the shore. The undisclosed narratives of the marooned flip-flops drew Tagoe-Turkson to their materiality. He derives pleasure from peeling and cutting away the faded and damaged surfaces of the sandals to reveal the colors and textures that remain preserved underneath. His choice to salvage plastic sandals inadvertently tethers his art to the history of plastic manufacturing in Ghana. One of the first plastic factories established in Ghana, a publicly owned enterprise that was part of the Ghana Industrial Holding Corporation, made cheap plastic footwear for schoolchildren.[57] The administration of Kwame Nkrumah, Ghana's first president, understood that plastic was an ideal material for the mass production of inexpensive and durable footwear. Impoverished families could buy this footwear for their children who needed shoes to attend school, where they would receive the education needed to contribute to the advancement of their newly independent country. Plastic footwear enabled mobility across space, of course, but it also signified movement toward prosperity and national development. Plastic production plants were among a range of small-scale industries courted by Nkrumah's government, and by 1972, ten private firms were making small plastic fabrications such as utensils, buckets, and pipes from molding machines imported from the US, Italy, the United

Kingdom, China, and Hong Kong.[58] Plastic production held steady until the late 1990s when the industry expanded significantly. The Ghana Plastic Manufacturer's Association reports that between 2013 and 2019, the industry grew by about 72 percent.[59] Today, most of these plants are locally owned and sell to both domestic markets and consumers in Togo, Mali, Niger, Burkina Faso, and Cote d'Ivoire.[60]

Plastic trash and microplastics as well as the toxins released by plastic breakdown, such as bisphenol A (BPA), permeate Earth's water. Ronda notes that "only around nine percent of plastic goods are recycled," and although a lot of plastic ends up dumped in landfills, vast amounts continually pollute the oceans.[61] Plastic has become a pervasive and monstrous sea creature that fish, turtles, birds, and other sea animals ingest and live with, and its stagnation and flow have transformed the ocean's ecosystem. Margaret Ronda writes that the presence of plastic substantiates "the ocean as an arena of capitalist extraction and as dumping ground, as consumer goods and waste from industrial fishing operations appear in uncanny forms, swirling alongside uncanny sea creatures."[62] Borne to Ghana's shore by ocean tides, the plastic sandals Tagoe-Turkson salvages lack evidence of origin or history. They are the anonymous, deterritorialized refuse of globalization and free trade. Plastic, "the material of a thousand uses," makes our "commodity society" possible.[63] It provides the packing essential to the safe, fast, clean, and convenient movement of commodities across the planet while also acting as the primary material from which many of these same commodities are derived. In a chapter discussing the use of flips-flops in work by Dominican artist Tony Capellán, DeLoughrey notes that this "mass-marketed piece of plastic and rubber footwear . . . becomes a sign of the commodification and disposal of global consumption" in art that repurposes it.[64] Tagoe-Turkson's dazzlingly colorful sculptures rely on and emphasize plastic's banality, ubiquity, mobility, and endurance. Lightweight yet strong, these ordinary and simple objects made from plastic travel thousands of miles and yet maintain some semblance of their original form. Although beached without history, the flip-flops have been molded by the weight of the unique human bodies that wore them. Simultaneously global and local, the discarded flip-flop carries its anonymity and singularity, which for Tagoe-Turkson makes it a fascinating thing from which to create.

Tagoe-Turkson's creative process is solitary. He works alone on the hundreds of pounds of plastic flip-flops he collects from local beaches and stores in his studio in Takoradi. He meticulously cuts them into square-shaped

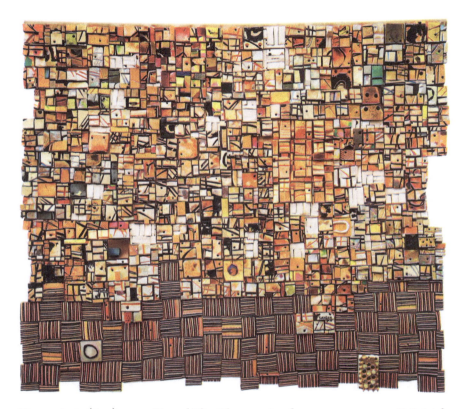

Fig. 5.1 *Awia* (Sun). 2020. Found Flip-Flops on Suede. 149 cm × 135 cm. © Patrick Tagoe-Turkson.

fragments, which he then glues or stitches into quilt-like hanging pieces of various sizes, colors, and forms. His tapestries have more dimension and texture than Clottey's. Some of his pieces suggest the movement of a body of water; others resemble stained-glass windows. He has also re-created the patterns of kente cloth in forms that are blocklike and thick.

Tagoe-Turkson's installations, like Clottey's, bring to mind the work of El Anatsui, an internationally recognized Ghanaian artist who has been living and teaching in Nigeria for decades. El Anatsui is best known for his immense, rippling metal hangings, which he began creating in 2004 with recovered materials such as aluminum bottle caps and copper wire. Anatsui has described a desire to explore "the sculptural possibilities of the sheet, and increasingly colors, textures, lines, dots, and other elements."[65] Clottey's and Tagoe-Turkson's

Fig. 5.2 *Menyankoba Basia* (*My Friend's Daughter*). 2021. Found Flip-Flops on Suede. 95 cm × 112 cm. © Patrick Tagoe-Turkson.

art reveals similar interests; indeed, their flowing plastic textures might be read as plastic reimaginings of Anatsui's "stunning textile-like-wrap-arounds and throw-overs."[66] Substituting plastic squares for aluminum caps highlights the materiality of plastic art. The fluidity and malleability of the tapestries of both artists emphasize the shapeless nature of plastic, the property that makes it useful as a chemical substance that can be formed into anything.

Clottey's artistic practice borrows heavily from what Vogel describes as Anatsui's "collective creativity."[67] Anatsui and Clottey produce their art with a team of paid apprentices who, within limits set by the artist, develop their own methods and styles of connecting and fastening plastic squares. They similarly share a fascination with the labor of artistic creation. The creative work begins with the collection of plastic materials from local refuse and recycling centers. In his workshop, Clottey and his team spend hours cutting these materials and then carefully fastening small squares together with hand-cut strings of copper wire. Clottey also shares Anatsui's interest in making art with everyday objects that have been touched by human hands. The recovered plastic has been touched again and again by those who used it as a jerrican. It is then remade by the hands of his apprentices and finally made again when hung by different sets of hands. This process of artistic production compels awareness of plastic objects entwined with human bodies.

Hyperobjects, like plastic, reveal that nature is not separate from culture and that human beings are not sealed off from the environments in which living and nonliving things coexist and intermingle. In his many books, Morton explores the connection between humans and nonhumans, analyzing contemporary art for suggestions of an ecological ethics appropriate to hyperobjects and our current ecological crisis. He highlights contemporary art that invites "an attunement" to hyperobjects in all of their weirdness, incomprehensibility, and darkness.[68] Such art, he insists, enables thinking and feeling that is planetary in scale, which in part means art that might help us recognize that we exist "inside an object, or rather a series of 'objects wrapped in objects': Earth, the biosphere, climate, global warming."[69] Clottey's Afrogallonism and Tagoe-Turkson's flip-flop art enact many of Morton's ideas, but their work goes further. In effect, they qualify Morton's ecological thought, which says very little about power and history and the disjunctures that slice across planetary interconnectivity. Clottey's and Tagoe-Turkson's trash art reminds us of a point made throughout this book, that humans are part of something vast across time and space (global warming and plastic waste) and that we live and experience these massive hyperobjects in historically and geographically particular contexts.

Take Clottey's 2016 *Yellow Brick Road* (*YBR*), which is among his largest public art installations. Created and displayed in the Labadi neighborhood of Accra, a residential area on the Gulf of Guinea and not far from Agbogbloshie, the yellow tapestry appears to flow over houses and down the neighborhood's narrow streets. It runs through and wraps around Clottey's family compound, encircling his ancestral home. The piece alludes to Dorothy's journey home in the *Wizard of Oz* (1939), a film that enchanted Depression-era audiences with the spectacle of Technicolor and a narrative that, like Clottey's waste art, spotlights recovered materials: a Tin Man made of junk and reanimated by Dorothy with a few drops of oil held in a small can. The reference to the film also underlines Clottey's engagement with global culture and the transnational discourse of waste art.[70] His artistic practice is highly self-conscious, showing an understanding of its involvement in the global processes it comments on. Clottey has publicly stated that he wants his sculptures to reflect back on a global waste-art economy that revives and redistributes in one part of the world what has been used and discarded in another. (We might place *Welcome to Sodom* within this circuit.) Clottey disrupts this postcolonial economy in part by making contemporary art in Ghana through a creative process that is collaborative and collective. He also exhibits his art in Ghana, in the communities where he collects discarded jerricans. In a small way, Clottey redirects the path of the art world's distinction, which often reaches its zenith in European museums. The construction of *YBR*, for instance, involved members of Clottey's GoLokal workshop, based in Labadi, as well as ordinary folks who live in his neighborhood.[71] They assembled large segments of the installation in the streets, and *YBR* grew as if alive, spreading a shimmering wave of color across the area. The people who attached *YBR* to their homes or walked across its surface were part of its ecology. *YBR* was about human bodies interacting with plastic fabrics, humans and plastic coming together in an unfixed form.

In 2021, Clottey was invited to participate in Desert X, a series of "public exhibitions of art that respond meaningfully to the condition of desert locations, the environment and indigenous communities."[72] The artist set up his installation *The Wishing Well* between a line of trees in a lush, public green space within sight of a series of wind turbines.[73] Two large boxes draped in Clottey's signature yellow-plastic tapestries were stood upside down and with their flaps opened. Clottey made no effort to blend his work of Afrogallonism into the space. The strange beauty of the huge, bright yellow, symmetrical objects comes partly from their incongruity with all that surrounds them. *The Wishing Well* seems to be in tune with the wind turbines far in the distance and somewhat indifferent to the nearby trees. These giant, human-made plastic objects, like the turbines behind them, encourage viewers to think about the connection between living and nonliving objects, but with a slight shift. *The Wishing Well*, like the other works mentioned here, reimagines the everyday ubiquity of plastic and its penetration into human ecologies. Clottey's installation, however, unsettles boundaries between fabricated and "natural" spaces. It asks why a fabricated public park is any more "natural" than a fabricated yellow plastic box. The piece also plays with our ideas about art and machines. Is it the plastic box or the giant turbine that counts as art? After all, both human-made creations are expressions of human interactions with energy, manifested in the turning blades of a turbine or art created from plastic, itself a waste product of petroleum processing. In 2022, Clottey erected another large-scale installation called *Gold Falls* for Desert X as part of the open-air AlUla Arts Festival in the Al Ula desert region in the Arabian Peninsula. Clottey created a gold waterfall from a massive yellow fabric made in his signature jerrican style. The piece appears to ripple down the side of a mountain, plastic water in a desert. Magical and dazzling, this installation comments on petroculture in relation to anthropogenic conditions such as water scarcity and drought, and like *The Wishing Well*, it invites us to contemplate how hyperobjects, like plastic, disrupt the human-centric categories that Morton argues blind us to planetary interconnectedness.

CONCLUSION

Art created from recovered plastic waste might be said to raise awareness about recycling, the need to consume less, the value of found materials, and the vast amounts of plastic trash that pollutes our oceans, air, and soil. But these are to my mind the least interesting observations we can make about the African trash art analyzed in this chapter. Like Morton's ecological thinking, these works reject the environmental fantasy perpetuated by projects like *Welcome to Sodom*, which maintain that energy's by-products can be hidden, eliminated, or reduced by moral edict and which keeps alive the idea of a Nature outside of history and culture. Clottey and Tagoe-Turkson bring plastic waste into view and, in form and presentation, work with its complex and contradictory materiality. They acknowledge that plastic both threatens and sustains life and that its toxicity and persistence create serious public health problems in Ghana even as plastic remains essential to providing vital products and services. Theirs is "political art" as it has been theorized by Rancière. These strange and beautiful installations transform the systems that bind humans to fossil fuels. Clottey, in particular, invites human bodies to interact with plastic. One is *inside* his work, and this connection brings to life the insight that "petroculture is lived from within."[74] (How unlike the authoritative and external gaze of *Welcome to Sodom*!) Engaging with the Ghanaian art discussed here

Fig. 5.3 *Gold Falls*. 2022. Photograph by Harry Parvin. © Serge Attukwei Clottey.

Fig. 5.4 *Gold Falls*. 2022. Close-up. Photograph by Harry Parvin. © Serge Attukwei Clo

means sensing human entanglements with the by-products of petroculture and reflecting on plastic as hyperobject. I tend to think, as do many others, that seeing and sensing these entanglements might assist us in finding "ways of living without the categories and fantasies of containment" that displace our responsibilities for creating a more just present, and for our planet's future.[75]

NOTES

1. Boetzkes, *Plastic Capitalism*, 77. Boetzkes's excellent book has inspired and shaped this chapter in too many ways to name. Boetzkes also leads me to a more careful engagement with the many books by Tim Morton, whom I cite throughout this chapter. I would like to imagine this chapter as building on and in conversation with their provocative thought and writing.
2. Boetzkes, "Plastic Vision and the Sight of Petroculture," 229.
3. DeLoughrey, *Allegories of the Anthropocene*, 98.
4. Ronda, "Organic Form, Plastic Forms," 115.
5. Lerner, "Africa's Exploding Plastic Nightmare," 22.
6. Irr and Kim, "Introduction," 2.
7. Morton, *The Ecological Thought*, 130.
8. Morton, *The Ecological Thought*, 130.
9. Morton, *Hyperobjects*, 15.
10. Weigensamer and Krönes, dirs., *Welcome to Sodom*, Austria and Ghana: Blackbox Film & Medienproduktion, 2019, DVD.
11. Wenzel, *The Disposition of Nature*, 55.
12. Press materials for *Welcome to Sodom*, http://www.welcome-to-sodom.com/wp-content/uploads/2018/04/EPK_WTS_eng_lq.pdf.
13. Van der Velden and Oteng-Ababio, "Six Myths about Electronic Waste in Agbogbloshie, Ghana."
14. Quayson, *Oxford Street, Accra*, 227–228.
15. "Agbogbloshie Dwellers Matter, Every Ghanaian Matters," 16.
16. Rancière, *Dissensus*, 136.
17. Boetzkes, *Plastic Capitalism*, 17.
18. Boetzkes, *Plastic Capitalism*, 15.
19. Boetzkes, *Plastic Capitalism*, 15.
20. Rancière, *Dissensus*, 136, 141–143.
21. For detailed chapters on the global circulation of e-waste, see Biswajit et al., *Paradigm Shift in E-Waste Management*.
22. Van der Velden and Oteng-Ababio, "Six Myths about Electronic Waste in Agbogbloshie, Ghana."
23. Wynter, "Unsettling the Coloniality of Being," 262.
24. Wynter, "Unsettling the Coloniality of Being," 321.

25. Later in the documentary, in one of his monologues, the boy explains that he was born a girl and that in the dump, he can live and work as the boy he is.
26. Boetzkes, *Plastic Capitalism*, 116.
27. Millar, *Reclaiming the Discarded*, 38.
28. Millar, *Reclaiming the Discarded*, 38.
29. Millar, *Reclaiming the Discarded*, 58.
30. Millar, *Reclaiming the Discarded*, 58.
31. Morton, *The Ecological Thought*, 5.
32. Morton, *Ecology without Nature*, 21, quoted in Patricia Yeager, "The Death of Nature and the Apotheosis of Trash; Or, Rubbish Ecology," *PMLA* 123, no. 2 (March 2008): 324 (321–339).
33. Said, *Orientalism*, 55.
34. Adams, "Nature and the Colonial Mind," 32–33.
35. Ghosh, *The Nutmeg's Curse*, 71.
36. Ghosh, *The Nutmeg's Curse*, 63.
37. Iheka, *African Ecomedia*, 82–92.
38. Yeboah, "Subaltern Strategies and Development Practice," 50–65.
39. Obeng-Odoom, "Do African Cities Have Markets for Plastic or Plastics for Markets?," 468.
40. Obeng-Odoom, "Do African Cities Have Markets for Plastics or Plastics for Markets?," 467.
41. Boetzkes, *Plastic Capitalism*, 182.
42. Boetzkes, *Plastic Capitalism*, 182.
43. Maja van der Veleden and Martin Oteng-Ababio raise the same complaint: "By portraying Agbogbloshie as an 'apocalyptic society,' [*Welcome to Sodom*] may even contribute to risks for those vulnerable people for whom it clearly seeks to generate sympathy: the Ghanaian authorities have shown in the past that they are not unwilling to use foreign media attention for 'the largest e-waste dump in the world' as the justification to forcefully evict people from the slum." See van der Veleden and Oteng-Ababio, "Six Myths about Electronic Waste in Agbogbloshie, Ghana," 4.
44. DuBois, *Plastics History*, 1.
45. Huber, *Lifeblood*, 66.
46. Huber, *Lifeblood*, 72.
47. Babyemi, et al., "Ensuring Sustainability in Plastics Use in Africa," 2.
48. Babyemi, et al., "Ensuring Sustainability in Plastics Use in Africa," 4.
49. It seems important to mention that plastic and copper are some of the materials most commonly recycled in Agbogbloshie.
50. Others include Jeremiah Quarshie, also from Ghana, Ugandan Martin Kharumwa, Beninois artist Romuld Hazoumé, and Cephas Mutua Muthini from Kenya. For images of works by these artists, see Kampire Bahana, "African Artists Reimagine the Humble Yellow Jerrycan," at https://vuga.wordpress.com/2017/03/23/african-artists-reimagine-the-humble-yellow-jerrycan/.

51. Sutton, "The Plastic Revolution?," 20–22.
52. Boetzkes, *Plastic Capitalism*, 185.
53. Zaato, "Look Before You Leap," 689. See this article for a detailed discussion of the history of water policy in Ghana.
54. For more information about private water delivery in urban areas in Ghana, see Twum and Abubakari, "Drops in the City," 417–434.
55. Stoler et al., "Piped Water Flows but Sachet Consumption Grows," 54.
56. Bier, "Serge Attukwei Clottey."
57. This information was found in file GH/PRAAD/SCO.6/3/457 in the archives at the Public Records Administration in Accra. It is confirmed in Grayson, "A Conglomerate in Africa," 317.
58. This information was found in file GH/PRAAD/SCO.6/3/457 in the archives at the Public Records Administration in Accra. See also Forsyth and Solomon, "Restrictions on Foreign Ownership," 286.
59. Kutten, "The Potential of Africa's Plastic Market," 27.
60. Kutten, "The Potential of Africa's Plastic Market," 30.
61. Ronda, "Organic Form, Plastic Forms," 128.
62. Ronda, "Organic Form, Plastic Forms," 130.
63. Davis, "Life and Death in the Anthropocene," 348.
64. DeLoughrey, *Allegories of the Anthropocene*, 108.
65. James, "Convergence," 43.
66. Boateng, "The Master of Hanging Pieces," 94.
67. Vogel, *El Anatsui: Art and Life*, 162.
68. Morton, *Hyperobjects*, 175.
69. Morton, *Hyperobjects*, 119.
70. In an August 2019 interview with the author in Accra Ghana, Clottey explained that he received his fine arts diploma from Ghanatta College of Art and Design in Ghana before studying at the Escola Guinard University of Art in Brazil. He has been called a multidisciplinary, experimental, mixed-media, political, materialist, and performance artist, and his work has appeared in galleries in Africa, Europe, and North America. In 2018, he received a commission from Facebook to create and mount an installation at the corporate headquarters in Menlo Park, San Francisco.
71. GoLokal names the space in Labadi where Clottey and the men and women who work with him as apprentices (and whom he pays a wage) assemble his pieces.
72. desertx.org.
73. See https://desertx.org/dx/desert-x-21/serge-attukwei-clottey.
74. Boetzkes, "Plastic Vision and the Sight of Petroculture," 226.
75. Davis, "Life and Death in the Anthropocene," 355.

CONCLUSION: READING FOR RENEWABLE FUTURES

IN THE *AFRICAN STUDIES REVIEW* Forum: What's New in African Cinema, MaryEllen Higgins suggests wind as a metaphor for describing change in African cinema. Unlike the commonly used *wave*, as in Manthia Diawara's description of a new wave of African cinema—which I referenced in the introduction—wind, Higgins argues, "defies impositions of linear history." Amorphous and lacking a center, wind "open[s] an alternative vision of African cinema" and loosens it from Western supports.[1] In this brief conclusion, I want to build on Higgins's reflection by considering wind not as a metaphor but as a material force in two films, both about electricity and both set in Africa: *The Boy Who Harnessed the Wind* (2019) and *Waiting for Happiness* (2002). Neither film is pedagogical or political in the same ways as African films of the first or even the second generation. They represent a new type of African cinema that could be placed along a spectrum that on one end includes commercial products, such as Nollywood, and on the other, overtly political and anticolonial productions in the tradition of Ousmane Sembène. Bringing these two films into conversation allows me to revisit some of the main points discussed in *African Energy Worlds*.

Writing about energy involves examining human relations with living and nonliving things—like uranium dust, oil, and wind—and thinking beyond human scales of time and space. Wind, a source of renewable energy, acts at human and planetary scales. Its source is solar radiation, which heats the atmosphere and the planet's surface unevenly. The hotter regions at the equator pull colder air from the poles, while rising hot air moves toward the colder polar regions. This planetary circulation of air generates "complex structures of high and low pressure systems that move through the atmosphere," creating wind.[2] Differential atmospheric pressures between land and sea as well as the rotation of the Earth's surface influence air currents, too. These complicated atmospheric interactions "mean that wind is by its nature both unpredictable and intermittent."[3] Anthropologist Cymene Howe describes wind as "a negotiation" among atmospheric forces.[4] It's a planetary movement of air currents compelled by forces that are challenging for humans to model and predict.

That a young boy overcomes major economic and social obstacles to capture the force of the wind and direct it toward social good surely accounts for the pleasure derived from watching *The Boy Who Harnessed the Wind*. Distributed internationally by Netflix and written and directed by British-Nigerian actor Chiwetel Ejiofor (who also stars), the film is based on the memoir of the same title by William Kamkwamba and Bryan Meale. It's a prestige film, a hybrid transnational coproduction intended to appeal to commercial and independent cinema audiences. The film, like the memoir, presents an uplifting and entertaining narrative about the real-life William Kamkwamba and the windmill he assembles from electronic junk and recovered wood during the 2001 food crisis in Malawi. William uses his machine to capture wind power and rotate the blades of a turbine, which creates electricity to run a water pump for the village. The pump draws water from a well and irrigates crops planted during the dry season to fend off starvation. Like many Netflix features, its story, although set in a particular historical context, is meant to be universal. The story is told from the perspective of a sympathetic protagonist who expresses strong beliefs about the power of education and the importance of family, community, and human ingenuity. The film's mimetic realism naturalizes those ideologies. The film is more polished and professional than *Black November* and *Blood and Oil* (analyzed in chapter 1) and less dark and gritty than *Viva Riva!* (discussed in chapter 3). But like those films, *The Boy Who Harnessed the Wind* is a product of the major changes that have reshaped cinema in the twenty-first century, including the wide availability of new digital technologies and Internet-based channels of distribution, among other developments described in this book.

To conform with Netflix standards, *The Boy Who Harnessed the Wind* condenses its political critique and historical depth, which the memoir elaborates on, to one scene involving a tobacco estate and its farmers, and one mention of the pressure international financial institutions leveraged to force Malawi's government to profit from grain held in storage. These scenes are nonetheless important: we learn that the industrial tobacco farm was responsible for the deforestation that exacerbated the cycle of drought and flooding that destroyed crops. We also find out that the previous year, the IMF and World Bank had insisted that Malawi sell off its state-owned food stores to neighboring countries. This outline of historical and political conditions, like the setting of the narrative, does background work; it places viewers in a context meant to spotlight the extraordinary achievements of the protagonist. This backdrop remains largely unchanged and out of focus to highlight the agency of William and the community he rallies in support of his electricity adventure. The wind, too, does background work. It is a feature of the setting, a natural resource that is captured and made useful by human intelligence and will.

From an ecological perspective, the film generates a central tension. On one hand, it calls out the damage caused by capitalism's regime of economic growth to human and nonhuman life. It is easy to recognize that the film aligns with Wangari Maathai's Green Belt Movement and its campaign against industrial deforestation and demands for energy and environmental justice for impoverished people.[5] Within the constraints of its production, the film attempts to act on the social. Yet, on the other hand, its ideological investment in the heroic individual who, using a book about electricity written by an American, transforms his unproductive environment into a useful resource, reflects the colonial, extractive mindset that sees humans as lords over the planet. Ecological thinkers like Maathai and Morton assert that this mindset must be dismantled to clear the way for a more just and sustainable energy future.

This brief look at the film is not meant to dismiss it. Indeed, I want to suggest that *The Boy Who Harnessed the Wind* makes an important contribution to the intellectual and artistic work required of us if we are to move away from petromodernity and, simultaneously, address energy injustice. Like other African films, as noted by Higgins, it "tell[s] us about the earth's unevenness—about gross colonial and neocolonial inequalities, uneven distribution of justice, the uneven impacts of neoliberalism."[6] The film generates questions about how we promote renewable energy and also imagine a politics that guarantees the security and health of all humans. It also alerts us to African entitlements to energy, countering the old, tired idea that Africans are helpless victims, that they cannot transform their own circumstances without outside intervention. Although it does not directly address global warming, the film raises awareness about the ecological violence inherent to development under neoliberal capitalism. If the film's energy imaginary is limited, those limits are products of its networks of production and distribution. Such limits ask film scholars and Africanists to make sense of its obvious weaknesses and highlight the tensions that might make possible other interpretations.

Waiting for Happiness (2002), written and directed by Abderrahmane Sissako, circulated through several A-level film festivals: Cannes, where it won the FIPRESCI Prize, Toronto, Rotterdam, and New York. As I have explained, Sissako is one of the very few African auteurs to be fully incorporated into world cinema networks. This film, like *Bamako* (discussed in chap. 2), adopts a realist mode of production and, in its form and presentation, stresses the material, temporal, and sensory features of its location, Nouadhibou, a transit village on the Mauritania coast. Like all of Sissako's work, *Waiting for Happiness* "fashion[s] a narrative style that bears the signature of a distinctive artistic temperament."[7] It is episodic, poetic, and open-ended, following four characters whose travels stall in the tiny town during the same short period. Two of these four figures, Maata, an elderly electrician, and Khatra, his young apprentice, work at the margins of electricity's reach, connecting villagers to an overburdened and overextended electrical grid. Through them, the film emphasizes energy's imbrication with modernity and remarks on the blockages that thwart connectivity and movement under globalization.

To highlight the differences between this film and the former, I employ an ecological analysis that decenters human agency and attends to energy as invisible and unwieldy potential, something that becomes perceptible only through contact with something else. Maata's narrative chronicles his many unsuccessful efforts to direct the flow of electricity. Electric current defies Maata's will. Wind, too, disrupts human intentions and plans. It is not domesticated, as it is in the Netflix production. It buries Makan's radio and blows sand into the carburetor of Abdallah's taxi, stalling it. The wind perhaps causes the disaster that drowns Michael at sea and brings his body back to shore, and it redirects the light bulb Khatra throws into the ocean after Maata's death. Wind is much more than a feature of the setting in the film; it acts on and influences the plot, and Sissako draws out this active materiality. The soundscape amplifies the sound of wind interacting with its surroundings and brushing across the microphone, especially in the opening. Long shots of a depopulated stretch of desert stress the impact of the wind on dunes of sand, which flow like liquid, and the camera follows a fist of tumbleweed that the wind has lifted from the ground. In these and other moments, the film also stresses wind's relationality, as described by Howe: "Wind is only ever made visible through its impact and influence on other matter, other materials, and other things. Wind's ontology refuses to take separateness as an inherent feature of the world. Its relationality exists as an inverse allegory to the teleology of extraction that operates in one direction, to one end for a singular purpose. And this is, in part, wind's value—it has an existential precondition that appears only in the context of contact. Wind is touching, mutual, moving."[8] This excerpt comes from Howe's study of the failed Mareña wind park project on the Isthmus of Tehuantepec, in Mexico. Her observations about wind's ontological relationality support her larger conclusions about wind, ecology, and renewable energy. She argues that the Mareña project fell apart because its investors and promoters failed to understand that energy systems, even those derived from wind and solar, are "mutual acts created between forces and materials, as well as humans and their others."[9] Wind has a crucial place in our energy future, Howe acknowledges, but wind alone won't save us. Without attunement to the "array of the-other-than-human relations including those with nonhuman beings, technomaterial artifacts, infrastructures, and geophysical forces" that compose all energy systems, we risk reproducing the human-dominant order and the resource-extraction model responsible for the anthropogenic climate crisis we are trying to slow or halt.[10] Sissako's film explores human entanglements with wind, waves, sand dunes, electricity, light bulbs, and birds (as in Khatra's song). Its energy imaginary can be made to reflect back on *The Boy Who Harnessed the Wind* not as a corrective but as a question. Both films comment on the limits of modernity and development, and each articulates African claims to lives of security and opportunity made possible by affordable energy. The differences are instructive and compel us to acknowledge energy as potential and as product engendered by interactions between humans and their environments.

In their introduction to "Fueling Capture: Africa's Energy Frontiers," which I cite in the introduction, Michael Degani, Brenda Chalfin, and Jamie Cross ask: "What sort of social and political formations find purchase in the technical and material affordances of air, sunlight, gas or recycled waste? And what are the stakes for theorizing the politics of energy that does not take fossil fuels as its paradigmatic case but rather begins with a complex field of global realignment, comprising multiple sites and sources?" These questions, which guide the excellent anthropology published in the issue, might also inspire African film and media scholars to read cinematic texts through the multiplicity of energy sources and flows emergent across the continent in the current period of "global energy realignment." In this book,

I have investigated the energetic ecologies and aesthetics animated by fossil fuels, hydropower, electricity, uranium, and wind in a range of films and visual media and highlighted cinema's unique ability to represent the human body as a site of energy potential (affect) and energy expenditure and to focus on the human and nonhuman connections experienced through energy sources, forms, waste, and infrastructures. In the context of "resurgent extractivism" in Africa, film scholars might do well to engage the finely tuned and deeply situated research of anthropologists, including those published in the "Fueling Capture" special issue of *Cambridge Anthropology*, whose work theorizes the swiftly changing African energy landscape, including postcarbon developments that promise to be the focus of or otherwise figure in African film and media in the future. More than merely representing what the scholarly literature describes, African cinema works alongside energy humanities and social science research to bring forth Africans' lived experiences with energy and to amplify their political and economic energy demands.

This book has presented African cinema as a resource singular in its capacities to explore the promise and limits of energetic modernity and the uneven distribution of prosperity and slow violence produced by global energy economies, from sites of extraction to plastic-littered waste dumps. I have used an energy analytics to focus on the ecological, affective, labor, and debt relations caused by particular energy sources and systems as found in postcolonial African cinema and to describe connections between electricity infrastructures and local movie assemblages, using Dagbani-language movies produced in northern Ghana as a case study. Very broadly, this book has tried to demonstrate that studying African cinema for energy raises important questions in the Anthropocene and provides an entry into the urgent process of articulating a post–fossil fuel politics that advances the health of the planet and critiques the grossly exploitative energy relationship to modernity's sacrifice zones. The book has read African films to clear space for us to imagine a politics for a world free of fossil fuels, one that dismantles the "human-dominant order" that produced slavery and colonialism, as well as the "modernizing nationalisms, and capitalist and consumerist globalization" of the last seven hundred years.[11] In the end, the book, like so many others before it and, I hope, after, affirms the central place of the humanities and the arts in facilitating the difficult transformations essential to transitioning away from hydrocarbons and toward renewable energy systems that work for all humans and, yet and crucially, also are less human-centered.

NOTES

1. Higgins, "Winds of African Cinema," 88.
2. Breeze, *Wind Power Generation*, 9.
3. Breeze, *Wind Power Generation*, 10.
4. Howe, *Ecologics*, 190.
5. See Maathai, *Replenishing the Earth*; *Unbowed*.
6. Higgins, "Winds of Change," 84.
7. Adesokan, "Abderrahmane Sissako and the Poetics of Engaged Expatriation," 146.
8. Howe, *Ecologics*, 11.
9. Howe, *Ecologics*, 190.
10. Howe, *Ecologics*, 2.
11. Chakrabarty, *The Climate of History*, 203.

FILMOGRAPHY

Abt, Danya, dir. *Quel Souvenir*. Distributed by Danya Abt, 2009. DVD.
Amata, Jeta, dir. *Black November: Struggle for the Niger Delta*. Amazon Prime Video, 2015.
Ejiofor, Chiwetel, dir. *The Boy Who Harnessed the Wind*. United Kingdom/Malawi. Participant Media, BBC Films and Netflix, 2019.
Graham, Curtis, dir. *Blood and Oil*. Netflix, 2015.
Haroun Mahamat-Saleh, dir. *Daratt (Dry Season)*. ArtMattan Productions, 2008. DVD.
———, dir. *Grigris*. Film Movement, 2013. DVD.
Jai, Ramesh, dir. *Life!* Stage 32, 2017. https://www.stage32.com/media/1850160 473576580020.
Kubaloe, Leonard A., dir. *Piele: Rise of Montana*. OBL Studios, 2017. DVD.
Makengo, Nelson, dir. *Up at Night*. Studio Olafur Eliasson, 2019. Vimeo.
Mambéty, Djibril Diop, dir. *Hyènes (Hyenas)*. Kino Video, 1992. DVD.
Mora Kpai, Idrissou, dir. *Arlit, deuxième Paris*. San Francisco, CA: California Newsreel, 2004. DVD.
Ousmane, Sembène, dir. *Faat Kiné*. Films Domirev and LC Purchase Collection. Paris: Organisation internationale de la francophonie, 2001. DVD.
Sissako, Abderrahmane, dir. *Bamako*. New Yorker Video, 2006. DVD.
———, dir. *Waiting for Happiness*. New Yorker Video, 2002. DVD.
Wa Munga, Djo Tunda, dir. *Viva Riva!* Music Box Films, 2011.
Weigensamer, Florian, and Christian Krönes, dirs. *Welcome to Sodom*. Stuttgart: Camino Filmverleih, 2019. DVD.

BIBLIOGRAPHY

Adams, William. "Nature and the Colonial Mind." In *Decolonizing Nature: Strategies for Conservation in a Post-Colonial Era*, edited by William M. Adams and Martin Mulligan, 16–50. Oxford, UK: Earthscan, 2003.

Adejunmobi, Moradewun. "Evolving Nollywood Templates for Minor Transnational Film." *Black Camera* 5, no. 2 (2014): 74–94.

Adesokan, Akin. "Abderrahmane Sissako and the Poetics of Engaged Expatriation." *Screen* 51, no. 2 (2010): 143–160. doi:10.1093/screen/hjq002.

Adom, Philip Kofi, and Samuel Adams. "Technical Fossil Fuel Energy Efficiency (TFFEE) and Debt-Finance Government Expenditure Nexus in Africa." *Journal of Cleaner Production* 271 (2020). doi:10.1016/j.jclepro.2020.122670.

Adunbi, Omolade. *Oil Wealth and Insurgency in Nigeria*. Bloomington: Indiana University Press, 2015. https://www.jstor.org/stable/j.ctt16gzkft.

"Agbogbloshie Dwellers Matter, Every Ghanaian Matters." *Graphic Online*, September 19, 2019a, 19. https://www.graphic.com.gh/news/politics/agbogbloshie-dwellers-matter-every-ghanaian-matters-bawumia.html.

Aghoghovwia, Philip. "Nigeria." In *Fueling Culture: 101 Words for Energy and Environment*, edited by Imre Szeman, Jennifer Wenzel, and Patricia Yaeger, 238–241. New York: Fordham University Press, 2017. https://www.graphic.com.gh/news/politics/agbogbloshie-dwellers-matter-every-ghanaian-matters-bawumia.html

Akpandjar, George, and Carl Kitchens. "From Darkness to Light: The Effect of Electrification in Ghana, 2000–2010." *Economic Development and Cultural Change* 66, no. 1 (October 2017): 31–54. doi:10.1086/693707.

Amatya, Alok, and Ashley Dawson. "Literature in an Age of Extraction: An Introduction." *MFS Modern Fiction Studies* 66, no. 1 (2020): 1–19.

Appel, Hannah. *The Licit Life of Capitalism: US Oil in Equatorial Guinea*. Durham, NC: Duke University Press, 2019.

Appel, Hannah, Arthur Mason, and Michael Watts, eds. *Subterranean Estates*. Ithaca, NY: Cornell University Press, 2015.

Arbogast, Stephen V. "Project Financing and Political Risk Mitigation: The Singular Case of the Chad-Cameroon Pipeline." *Texas Journal of Oil, Gas, and Energy Law* 4, no. 2 (2008): 269–298.

Babayemi, Joshua O., Innocent C. Nnorom, Oladele Osibanjo, and Roland Weber. "Ensuring Sustainability in Plastics Use in Africa: Consumption, Waste Generation, and Projections." *Environmental Sciences Europe* 31, no. 1 (2019): 1–20. doi:10.1186/s12302-019-0254-5.

Baker, Jonathan. "Oil and African Development." *Journal of Modern African Studies* 15, no. 2 (June 1977): 175–212. doi:10.1017/S0022278X00053908.

Barad, Karen. "No Small Matter." In *Arts of Living on a Damaged Planet*, edited by Anna Tsing, Heather Swanson, Elaine Gan, and Nils Bubandt, 103–120. Minneapolis: University of Minnesota Press, 2017.

Barr, Burlin. "Dependency, Appetite, and Iconographies of Hunger in Mambéty's *Hyenas*." *Social Text* 28, no. 2 (2010): 57–83.

Bassey, Nnimmo. *To Cook a Continent*. Alexandria: Pambazuka, 2012.

Baucom, Ian. *History 4° Celsius: Search for a Method in the Age of the Anthropocene*. Durham, NC: Duke University Press, 2020.

Beck, Ulrich. *Risk Society: Towards a New Modernity*. Translated by Mark Ritter. Sage, 1992.

Bellamy, Brent Ryan, Stephanie LeMenager, and Imre Szeman. "When Energy Is the Focus: Methodology, Politics, and Pedagogy." *Postmodern Culture* 26, no. 2 (2016). doi:10.1353/pmc.2016.0004.

Bennett, Jane. *Vibrant Matter*. Durham, NC: Duke University Press, 2010.

Bier, Arielle. "Serge Attukwei Clottey: In Conversation with Arielle Bier." *NYAQ/LXAQ/SFAQ: International Art and Culture* (March 18, 2016).

Biswajit, Debnath, Siddhartha Bhattacharyya, Abhijit Das, and Polturi Anil Chowdary. *Paradigm Shift in E-Waste Management*. Boca Raton, FL: CRC, 2022. doi:10.1201/9781003095972. http://digital.casalini.it/9781000568578.

Boateng, Osei. "The Master of Hanging Pieces . . . How El Anatsui Rose to Fame." *New African*, June 1, 2013. https://search.ebscohost.com/login.aspx?direct=true&db=edsbig&AN=edsbig.A334946606&authtype=shib&site=eds-live&scope=site.

Boetzkes, Amanda. *Plastic Capitalism*. Cambridge, MA: MIT Press, 2019.

———. "Plastic Vision and the Sight of Petroculture." In *Petrocultures: Oil, Politics, Culture*, edited by Sheena Wilson, Adam Carlson, and Imre Szeman, 222–241. Montreal: McGill-Queen's University Press, 2017. doi:10.1515/9780773550391-012.

Bouwer, Karen. "Life in Cinematic Urban Africa." In *A Companion to African Cinema*, edited by Kenneth W. Harrow and Carmela Garritano, 69–87. Hoboken, NJ: John Wiley & Sons, 2018.
Boyer, Dominic. *Energopolitics: Wind and Power in the Anthropocene*. Durham, NC: Duke University Press, 2019.
Breeze, Paul. *Wind Power Generation*. Cambridge: Academic Press, 2016.
Brinkema, Eugenie. *The Forms of the Affects*. Durham, NC: Duke University Press, 2014.
Brøvig-Hanssen, Ragnhild, and Anne Danielsen. *Digital Signatures*. Cambridge, MA: MIT Press, 2016.
Buell, Frederick. *From Apocalypse to Way of Life*. 1st ed. Florence: Routledge, 2003.
Butler, Judith. *Precarious Life*. London: Verso, 2006.
Caminero-Santangelo, Byron. *Different Shades of Green: African Literature, Environmental Justice, and Political Ecology*. Charlottesville: University of Virginia Press, 2014.
Caminero-Santangelo, Byron, and Garth Myers. *Environment at the Margins*. 1st ed. Athens: Ohio University Press, 2011. https://www.jstor.org/stable/j.ctt1j7x72r.
Canavan, Gerry. "Debt, Theft, Permaculture." In *Debt: Ethics, the Environment, and the Economy*, edited by Peter Y. Paik and Merry Wiesner-Hanks, 210–224. Bloomington: Indiana University Press, 2013.
"Chad: Fuel Shortages in N'Djaména." *African Manager*, 2014. https://en.africanmanager.com/chad-serious-fuel-shortage-reported-in-chadian-capital.
Chad Prepays World Bank Pipeline Debt. Euromoney Trading Limited, 2008. https://proxy.library.tamu.edu/login?url=https://search.ebscohost.com/login.aspx?direct=true&db=edsinc&AN=edsinc.A186374919&site=eds-live.
Chakrabarty, Dipesh. *The Climate of History in a Planetary Age*. Chicago: University of Chicago Press, 2021.
Collier, Stephen J. *Post-Soviet Social: Neoliberalism, Social Modernity, Biopolitics*. Princeton NJ: Princeton University Press, 2011.
Comaroff, Jean, and John L. Comaroff. *Theory from the South (The Radical Imagination)*. London: Routledge, 2012. doi:10.4324/9781315631639.
Conde, Marta, and Giorgos Kallis. "The Global Uranium Rush and Its Africa Frontier. Effects, Reactions and Social Movements in Namibia." *Global Environmental Change* 22, no. 3 (August 2012): 596–610. doi:10.1016/j.gloenvcha.2012.03.007.
"Country Energy Report." *Global Energy Market Research: DR Congo* (2019): 1–13. https://proxy.library.tamu.edu/login?url=https://search.ebscohost.com/login.aspx?direct=true&db=enr&AN=137156549&site=eds-live.
Daggett, Cara New. *The Birth of Energy: Fossil Fuels, Thermodynamics, and the Politics of Work*. Durham, NC: Duke University Press, 2019.

Davies, Thom. "Slow Violence and Toxic Geographies: 'Out of Sight' to Whom?" *Environment and Planning C: Politics and Space* 40, no. 2 (2022): 409–427. doi:10.1177/2399654419841063.

Davis, Heather. "Life and Death in the Anthropocene." In *Art in the Anthropocene: Encounters among Aesthetics, Politics, Environments and Epistemologies*, 347–358. London: Open Humanities, 2015.

De Boeck, Filip. "'Divining' the City: Rhythm, Amalgamation and Knotting as Forms of 'Urbanity.'" *Social Dynamics* 41, no. 1 (January 2015): 47–58. doi:10.1080/02533952.2015.1032508.

De Luca, Tiago, and Jorge Nuno Barradas. *Slow Cinema*. Traditions in World Cinema. Edinburgh: Edinburgh University Press, 2016.

Degani, Michael. *The City Electric*. Durham, NC: Duke University Press, 2022.

Degani, Michael, Brenda Chalfin, and Jamie Cross. "Introduction: Fueling Capture: Africa's Energy Frontiers." *Cambridge Anthropology* 38, no. 2 (September 2020): 1. doi:10.3167/cja.2020.380202.

Deleuze, Gilles, *Cinema 1*. Translated by Hugh Tomlinson and Barbara Habberjam. Minneapolis: University of Minnesota Press, 1986.

DeLoughrey, Elizabeth M. *Allegories of the Anthropocene*. Durham, NC: Duke University Press, 2019.

Diawara, Manthia. *African Film: New Forms of Aesthetics and Politics*. Munich: Prestel, 2010.

Dittgen, Romain. "Of Other Spaces? Hybrid Forms of Chinese Engagement in Sub-Saharan Africa." *Journal of Current Chinese Affairs* 44, no. 1 (2015): 43–73. doi:10.1177/186810261504400103.

Dittgen, Romain, and Dan Large. *China's Growing Involvement in Chad: Escaping Enclosure?* Unpublished manuscript, 2012. doi:10.13140/rg.2.2.30222.08009.

Dovey, Lindiwe. *Curating Africa in the Age of Film Festivals*. New York: Palgrave Macmillan, 2015.

DuBois, J. H. *Plastics History*. Boston: Cahners Books, 1972.

Egya, Sule E. *Nature, Environment, and Activism in Nigerian Literature*. Paperback ed. London: Routledge Taylor & Francis Group, 2021.

El-Gamal, Mahmoud A., and Amy Jaffe. *Oil, Dollars, Debt, and Crises*. Cambridge: Cambridge University Press, 2010.

Farahmand, Azadeh. "Disentangling the International Festival Circuit: Genre and Iranian Cinema." In *Global Art Cinema: New Theories and Histories*, edited by Rosalind Galt and Karl Schoonover, 263–281. Oxford: Oxford University Press, 2012.

Ferguson, James. *Global Shadows*. Durham, NC: Duke University Press, 2007.

Forsyth, D. J. C., and R. F. Solomon. "Restrictions on Foreign Ownership of Manufacturing Industry in a Less Developed Country." *Journal of Developing Areas* 12, no. 3 (1978): 281–296. http://www.econis.eu/PPNSET?PPN=392772906.

Frassinelli, Pier Paolo. "Heading South: Theory, *Viva Riva!* and *District 9*." *Critical Arts* 29, no. 3 (May 2015): 293–309. doi:10.1080/02560046.2015.1059545.

Gabara, Rachel. "Abderrahmane Sissako: Second and Third Cinema in the First Person." In *Global Art Cinema: New Theories and Histories*, 320. Oxford: Oxford University Press, 2012.

Galt, Rosalind, and Karl Schoonover, eds. *Global Art Cinema: New Theories and Histories*. Oxford: Oxford University Press.

Garritano, Carmela. *African Video Movies and Global Desires*. Athens: Ohio University Press, 2013. https://www.jstor.org/stable/j.ctt24joor.

———. "Introduction: Nollywood—An Archive of African Worldliness." *Black Camera: The Newsletter of the Black Film Center/Archives* 5, no. 2 (April 2014): 44–52. doi:10.2979/blackcamera.5.2.44.

———. "Living Precariously in the African Postcolony: Debt and Labor Relations in the Films of Mahamat-Saleh Haroun." *Cinema Journal* 58, no. 2 (2019a): 23–45. doi:10.1353/cj.2019.0001. https://muse.jhu.edu/article/717121.

Gauch, Suzanne. "Darker Vision." In *A Companion to African Cinema*, edited by Kenneth W. Harrow and Carmela Garritano, 337–357. Hoboken, NJ: John Wiley & Sons, 2019.

Ghazvinian, John. *Untapped: The Scramble for Africa's Oil*. San Diego: Harcourt, 2007.

Ghosh, Amitav. *The Great Derangement: Climate Change and the Unthinkable*. Chicago: University of Chicago Press, 2016.

———. *The Nutmeg's Curse*. Chicago: University of Chicago Press, 2021.

Gnassou, Laure. "Addressing Renewable Energy Conundrum in the DR Congo: Focus on Grand Inga Hydropower Dam Project." *Energy Strategy Reviews* 26 (November 2019): 100400. doi:10.1016/j.esr.2019.100400.

Goldstone, Brian, and Juan Obarrio. *African Futures: Essays on Crisis, Emergence, and Possibility*. Chicago: University of Chicago Press, 2017.

Gore, Christopher. *Electricity in Africa*. Woodbridge, UK: James Currey, 2017.

Gorfinkel, Elena. "Weariness, Waiting: Endurance and Art Cinema's Tired Bodies." *Discourse: Journal for Theoretical Studies in Media and Culture* 34, nos. 2–3 (2012): 311–347. doi:10.13110/discourse.34.2-3.0311.

Graeber, David. *Debt*. Brooklyn, NY: Melville House, 2011.

Grayson, L. E. "A Conglomerate in Africa." *African Studies Review* 16, no. 3 (1973): 315–345. http://www.econis.eu/PPNSET?PPN=477824684.

Green-Simms, Lindsey. *Postcolonial Automobility: Car Culture in West Africa*. Minneapolis: University of Minnesota Press, 2017.

Günel, Gökçe. *Spaceship in the Desert*. Durham, NC: Duke University Press, 2019. doi:10.1515/9781478002406.

Gustafsson, Henrik. "A Wet Emptiness." In *A Companion to Film Noir*, edited by Andrew Spicer and Helen Hanson, 50–66. Oxford, UK: Blackwell, 2013.

Guyer, Jane I. *Legacies, Logics, Logistics: Essays in the Anthropology of the Platform Economy*. Chicago: University of Chicago Press, 2016.

Hage, Ghassan. "Waiting Out the Crisis: On Stuckedness and Governmentality." In *Waiting*, edited by Ghassan Hage, 97–106. Carlton, Australia: Melbourne University Press, 2009.

Hale, R. "Offering Tales They Want to Hear: Transnational European Film Funding as Neo-orientalism." In *Global Art Cinema: New Theories and Histories*, edited by Rosalind Galt and Karl Schoonover, 303–319. New York: Oxford University Press, 2010.

Harrow, Kenneth W. *Trash: African Cinema from Below*. Bloomington: Indiana University Press, 2013.

Harrow, Kenneth W., and Carmela Garritano. "Introduction." In *A Companion to African Cinema*, edited by Kenneth W. Harrow and Carmela Garritano, 1–20. Hoboken, NJ: Wiley-Blackwell, 2019.

Haynes, Jonathan. *Nollywood*. Chicago: University of Chicago Press, 2016.

Hecht, Gabrielle. *Being Nuclear: Africans and the Global Uranium Trade*. Cambridge, MA: MIT Press, 2014.

———. "Interscalar Vehicles for an African Anthropocene: On Waste, Temporality, and Violence." *Cultural Anthropology* 33, no. 1 (February 2018): 109–141. doi:10.14506/ca33.1.05.

Hicks, Celeste. *Africa's New Oil*. African Arguments. Vol. 6. London: NBN International, 2015.

Higgins, MaryEllen. "At the Intersection of Trauma, Precarity, and African Cinema: A Reflection on Mahamat-Saleh Haroun's *Grigris*." In *A Companion to African Cinema*, edited by Kenneth W. Harrow and Carmela Garritano, 91–111. Hoboken, NJ: Wiley-Blackwell, 2019.

———. "The Winds of African Cinema." *African Studies Review* 58, no. 3 (2015): 77–92.

Hitchcock, Peter. "Velocity and Viscosity." In *Subterranean Estates: Life Worlds of Oil and Gas*, edited by Hannah Appel, Arthur Mason, and Michael Watts, 45–60. Ithaca, NY: Cornell University Press, 2015.

Horta, Korinna. "Public-Private Partnership and Institutional Capture: The State, International Institutions, and Indigenous Peoples in Chad and Cameroon." In *The Politics of Resource Extraction: Indigenous Peoples, Multinational Corporations, and the State*, edited by Suzana Sawyer and Edward Terence Gomez, 204–229. London: Palgrave Macmillan UK, 2012.

Howe, Cymene. *Ecologics: Wind and Power in the Anthropocene*. Durham, NC: Duke University Press, 2019.

Huber, Matthew T. *Lifeblood: Oil, Freedom, and the Forces of Capital*. Minneapolis: University of Minnesota Press, 2013.

Ian, Gary, and Reisch Nikki. *Chad's Oil: Miracle or Mirage? Following the Money in Africa's Newest Petro-State*. Baltimore: Catholic Relief Services, 2005. http://www.internationalbudget.org/wp-content/uploads/Chads-Oil-Miracle-or-Mirage.pdf.

Iheka, Cajetan Nwabueze. *African Ecomedia*. 1st ed. Durham, NC: Duke University Press, 2021. doi:10.1515/9781478022046.

———. *Naturalizing Africa*. 1st ed. Cambridge: Cambridge University Press, 2018.

Ince, Kate. "Ethics, Universality and Vulnerability in Abderrahmane Sissako's *Bamako* (2006) and *Timbuktu* (2014)." *Paragraph: A Journal of Modern Critical Theory* 41, no. 2 (2018): 167–183. doi:10.3366/para.2018.0261.

Iocchi, Alesso. "Informality, Regulation and Predation: Governing Déby's Chad." *Politique Africaine* 154 (2019): 179–197.

Irr, Caren, and Nayoung Kim. "Introduction: Concepts and Consequences of Plastic." In *Life in Plastic*, edited by Caren Irr, 1–8. Minneapolis: University of Minnesota Press, 2021. doi:10.5749/j.ctv2382dx1.4.

Izzo, Justin. "Cinematic Economies of the Hypercontemporary in Haroun and Sissako." In *A Companion to African Cinema*, edited by Kenneth W. Harrow and Carmela Garritano, 23–43. Hoboken, NJ: Wiley-Blackwell, 2019.

James, Laura Leffler. "Convergence: History, Materials, and the Human Hand—An Interview with El Anatsui." *Art Journal* 67, no. 2 (2008): 36–53. doi:10.1080/00043249.2008.10791303.

Jamieson, Dale. "Ethics for the Anthropocene." In *Energy Humanities*, edited by Imre Szeman and Dominic Boyer, 389–398. Baltimore: Johns Hopkins University Press, 2017.

Johnson, Willard R., and Ernest J. Wilson. "The 'Oil Crises' and African Economies: Oil Wave on a Tidal Flood of Industrial Price Inflation." *Daedalus* 111, no. 2 (1982): 211–241.

Kaposy, Tim. "Petroleum's Longue Durée: Writing Oil's Temporalities into History." In *Petroculture: Oil, Politics, Culture*, edited by Sheena Wilson, Adam Carlson, and Imre Szeman, 389–406. Toronto: McGill-Queen's University Press, 2017.

Keating, Patrick. "Film Noir and the Culture of Electric Light." *Film History* 27, no. 1 (2015).

Kemausuor, Francis, and Emmanuel Ackom. "Toward Universal Electrification in Ghana." *WIREs: Energy & Environment* 6, no. 1 (January 2017). doi:10.1002/wene.225.

Klein, Naomi. *This Changes Everything*. New York: Simon & Schuster, 2014.

Kretzmann, Stephan, and Irfan Nooruddin. *Drilling into Debt: An Investigation into the Relationship between Debt and Oil*. Washington, DC: Oil Change International, 2005.

Kumi, Ebenezer. *The Electricity Situation in Ghana: Challenges and Opportunities.* Washington, DC: Center for Global Development, 2017.
Kutten, Kenneth. "The Potential of Africa's Plastic Market and Its Impact on Plastic Waste Management." Master's thesis, LUT University, 2019.
Larkin, Brian. *Signal and Noise: Media, Infrastructure, and Urban Culture in Nigeria.* Durham, NC: Duke University Press, 2008.
Larsen, Rasmus Kløcker, and Christiane Alzouma Mamosso. "Aid with Blinkers: Environmental Governance of Uranium Mining in Niger." *World Development* 56 (April 2014): 62–76. doi:10.1016/j.worlddev.2013.10.024.
Lazzarato, Maurizio. *The Making of the Indebted Man.* Translated by Joshua David Jordan. Semiotext(E) Intervention Series. Vol. 13. Cambridge, MA: MIT Press, 2012.
Le Gallic, Stéphanie, Léonard Laborie, and Pierre Lanthier, eds. *Electric Worlds / Mondes Électriques.* History of Energy / Histoire De L'Energie. Vol. 8. Bern: Peter Lang, 2017.
LeMenager, Stephanie. *Living Oil: Petroleum Culture in the American Century.* Oxford: Oxford University Press, 2014.
Leonard, Lori. *Life in the Time of Oil.* Bloomington: Indiana University Press, 2016.
Lerner, Sharon. "Africa's Exploding Plastic Nightmare." *The Intercept,* April 19, 2020. https://theintercept.com/2020/04/19/africa-plastic-waste-kenya-ethiopia/.
Lim, Song Hwee. "Temporal Aesthetics of Drifting: Tsai Ming-Liang and a Cinema of Slowness." In *Slow Cinema,* edited by Tiago de Luca and Nuno Barradas, 87–98. Edinburgh: Edinburgh University Press, 2015.
Lorey, Isabell. *State of Insecurity.* London: Verso, 2015.
Maathai, Wangari. *Replenishing the Earth: Spiritual Values for Healing Ourselves and the World.* New York: Random House, 2010.
———. *Unbowed.* New York: Anchor Books, 2007.
MacGaffey, Wyatt. *Chiefs, Priests, and Praise-Singers.* Charlottesville: University of Virginia Press, 2013.
Masquelier, Adeline. "Teatime: Boredom and the Temporalities of Young Men in Niger." *Africa* 83, no. 3 (2013): 470–491. doi:10.1017/S0001972013000272.
Massumi, Brian. *The Power at the End of the Economy.* Durham, NC: Duke University Press, 2015.
Matthews, William. "Opportunities and Challenges for Petroleum and LPG Markets in Sub-Saharan Africa." *Energy Policy* 64 (2014): 78–86.
Mbembe, Achille. "Necropolitics." *Public Culture* 15, no. 1 (2003): 11–40. doi:10.1215/08992363-15-1-11.
———. *On the Postcolony.* Studies on the History of Society and Culture. 1st ed. Vol. 41. Berkeley: University of California Press, 2001. doi:10.1525/j.ctt1ppkxs.

———. *Out of the Dark Night*. Translated by Daniela Ginsburg. New York: Columbia University Press, 2021. doi:10.7312/mbem16028.

McClennen, Sophia A. "The Rights to Debt." In *The Debt Age*, edited by Jeffrey R. Di Leo, Peter Hitchcock, and Sophia A. McClennen, 11–26. New York: Routledge, 2018.

McDermott Hughes, David. *Energy without Conscience: Oil, Climate Change, and Complicity*. Durham, NC: Duke University Press, 2017.

McDonald, David A. "Introduction: The Importance of Being Electric." In *Electric Capitalism: Recolonising Africa on the Power Grid*, edited by David A. McDonald, xv–xxiii. Oxford, UK: Earthscan, 2009.

Miescher, Stephan F. "The Akosombo Dam and the Quest for Rural Electrification in Ghana." In *Electric Worlds / Mondes Électriques: Creations, Circulations, Tensions, Transitions (19th–21st C.)*, edited by Alain Beltran, Léonard Laborie, Pierre Lanthier, and Stéphanie Le Gallic, 317–342. Peter Lang, 2016.

———. *A Dam for Africa*. Bloomington: Indiana University Press, 2022. doi:10.2307/j.ctv2q06gzt.

———. "'Nkrumah's Baby': The Akosombo Dam and the Dream of Development in Ghana, 1952–1966." *Water History* 6, no. 4 (2014): 341–366. doi:10.1007/s12685-014-0112-8. https://link.springer.com/article/10.1007/s12685-014-0112-8.

Miescher, Stephan F., and Dzodzi Tsikata. "Hydro-Power and the Promise of Modernity and Development in Ghana: Comparing the Akosombo and Bui Dam Projects." *Ghana Studies* 12, no. 1 (2009): 15–53.

Millar, Katharine M. *Reclaiming the Discarded*. Durham, NC: Duke University Press, 2018.

Mitchell, Timothy. *Carbon Democracy: Political Power in the Age of Oil*. New York: Verso, 2013.

Mohammed, Wunpini Fatimata. "Globalisation and Indigenous Cinemas: A History of Ghanaian Dagbanli Films." *Journal of International Communication* (May 2022): 1–20. doi:10.1080/13216597.2022.2073256.

Morton, Timothy. *Dark Ecology: For a Logic of Future Coexistence*. New York: Columbia University Press, 2016.

———. *The Ecological Thought*. Cambridge, MA: Harvard University Press, 2010.

———. *Hyperobjects: Philosophy and Ecology after the End of the World*. Minneapolis: University of Minnesota Press, 2013.

Nagib, Lúcia. *Realist Cinema as World Cinema: Non-Cinema, Intermedial Passages, Total Cinema*. Amsterdam: Amsterdam University Press, 2020. https://openresearchlibrary.org/viewer/ac667c27-d634-4ede-9205-c407e218b73e.

Nixon, Rob. *Slow Violence and the Environmentalism of the Poor*. Cambridge, MA: Harvard University Press, 2011a. https://www.jstor.org/stable/j.ctt2jbsgw.

Nooruddin, Irfan. "The Political Economy of National Debt Burdens, 1970–2000." *International Interactions* 34, no. 2 (June 2008): 156–185. doi:10.1080/03050620802083228.

Obeng-Odoom, Franklin. "Do African Cities Have Markets for Plastics or Plastics for Markets?" *Review of African Political Economy* 40, no. 137 (September 2013): 466–474. doi:10.1080/03056244.2013.817087.

Ogude, James, and Tafadzwa Mushonga. *Environmental Humanities of Extraction in Africa*. London: Routledge, Taylor & Francis, 2023.

Okuyade, Ogaga, ed. *Eco-Critical Literature: Regreening African Landscapes*. Trenton, NJ: African Heritage Press, 2013.

Olaniyan, Tejumola. "Of Rations and Rationalities: The World Bank, African Hunger, and Abderrahmane Sissako's *Bamako*." *Global South* 2, no. 2 (2008): 130–138.

Onishi, Norimitsu, and Neela Banerjee. "The Perils of Plenty: A Special Report; Chad's Wait for Its Oil Riches May Be Long." *New York Times*, May 16, 2001, Section A, 1.

Oscherwitz, Dayna. "Daratt." *African Studies Review* 57, no. 2 (September 2014): 237–239. doi:10.1017/asr.2014.76.

Osseo-Asare, Abena Dove. *Atomic Junction*. Cambridge: Cambridge University Press, 2019.

Oyewo, Ayobami Solomon, Javier Farfan, Pasi Peltoniemi, and Christian Breyer. *Repercussion of Large Scale Hydro Dam Deployment: The Case of Congo Grand Inga Hydro Project*. Vol. 11. 2018. doi:10.3390/en11040972.

Paik, Peter Y., Merry Wiesner-Hanks, Richard D. Wolff, Elaine Lewinnek, Mary Poovey, Michael A. Gillespie, Joel Magnuson, Stephen Gardner, Julianne Lutz Warren, and Genese Marie Sodikoff. *Debt*. 21st Century Studies. Bloomington: Indiana University Press, 2013.

Pendakis, Andrew. "Being and Oil." In *Petrocultures: Oil, Politics, Culture*, edited by Sheena Wilson, Adam Carlson, and Imre Szeman, 377–388. Montreal: McGill-Queen's University Press, 2017. doi:10.1515/9780773550391-018.

Petty, Sheila. "Sacred Places and *Arlit: Deuxième Paris*: Reterritorialization in African Documentary Films." *NKA (Brooklyn, NY)*, no. 32 (2013): 70–79. doi:10.1215/10757163-2142269.

Phillips, Kristin D. "Prelude to a Grid: Energy, Gender and Labour on an Electric Frontier." *Cambridge Anthropology* 38, no. 2 (September 2020): 71. doi:10.3167/cja.2020.380206.

Piot, Charles. *Nostalgia for the Future: West Africa after the Cold War*. Chicago: University of Chicago Press, 2010.

Pörtner, H.-O., D. C. Roberts, M. Tignor, E. S. Poloczanska, K. Mintenbeck, A. Alegría, M. Craig, S. Langsdorf, S. Löschke, V. Möller, A. Okem, and B. Rama, eds. *IPCC, 2022: Climate Change 2022: Impacts, Adaptation, and Vulnerability. Contribution of Working Group II to the Sixth Assessment Report of the Intergovernmental Panel on Climate Change.* Cambridge: Cambridge University Press, 2022.

Quayson, Ato. *Oxford Street, Accra: City Life and the Itineraries of Transnationalism.* Durham, NC: Duke University Press, 2014.

Rancière, Jacques. *Dissensus.* London: Bloomsbury, 2015.

Rodowick, D. N. *The Virtual Life of Film.* Cambridge, MA: Harvard University Press, 2009.

Roitman, Janet. "The Ethics of Illegality in the Chad Basin." In *Law and Disorder in the Postcolony,* 247–272. Chicago: University of Chicago Press, 2006. doi:10.7208/9780226114101-008.

———. *Fiscal Disobedience.* Princeton, NJ: Princeton University Press, 2004.

Ronda, Margaret. "Organic Form, Plastic Forms: The Nature of Plastic in Contemporary Ecopoetics." In *Life in Plastic,* edited by Caren Irr, 115. Minneapolis: University of Minnesota Press, 2021. doi:10.5749/j.ctv2382dx1.10.

Rosen, Philip. "Notes on Art Cinema and the Emergence of Sub-Saharan Film." In *Global Art Cinema: New Theories and Histories,* edited by Rosalind Galt and Karl Schoonover, 252–262: Oxford: Oxford University Press, 2012.

Said, Edward W. *Orientalism.* Penguin classics ed. London: Penguin Books, 2019.

———. *The World, The Text and the Critic.* Cambridge: Harvard University Press, 1983.

Sangare, Saadatou, and Hélène Maisonnave. "Mining and Petroleum Boom and Public Spending Policies in Niger: A Dynamic Computable General Equilibrium Analysis." *Environment and Development Economics* 23, no. 5 (October 2018): 580–590. doi:10.1017/S1355770X18000104.

Sawadogo, Boukary. *West African Screen Media.* East Lansing: Michigan State University Press, 2019.

Schareika, Nikolaus. "Creative Encounters: African Trade and Chinese Oil Production in Western Chad." *Social Analysis: International Journal of Social and Cultural Practice* 61, no. 3 (2017): 41–55.

Slaymaker, William. "Ecoing the Other(s): The Call of Global Green and Black African Responses." *PMLA: Publications of the Modern Language Association of America* 116, no. 1 (January 2001): 129–144.

Spicer, Andrew, and Helen Hanson, eds. *A Companion to Film Noir.* Hoboken, NJ: Wiley-Blackwell, 2013.

Staniland, Martin. *The Lions of Dagbon: Political Change in Northern Ghana.* African Studies Series: 16. New York: Cambridge University Press, 1975.

Stoler, Justin, Raymond A. Tutu, and Kiana Winslow. "Piped Water Flows but Sachet Consumption Grows: The Paradoxical Drinking Water Landscape of an Urban Slum in Ashaiman, Ghana." *Habitat International* 47 (June 2015): 52–60. doi:10.1016/j.habitatint.2015.01.009.

Sutton, Sally. "The Plastic Revolution?" *Waterlines* 19, no. 2 (October 2000): 20–22. doi:10.3362/0262-8104.2000.047.

Szeman, Imre. "Crude Aesthetics: The Politics of Oil Documentaries." *Journal of American Studies* 46, no. 2 (May 2012): 423–439. doi:10.1017/S0021875812000151.

Szeman, Imre, and Dominic Boyer, eds. *Energy Humanities: An Anthology*. Baltimore: Johns Hopkins University Press, 2017.

Szeman, Imre, Jennifer Wenzel, and Patricia Yaeger, eds. *Fueling Culture*. New York: Fordham University Press, 2017.

Tamakloe, Emmanuel F. *A Brief History of the Dagbamba People*. Accra: Government Printing Office, 1931.

Tchouaffe, Olivier-Jean. *The Poetics of Radical Hope in Abderrahmane Sissako's Film Experience*. Lanham, MD: Lexington Books, 2017.

Thrift, Nigel J. *Non-Representational Theory*. London: Routledge, 2008. doi:10.4324/9780203946565.

Toussaint, Eric, Damien Millet, Judith Abdel Gadir, Elizabeth Anne, Vicki Briault, and Judith Harris. *Debt, the IMF, and the World Bank*. New York: Monthly Review Press, 2010. doi:10.2307/j.ctv12pnqv6.

Tsikata, Dzodzi. *Living in the Shadow of the Large Dams*. African Social Studies Series. Vol. 11. Leiden: Brill, 2006.

Twum, Kwaku Owusu, and Mohammed Abubakari. "Drops in the City: The Puzzle of Water Privatization and Consumption Deficiencies in Urban Ghana." *Water Policy* 22, no. 3 (June 2020): 417–434. doi:10.2166/wp.2020.175.

Ugochukwu, Françoise. "Nollywood and the Niger Delta Conflict—Media in an Advisory Capacity." *AFFRIKA Journal of Politics, Economics and Society* 8, no. 2 (December 2018): 123–141. doi:10.31920/2075-6534/2018/v8n2a7.

van der Velden, Maja, and Martin Oteng-Ababio. "Six Myths about Electronic Waste in Agbogbloshie, Ghana." *Africa Is a Country*, March 26, 2019. https://africasacountry.com/2019/03/six-myths-about-electronic-waste-in-agbogbloshie-ghana.

Villiers, Jacques de. "Approaching the Uncertain Turn in African VideoMovies." In *A Companion to African Cinema*, 44–68. Hoboken, NJ: John Wiley & Sons, 2018. doi:10.1002/9781119100577.ch2.

Vogel, Susan Mullin, and El Anatsui. *El Anatsui: Art and Life*. 2nd ed. London: Prestel, 2020.

Watkins, Neil. "Oil: Fueling Another Debt Crisis?" *Multinational Monitor* 28, no. 4 (2007): 15–18.

Watts, Michael. "Frontiers: Authority, Precarity, and Insurgency at the Edge of the State." *World Development* 101 (January 2018): 477–488. doi:10.1016/j.worlddev.2017.03.024.

———. "Righteous Oil? Human Rights, the Oil Complex, and Corporate Social Responsibility." *Annual Review of Environment & Resources* 30, no. 1 (2005): 373–407. doi:10.1146/annurev.energy.30.050504.144456.

———. *Space, Oil and Capital*. Vol. 100. 2010. doi:10.1080/00045608.2010.485479.

———. "There Will Be Blood: Oil Curse, Fossil Dependency and Petro-Addiction." *New Formations* no. 103 (2021): 10–42. doi:10.3898/NEWF:103.02.2021.

Wengraf, Lee. *Extracting Profit*. Chicago: Haymarket Books, 2018.

Wenzel, Jennifer. "Afterword: Improvement and Overburden." *Postmodern Culture* 26, no. 2 (2016). doi:10.1353/pmc.2016.0003.

———. *The Disposition of Nature*. New York: Fordham University Press, 2019. https://muse.jhu.edu/book/71955.

———. "Introduction." In *Fueling Culture: 101 Words for Energy and Environment*, edited by Imre Szeman, Jennifer Wenzel, and Patricia Yaeger, 1–16. New York: Fordham University Press, 2017. muse.jhu.edu/book/49054.

———. "Petro-Magic-Realism: Toward a Political Ecology of Nigerian Literature." *Postcolonial Studies* 9, no. 4 (2006): 449–464. doi:10.1080/13688790600993263.

Whissel, Kristen. *Spectacular Digital Effects*. Durham, NC: Duke University Press, 2014. https://muse.jhu.edu/book/70082.

Williams, James S. "Neoliberal Violence and Aesthetic Resistance in Abderrahmane Sissako's *Bamako* (2006)." *Studies in French Cinema* 19, no. 4 (October 2019): 294–313. doi:10.1080/14715880.2017.1356136.

Williams, Patrick, and Laura Chrisman. "Teshome H. Gabriel Towards a Critical Theory of Third World Films." In *Colonial Discourse and Post-Colonial Theory*, 352–370. New York: Routledge, 1994.

Wilson, Sheena, Adam Carlson, and Imre Szeman. *Petrocultures: Oil, Politics, Culture*, edited by Sheena Wilson, Adam Carlson, and Imre Szeman. Montreal: McGill-Queen's University Press, 2017.

Winde, Frank, Doug Brugge, Andreas Nidecker, and Urs Ruegg. "Uranium from Africa—An Overview on Past and Current Mining Activities: Re-Appraising Associated Risks and Chances in a Global Context." *Journal of African Earth Sciences (1994)* 129 (May 2017): 759–778. doi:10.1016/j.jafrearsci.2016.12.004.

Wynter, Sylvia. "Unsettling the Coloniality of Being/Power/Truth/Freedom: Towards the Human, After Man, Its Overrepresentation—An Argument." *CR: The New Centennial Review* 3, no. 3 (2003): 257–337. doi:10.1353/ncr.2004.0015.

Yaeger, Patricia, Laurie Shannon, Vin Nardizzi, Ken Hiltner, Saree Makdisi, Michael Ziser, and Imre Szeman. "Editor's Column: Literature in the Ages of Wood, Tallow, Coal, Whale Oil, Gasoline, Atomic Power, and Other Energy

Sources." *PMLA: Publications of the Modern Language Association of America* 126, no. 2 (2011): 305–326. doi:10.1632/pmla.2011.126.2.305.

Yeboah, Ian. "Subaltern Strategies and Development Practice: Urban Water Privatization in Ghana." *Geographical Journal* 172, no. 1 (March 2006): 50–65. doi:10.1111/j.1475-4959.2006.00184.x.

Yoshimoto, Mitsuhiro. "Nuclear Disasters and Invisible Spectacles." *Asian Cinema* 30, no. 2 (2019): 169–185.

Yusoff, Kathryn. *A Billion Black Anthropocenes or None*. Minneapolis: University of Minnesota Press, 2018.

Zaato, Joshua Jebuntie. "'Look Before You Leap': Lessons from Urban Water Sector Reforms in Ghana." *Journal of Asian and African Studies* 50, no. 6 (December 2015): 683–701. doi:10.1177/0021909614541077.

INDEX

Page locators in italics indicate figures

Abacha, Sani, 38, 75
absence made present, 67–69
Abt, Danya, 55–56, 75–76
Accra, Ghana, 14, 108; Korle Lagoon, 132; moviemaking compared with Tamale, 111. *See also* Agbogbloshie waste dump (Accra, Ghana); Ghana
action cinema, 18, 19, 33–36
adjusting, experiential dimensions of, 80
Adunbi, Omolade, 34
affective potential, 56, 74, 76, 162
Africa: austerity and economic insecurity normalized, 49–50; economic liberalization policies imposed on, 71; exploration licenses to mining firms, 24; "new scramble for," 23, 53; racist stereotypes, 36; refining capacity, lack of, 89, 93–94. *See also specific countries and locations*
African Ecomedia (Iheka), 6–7
African Film: New Forms of Aesthetics and Politics (Diawara), 9

African Studies Review forum, 157
Afrogallonism (Clottey), 14, 130, 141–43, 145–49, *150–53*; human-centric categories disrupted by, 148–49. *See also* jerricans, plastic
Agbogbloshie waste dump (Accra, Ghana), 131–37, 139; not called "Sodom" by workers, 131–32; violent eviction of workers from, 141, 155n43; waste produced in West Africa sent to, 134
agency, 11, 73, 121; of Africans, 5, 6, 134, 136, 159–60
Aghoghovwia, Philip, 36
Akosombo Dam and hydroelectric power plant (Ghana), 105–8, 127n13
Akufo-Addo, Nana Addo Dankwa, 3
Alhacen, Almoustapha, 31, 42, 44n32
AlUla Arts Festival (Arabian Peninsula), 149
Amata, Jeta, 18, 40
Anatsui, El, 145–47

Anthropocene, 1–7, 45n70; African, 2–7; multiple time scales of, 4, 34, 42–43
"any-space-whatever," 69
Appel, Hannah, 36
Arab-Israeli War, 48
AREVA (French parastatal mining company), 21, 31, 44n20
Arlit (Niger), 17, 19, 20–32; as extraction enclave, 22, 25–26; former prosperity, 26–27; migrants to, 27–28
Arlit, Deuxième Paris (Mora-Kpai), 12, 17, 19; depopulated landscape scenes, 18, 30; durational aesthetic, 32, 34, 42; "geographies of exploitation" in, 22; interlocutors, positioned as witnesses and experts, 21, 31; juxtaposition between mobility and waiting, 27–28; movement in, 22–23, 27; radiation exposure documented in, 21, 30–31; stasis in, 27–28; structure of, 20–21; testimonies in, 21, 24–25; uranium futures in, 20–32; viewers invited to "dwell in crisis," 31–32; waiting in, 26–30
armed conflict, 12; in Chad, 56, 66–67, 93; historicized in Nollywood films, 36–38, 41; resource wars, 19, 34. *See also* violence
art: "collective creativity," 148; pedagogical model of efficacy, 132–34, 139–40, 149; political, 136, 149
art cinema, 9–10, 95. *See also Grigris* (Haroun, 2013)
Arte (Franco-German TV Network), 10
art from waste, 126, 129–56; Afrogallonism, 14, 130, 141–43, 145–49, *150–53*; discourse of, 130–31; flip-flop tapestries, 130; global economy of, 148. *See also* waste

audience/viewers, 7–8, 11, 148, 158; attempts to mobilize, 14, 33, 35, 39, 42, 131–35; and Dagbani-language films, 112, 115, 120; doubling of performers, 54–55; international, 9, 20; invited to "dwell in crisis," 31–32; local, 32, 108, 110, 112; and pedagogical model of efficacy of art, 132–34, 139–40; and "political pedagogy," 33; as witnesses to acts of intimidation, 64–65
austerity programs, 49–50
auteurs, African, 10, 88
Awia (Sun) (Tagoe-Turkson), 145

back-to-the-source movies, 107, 115–16
Baker, Jonathan, 48–49
Bamako (Sissako, 2006), 12–13, 47, 53–55
Banda Islands, 138
Barad, Karen, 21–22
Barkai, Ali, 74
Barney, Darin, 97
Barr, Burlin, 51, 52
Bassey, Nnimmo, 45n73
Baucom, Ian, 2–4
Bawa, Rasheed, 108
Beck, Ulrich, 18–19, 24
Being Nuclear: Africans and the Global Uranium Trade (Hecht), 25
Benjamin, Walter, 3
Bennett, Jane, 121, 124
biopolitics, 3, 26, 81
Black November (2015), 12, 17, 18, 19, 158; armed conflict historicized in, 36–38, 41; funding of, 34–35
Blood and Oil (2015), 12, 17, 18, 19, 35, 39–42, 158
bodies: and affective contagion, 72; and affective potential, 56, 74, 76; and disability, 67, 75, 83, 95–96, 99; energy

generated by, 71–72; "grievable life," 72; labor of, 11, 56, 70–72; male, 29, 56, 66, 72, 83, 94–95, 99–101; male, as fuel-transport machines, 13, 99; "new discernment" concept, 124
Boetzkes, Amanda, 132–33, 135, 140–41, 154n1
Bollywood, 33, 110
Bouwer, Karen, 91
Boyer, Dominic, 8
The Boy Who Harnessed the Wind (Ejiofor, 2019), 157–60, 161
The Boy Who Harnessed the Wind (Kamkwamba and Meale), 158
Brazil, waste pickers, 135
Bretton Woods agreement, 48
Brinkema, Eugenie, 67–68
British Petroleum, 41
Brøvig-Hanssen, Ragnhild, 113
Buell, Frederick, 31
"bunkering" of oil, 35–36
Butler, Judith, 72

Cambridge Journal of Anthropology, 1, 161–62
Cameroon, 55–61, 104n52; cartoons and comics, 120. See also Chad-Cameroon Petroleum Development and Pipeline Project (CCPDPP)
Cameroon Oil Transportation Company (COTCO), 60
Canal Plus, 89
Cancer Alley, Louisiana, 11
Capellán, Tony, 144
capitalism: ecological violence under, 159–60; "ghosted communities" produced by, 28; ocean as arena of, 144; petrocapitalism, 2, 6, 56, 89, 94, 131. See also colonialism; petrocapitalism

Carbon Democracy (Mitchell), 97–98
carbon periphery, 67
care and support obligations, 73–75, 77, 83, 100
cartoons and comics (Cameroon), 120
Chad, 13, 47, 55–61, 103n36, 104n52; amnesty for war crimes, 56, 66–67; dependence on China, 58–59, 93–94; Djérmaya refinery, 59, 93–94; "Future Generations Fund," 57, 93; Law 001, 57, 58, 93; payment of debt, 58–59, 78n42; promises of oil pipeline, 57–58, 93; unregulated commercial networks in Chad Basin, 96; war economy of, 71. See also Chad-Cameroon Petroleum Development and Pipeline Project (CCPDPP); debt relations; *Grigris* (Haroun, 2013)
Chad-Cameroon Petroleum Development and Pipeline Project (CCPDPP), 12, 13, 47, 55–59, 64, 75; Compensation and Resettlement Plan, 61–63, 64; embeddedness of, 62, 64; extent and cost of, 92–93; violence used to suppress citizen protest, 63–65
Chakrabarty, Dipesh, 4, 5, 101–2
Chalfin, Brenda, 1, 161–62
Chase, The (2011), 114
Chevalier, Pierre, 10
China National Petroleum Corporation International Chad (CNPCIC), 59, 93–94, 103n33
cinema: action cinema, 18, 19, 33–36; art cinema, 9–10, 95; grief tableau in, 67–69; independent, 9–10, 88, 114–25; sensorium of, 8, 137; transnational films and transnationalization, 8–9, 88; world cinemas, 9–10, 160

cinema, African, 4–5; anticolonialism as founding objective of, 17; back-to-the-source movies, 107, 115–16; changes to in twenty-first century, 157–58; electricity access as foundational to, 107, 113, 124–25; expansion of objects of study, 88; and film festivals, 9–10, 32–33, 88–89, 149, 160; genre repurposed, 80; as interscalar vehicle, 5, 12; materiality of production, 7, 55, 87–88; quest movies, 56, 115–18; socialist-realist approach to, 88; soundscapes, 85–87, 134–35, 160; twenty-first-century, 8–11. *See also* petronoir; video films

Cinema 1 (Deleuze), 69

citizens: as credit-bearing subjects, 50; debt borne by, 67; debt owed to, 62–63, 75–76

climate crisis, 2–3, 6, 10, 101–2, 124, 161; climate debt, 76–77

Climate of History in a Planetary Age, The (Chakrabarty), 101–2

Clottey, Serge Attukwei, 14, 129, 130, 141–43, 145–49, 156n70; GoLokal workshop, 148, 156n71; *The Wishing Well*, 148–49; *Works: Gold Falls*, 149, 150–53; *Yellow Brick Road (YBR)*, 147–48

Collier, Stephen, 80

colonialism: advanced by sustainability discourse, 133–34; environmentalist thinking of, 138–39; extractive methods and mindset of, 6, 11, 15, 159; human-dominant order, 101, 161, 162; "imaginative geographies" of, 138; legacies of, 4, 11, 15, 25; "new scramble for" Africa, 23, 53; ongoing sovereign debt, 50, 77n19; radio as technology of, 86; terraforming, 138–39

Comaroff, Jean, 50
Comaroff, John, 50
Compensation and Resettlement Plan, 61–63, 64
COVID-19 pandemic, 125
Cross, Jamie, 1, 161–62

Dagbamba culture: Dagbani language, 111, 120, 127n13; drama groups, 108; "invasion model," 117; origin narratives and drum histories, 14, 107, 115–17, 124; precolonial Dagbon, 116, 120; vital materialism, 124

Dagbani-language video production and exhibition, 13–14, 162; back-to-the-source movies, 107, 115–16; DVD distribution, 110–13; electricity and movies in Tamale, 107–14; electrified effects and epic tales, 114–25, *119*, *122*, *123*; pen drive piracy, 125–26

Dakar (Senegal), 81–82
Danielsen, Anne, 113
Daratt (Haroun, 2008), 55–56, 66–75, 94; labor types in, 70–71; spatial arrangement in, 67–68
Dardenne, Jean Pierre, 29
Dardenne, Luc, 29
Davies, Thom, 11
De Boeck, Filip, 84
debt: Chad, 58–59, 78n42; climate debt, 76–77; and gender, 66; and gifts, 51–52, 60, 83; life as instrument of, 52; moral, 67; personal, 13, 50; and petrodollar recycling, 48–50; refusal of, 74–75; responsibilities owed to citizens, 62–63, 75–76; social bonds destroyed by creditor-debtor connections, 51–52, 61, 75
Debt (Graeber), 61

debt relations, 8, 12–13, 47–79; and 2008 subprime crisis, 49; asymmetry of, 57–58; care and support obligations, 73–75, 77, 83; Chad, 58–59, 78n42; community-based credit-debt networks, 66; and credit, 49–54, 61; debt economy, neoliberal, 49–50; detachment, relational ethic of, 60–62; DRC, 84; ethico-political labor of repayment, 70; as feature of public life, 51; and foreign currencies, 58; future beyond creditor-debtor conflict, 75; *homo debitor*, 50; livelihoods affected, 54, 56, 58, 65–66; loan payments and interest, 58, 73; and oil, 12, 48–50, 52; ongoing since colonial period, 50, 77n19; as perversion of promise, 51; social connections altered by, 52, 66–67; sovereign debt in the time of oil, 50–55; and structural adjustment policies, 8, 20, 49–50, 80

Déby, Idriss, 56, 66, 93

Degani, Michael, 1, 161–62

Deleuze, Gilles, 69

DeLoughrey, Elizabeth, 130, 144

de Luca, Tiago, 10, 55

Democratic Republic of the Congo (DRC): infrastructure, 84–87. See also *Up at Night* (Makengo, 2019); *Viva Riva!* (Wa Munga, 2011)

Desert X exhibitions, 148–49

detachment, relational ethic of, 60–62

development, 22, 25, 28, 52–53, 57–61, 66–67, 161; ecological violence inherent to, 159–60; Ghana, 107–8; resettlement programs, 61; social and health not addressed, 49, 97; temporary benefit, 60–61; unequal, 85–86, 92–94, 97, 101. See also debt relations

Diawara, Manthia, 9, 157

digital effects, 14, 114–25, *119*, *122*, *123*; "analog-digital hybrid," 119–21; "effects emblem," 115, 120; electricity allegorized by, 121–24; and system of double meaning, 120–21. See also electricity

distribution of cinema, 7–11; of DVDs, 110–13; European structures of, 9–10; multiplex cinemas, 32; Nollywood films, 32–33; parlors for viewing video films, 110; pen drive, 125–26; straight-to-video movie industry, 8–9, 13–14, 32, 111

Doba Basin (Chad), 55

documentaries: about oil, 33; interlocutors positioned as witnesses and experts, 21, 31; intertitles, 36, 132; threat of physical danger to participants, 65; visual representations of Niger Delta in, 35–36. See also *Arlit, Deuxième Paris* (Mora-Kpai); *Quel Souvenir* (Abt, 2009); *Welcome to Sodom* (2019)

Drilling into Debt report, 57–58

durational aesthetic, 20, 32, 42

Dutch "colonial terraforming," 138

dwelling in crisis, metaphor of, 31–32

ecocriticism, 5–6, 133

ecological thought, 10–11, 15, 130, 141, 147, 149

Ecology without Nature (Morton), 138

Edwards, Paul, 80–81

Ejiofor, Chiwetel, 158

electricity, 13, 52, 70; access as foundational to African cinema, 107, 113, 124–25; allegorized by digital effects, 121–24; *dumsor* crisis in Ghana, 105–6, 108; as inspiration, 106–7; local screen media formation made possible by,

electricity (*cont.*)
  106; and movies in Tamale, 107–14; power outages, 59, 84–87; withdrawn after project completed, 60. See also Akosombo Dam and hydroelectric power plant (Ghana); digital effects
Electricity Corporation of Ghana, 107
El-Gamal, Mahmoud A., 48
enclaves, energy, 22, 25–26, 61–62
enduration, 29
energopolitics, 8, 13, 48
energy: as affective potential, 56, 74, 76, 162; conceptualization of, 5; enclaves, 22, 25–26, 61–62; hydropower, 105–7, 127n13; postcarbon developments, 162; theorization of, 161. See also electricity; infrastructures, energy; justice, energy and climate; oil; shortage, energy; uranium extraction; wind
energy analytics, 7–8, 17, 76, 160–62
energy commodity chain, 12
energy humanities, 1–2, 6, 15, 72, 100
energy poverty, 11
energy sink and source, 1
energy worldliness, 4
entrepreneurial subject, 82–83
environmentalism, critiques of, 137–39, 149
Esso/Exxon, 59–65, 63
"ethical attention span," 32
Exim Bank of China, 59
Expectations (Haroun, 2010), 66
extraction: colonial methods and mindset of, 11, 15, 159; enclaves of, 22, 25–26; "new scramble for Africa," 23, 53; place, transnational ethics of, 42; "resurgent extractivism," 162; sites/zones of, 12, 25, 42–43, 162; violence of, 12, 17–19, 138; wind as inverse allegory to, 161. See also Arlit (Niger); Chad-Cameroon Petroleum Development and Pipeline Project (CCP-DPP); debt relations; Niger Delta; oil industry; uranium extraction
ExxonMobil, 56, 77n19, 92

Faat Kiné (Ousmane, 2001), 13, 80–84, 100–102; movement in, 82–83
Ferguson, James, 4, 101
film festivals, 9–10, 32–33, 88–89, 149, 160
film noir, 13; darkness, function of, 85, 92; elements of, 88–89; as material experience, 87; movement in, 89–91. See also petronoir
Film Producers Association of Ghana (FIPAG), 111
flip-flop tapestries (Tagoe-Turkson), 130, 141, 143–44, *145*, *146*
Forms of the Affects, The (Brinkema), 66–67
Foucault, Michel, 81
France: AREVA (parastatal mining company), 21, 31, 44n20; as consumer of uranium energy, 23–24; decolonization treaties, 25; as supporter of African cinema, 10, 89
Frassinelli, Pier Paolo, 89
"Fueling Capture: Africa's Energy Frontiers" (Degani, Chalfin, and Cross), 161–62
Fueling Culture: 101 Words for Energy and Environment (ed. Szeman, Wenzel, and Yaeger), 7
Fusheini, Hamidu, 108

Gabon, 5
Gabriel, Teshome, 20
Ga language, 143

Gauch, Suzanne, 88, 90
generators, 86–87
"geographies of exploitation," 22
geography of power, 22
Ghallywood, 108
Ghana: Akosombo Dam and hydroelectric power plant, 105–8, 127n13; COVID-19 pandemic, 125; electricity crisis (*dumsor*), 2014–2017, 105–6, 108; electrification programs, 13, 107, 111–12, *112*; as energy success story, 106; Internet access, 13, 110, 111–13; lack of recycling facilities, 126; National Electrification Program, 13, 107; NEDCo network, 108, *109*; off-shore oil, 4; plastic manufacturing, 142, 143–44; Self-Help Electrification Programme, 13, 107; solar energy, 108, 126n9; Tamale area, 13–14, 106–14; water infrastructure, 140, 142–43; Western Region and climate change, 3. See also Accra, Ghana; Agbogbloshie waste dump (Accra, Ghana); Dagbani-language video production and exhibition; Nollywood films; Tamale, Ghana
Ghana Broadcasting Corporation, 108
Ghana Industrial Holding Corporation, 143
Ghana National Petroleum Company, 4
Ghana Plastic Manufacturer's Association, 144
Ghazvinian, John, 94, 103n36
Ghosh, Amitav, 15, 138
"ghosted communities," 28
gifts, and debt, 51–52, 60, 83
global North, 2, 31, 56–57; addressed in *Welcome to Sodom*, 14, 133–35; art discourse of waste in, 130; consumption normalized in, 102; and debt relations, 48, 50, 76; role of plastics in, 141–42; shift of mining activities to, 24. See also France; United States
global South, 2–3; "culture of masculine waiting," 29; debt owed to, 76; plasticity as condition of life in, 14, 129; risk transferred to, 19, 24
Gold Falls (Clottey), 149, *150–53*
GoLokal workshop (Labadi), 148, 156n71
Gonda Sheje (OBL, 2013), 114, 116, 127n25
Goodwill, Tamuno, 38
Gorfinkel, Elena, 29
Graeber, David, 51, 61, 75
Graham, Curtis, 18, 40
Green Belt Movement, 159
Green-Simms, Lindsey, 82
grief tableau in cinema, 67–69
Grigris (Haroun, 2013), 13, 66, 80, 87, 92, 94–101
Gustafsson, Henrik, 90
Guyer, Jane, 20

Habré, Hissene, 56, 66
Hage, Ghassan, 26
half-second delay, 69
Haroun, Mahamat-Saleh, 9, 12–13, 47; Films: *Daratt* (2008), 55–56, 66–75, 94; *Expectations* (2010), 66; French support for, 10; *Lingui: The Sacred Bonds* (2021), 66; *Un Homme Qui Crie* (2010), 66. See also *Grigris* (Haroun, 2013)
Harrow, Kenneth W., 8–9, 74–75
Haynes, Jonathan, 32, 33
Hecht, Gabrielle, 5, 25, 31, 34, 45n70
Hicks, Celeste, 53, 58, 93, 103n33
Higgins, Mary Ellen, 94, 157, 159
History 4° Celsius (Baucom), 2–4
Hollywood, 18, 115, 120

Howe, Cymene, 158, 160–61
Huber, Matthew, 82, 141–42
Hugo, Pieter, 133, 139
human, "ethnoclass" of Man as, 134
human-dominant order, 101, 161, 162
humanities, 14–15, 162; energy humanities, 1–2, 6, 15, 72, 100
"Human Otherness," 134, 136
human smuggling, 28, 44–45n47
Hyenas (Mambety, 1992), 12, 47, 50–53
hyperobjects, 130, 137–41, 147, 149; environmentalism as inadequate for, 137–38
hyperrealism, 10, 54, 118

Ibrahima, Nana, 63, 64
Iheka, Cajetan, 5–7, 133, 139
impermanence, 138
Ince, Kate, 54
independent cinema, 9–10, 88; and Kubaloe (OBL), 114–25
industrialization, 11
inequalities, 3, 18, 80, 94, 134, 159
infrastructures: infrastructural modernity, 80–81, 112; as political technology, 81, 89; technologies indicating failure of, 86–87; water, 142–43
infrastructures, energy, 80; carbon periphery, 67; deterioration of, 91–92; frontier markets, 96, 97; incomplete, failed, or underdeveloped, 8, 11, 13, 80, 84–87, 94; infrastructural demands made by films, 80; positive portrayals of, 82–84; unregulated commercial networks in Chad Basin, 96
Inga Dam site (Congo River), 84
Intergovernmental Panel on Climate Change (IPCC), 76
"intermedial passage," 54

international financial institutions, 47–49; damage caused by, 158–59; and water infrastructure, 142–43. *See also* International Monetary Fund; World Bank
International Monetary Fund, 23, 53, 107, 159
Internet access, 13, 33, 110, 111–13
interscalar vehicles, 5, 12
intertitles, 36, 40, 42; in *Welcome to Sodom*, 132, 137, 139
Iocchi, Alesso, 104n52
Izzo, Justin, 94

Jaffe, Amy Myers, 48
Jai, Ramesh, 105–6
Jardim Gramacho (Rio de Janeiro, Brazil), 135, 136–37
Jedlowski, Alessandro, 88
jerricans, plastic, 87, 97–99, 104n51, 141–43, 147. *See also* Afrogallonism (Clottey)
Journal of Modern African Studies, 48
Jubilee Oil Fields, 4
justice, energy and climate, 4, 13, 76, 101, 159; and Abt's documentary, 61; in Nollywood films, 19–20, 33, 36–38, 4042; slow erosion of, 19; transnational collaboration promoted, 40–42

Kabila, Joseph, 84, 86
Kamkwamba, William, 158–61
Kaposy, Tim, 33
Kashi, Ed, 35–36
Keating, Patrick, 87
Kinshasa (DRC), 84–87, 92
Klein, Naomi, 76
kòbòlò, 29
Kosmos Energy, 4

Kubaloe, Leonard Atawugeh (OBL), 114–25; Films: *Biegni* (*Tomorrow*, 2015), 114; *Gangdu* (in production), 114–15, 127n25; *Gonda Sheje* (2013), 114, 116, 127n25. See also *Pieli: The Rise of Montana* (OBL, 2017)
Kufuor, John, 143

Lagos (Nigeria), 32
Larkin, Brian, 86
Lazzarato, Maurizio, 49–50, 69
leisure, dependence on energy, 52
LeMenager, Stephanie, 2, 81
Leonard, Lori, 56, 60–62, 75, 92, 94
Lévi-Strauss, Claude, 3
Life! (Jai, 2017), 105–6
Life in the Time of Oil: A Pipeline and Poverty in Chad (Leonard), 57, 92
Lim, Song Hwee, 20
Lingui: The Sacred Bonds (Haroun, 2021), 66
load-shedding, 84, 105–6
Logone River, 99
Lorey, Isabel, 26
loss, cinematic conventions of, 66–69
low-carbon environments, labor in, 71–72
Lumière, 23

Maathai, Wangari, 42, 159
MacGaffey, Wyatt, 116–17
Macky, Aicha, 103n26
Maikeri, Chad, 62
Makengo, Nelson, 9, 13, 80, 84–87
Making of the Indebted Man, The (Lazzarato), 49–50
Malawi, 2001 food crisis, 158–59
Mambety, Djibril Diop, 9, 75; *Hyenas* (1992), 12, 47, 50–53

Man, 134
Mareña wind park (Isthmus of Tehuantepec, Mexico), 161
Mason, Arthur, 36
Masquelier, Adeline, 29
Massumi, Brian, 74
Mataai, Wangari, 15
Mbembe, Achille, 15n3, 20, 25–26, 120–21
McClennen, Sophia A., 47, 50
Meale, Bryan, 158
Menyankoba Basia (*My Friend's Daughter*) (Tagoe-Turkson), 146
"mesh of the real," 54
Millar, Kathleen M., 136–37
Millet, Damien, 49
Ming-liang, Tsai, 20
Mitchell, Timothy, 13, 47, 97–98
modernity: African desires for, 101–2; artificial light used to comment on, 87; biopolitical systems, 81; human-centric ideologies of, 6; infrastructural, 80–81, 112; "modern" life, 4–5, 7; Nature as integral to, 138–39; petromodernity, 76; risk as product of, 18
Mohammed, Wunpini Fatimata, 108
Mora-Kpai, Idrissou, 12, 19, 20–32
Morton, Timothy, 10, 15, 130, 137, 147, 149, 154n1
movement, 22–23, 27, 82–83; in film noir, 89–91; and materiality of oil, 97–98
Movement for the Emancipation of the Niger Delta (MEND), 38
Movement for the Survival of the Ogoni People, 38
M'ramarde, Keiro, 65
Muniz, Vik, 135
muscularity, 11

Nagib, Lúcia, 9–10, 54, 55, 65
Na Nyagse, 116
National Electrification Program (NEP, Ghana), 13, 107
Nature, as integral to modernity, 138–39
Nelambaye, Nadji, 64–65
neoliberalism, 11, 20, 23, 25, 36; debt creation at heart of, 49–50
Netflix, 158
Nguiffo, Samuel, 75
Niger, 23–24, 29
Niger Delta, 2, 12, 17–20; liberal public sphere irrelevant in, 38–39; Nollywood films about, 32–43; nonfiction representations of, 35; oil spills, 34, 36, 40, 43, 45n73
Niger Delta Avengers, 38
Nigeria: commercial movie industry, 9; critiqued in Nollywood films, 36–38, 40–42; infrastructure, 86. See also Nollywood films
Nixon, Rob, 12, 18–19, 28, 32, 42
Nkrumah, Kwame, 102, 107, 143
Nollywood films, 8–9, 12, 17, 19, 157; action genre, 33–36; American oil executives portrayed in, 40; armed conflict portrayed in, 36–38, 41; black-and-white to indicate memories, 41; as commercial creative practice, 33; "contextual" images in, 36; corrupt Big Man in, 39–40; electricity access as foundational to, 107; energy and environmental justice in, 33, 36–38, 40, 48; establishing shots, 36, 42; intertitles, 36, 40, 42; landscape montage in, 36; multiple time scales in, 34, 42–43; about Niger Delta, 32–43; Nigerian government critiqued in, 36–38, 41–42; transnational collaboration promoted in, 32–33, 40–42. See also *Black November* (2015); *Blood and Oil* (2015); video films
nonhuman, the, 5, 13–14, 99, 101, 147, 162
nonviolent activism, 38
Nooruddin, Irfan, 58
nuclear bombs, 21–22
ŋuni Taali (*Whose Fault?*, 1989), 108, 110
Nutmeg's Curse, The (Ghosh), 138

OBL. *See* Kubaloe, Leonard Atawugeh (OBL)
OBL Studios (Tamale, Ghana), 14, 114
oil: and debt relations, 12, 48–50, 52; destructive potential of, 99; "image world" of, 36; materiality of, 97–98; "petroutopia," 81; petroviolence, 41. *See also* petrocapitalism; petroculture; petroleum smuggling
oil crisis of 1970s, 8, 12, 47–48
oil industry: "Africa's new oil," 53; differential manifestations of, 34; "duality of violence," 34; historical context, 40–41; "new scramble for Africa," 23, 53
oil time, 33–34
On the Postcolony (Mbembe), 120
oral tradition, 116–18; cliché of in *Welcome to Sodom*, 139
Oscherwitz, Dayna, 70, 72
Oteng-Ababio, Martin, 155n43
"overrepresentation," 134

pen drive piracy, 125–26
Permanent Error (Hugo), 133, 139
Peters, John Durham, 6
petrocapitalism, 2, 6, 56, 89, 94, 131. *See also* capitalism
petroculture, 6; byproducts of, 126; lived from within, 149–54; plasticity

as condition of life, 14, 129; and sustainability discourse, 133–34
petrodollar recycling, 48–50
petroleum smuggling, 9, 13, 89–90, 94, 96–99, 142
petromodernity, 76
petronoir, 13, 80–104; in African cinema, 87–92; chiaroscuro lighting, 85; Moroccan films noir, 88; petroleum smuggling in, 9, 13, 89–90, 94, 96–99; urban crime films and dark thrillers, 88. *See also* cinema, African; *Faat Kiné* (Ousmane, 2001); film noir; *Grigris* (Haroun, 2013); *Up at Night* (Makengo, 2019); *Viva Riva!* (Wa Munga, 2011)
Petty, Sheila, 21
Phillips, Kristin D., 67, 72
photography, art, 35–36
Pieli: The Rise of Montana (OBL, 2017), 14; effects in, 114–25, *119*, *122*, *123*; as pilot for Internet series, 115; unelectrified rural landscape in, 118
place, transnational ethics of, 42
plastic: as "anthropogenic ruin," 130; bisphenol A (BPA), 144; complexity of, 140–42, 147, 148–49; as hyperobject, 130; jerricans, 87, 97–99, 104n51, 141–43, 147; made from natural materials, 141; microplastics, 130, 144; nonbiodegradable permanence of, 129–30; pervasiveness of on planetary scale, 129; plasticity as condition of life, 14, 129; space-time ubiquity of, 130; water sachet, 140
Plastic Capitalism (Boetzkes), 132–33, 154n1
plutonium, 130
political pedagogy, 33, 39
"postwar petroleum order," 13, 47
precarity, 26, 31, 47, 53, 80
"props," 8

Quarmyne, Nyani, 3
Quayson, Ato, 29
Quel Souvenir (Abt, 2009), 55–56, 59–65, 75–76, 78n45, 94

radiation poisoning, 30–31
radical coexistence, 10–11
radio, as colonial technology, 86
radioactive contamination, 21–22
Rancière, Jacques, 132, 133, 149
Rawlings, Jerry John, 107
realism, 106, 119, 158, 160; ethical, 55, 65; hyperrealism, 10, 54, 118
Reclaiming the Discarded: Life and Labor on Rio's Garbage Dump (Millar), 136–37
Reichardt, Kelly, 29
Relufa (Cameroonian nonprofit organization), 55, 78n31
risk, 18–19, 24, 31
Risk Society: Towards a New Modernity (Beck), 18–19, 24
Rodowick, D. N., 113
Roitman, Janet, 96, 97
Ronda, Margaret, 144
Rosen, Philip, 9
Rosetta (Dardennes), 29
Royal Dutch/Shell Group, 40–41
Ruiz, Raúl, 54

Safo, Socrate, 111
Said, Edward, 4, 138
Santangelo, Byron, 5–6
Saro-Wiwa, Ken, 38, 42
Sartre, Jean-Paul, 3

Sawadogo, Boukary, 88
scale, 45n70; African cinema as interscalar vehicle, 5, 12; multiple time scales of Anthropocene, 4, 34, 42–43; pervasiveness of plastic, 129
Self-Help Electrification Programme (SHEP, Ghana), 13, 107
Sembène, Ousmane, 9, 13, 80–84, 100–102, 157
Senegal, 81
Senghor, Leopold, 102
shortage, energy, 13; darkness as condition of, 85; in DRC, 84; electricity crisis (Ghana, 2014–2017), 105–6, 108; load-shedding, 84, 105–6; new labor and social relationships in response to, 80, 84–87, 91; power outages, 59, 84–87. *See also* energy
Singida, Tanzania, 67
Sissako, Abderrahmane, 9, 10, 47, 75; *Films: Bamako* (2006), 12–13, 53–55; *Waiting for Happiness*, 160–61
Sitobu, 116
Sixth Assessment Report (IPCC), 76
slavery, legacies of, 4, 11, 15, 23
Slaymaker, William, 5–6
slow cinema, category of, 20
slow violence, 6, 12, 18–19, 32–33, 42–43
Slow Violence and the Environmentalism of the Poor (Nixon), 18–19
"socialist biopolitics," 81
sociotechnical apparatus, 81
soundscapes, 85–87, 134–35, 160
South Africa, 28
straight-to-video movie industry, 8–9, 13–14, 32, 111
streaming, 33, 110, 112
structural adjustment policies, 8, 20, 49–50, 80
structures of feeling, 101, 133

"stuckedness," 26, 28
Subterranean Estates (ed. Appel, Mason, and Watts), 36
Sudan, 93
"surplus people," 28
"suspensive interval," 74
sustainability discourse, 14; "bad duality" of, 132–33, 135; moral constraint on consumption as focus of, 132–33
Szeman, Imre, 33

Tagoe-Turkson, Patrick, 14, 129, 141, 143–47; *Works: Awia* (Sun), *145*; *Menyankoba Basia* (*My Friend's Daughter*), *146*
Tamakloe, Emmanuel Forster, 116
Tamale, Ghana, 13–14, 106–14; electricity and movies in, 107–14
Tanzania, 67
Tchouaffe, Olivier, 54
technologies of power, 25–26
temporality: Africanist scholarship on, 20; of benefits, 60–61; human and unhuman, 43; oil time, 33–34; of uranium breakdown, 21–22; violence at multiple temporalities, 12, 18, 34; waiting, 12, 21, 26–30
terraforming, colonial, 138–39
Third Cinema and Second Cinema, 9
Thrift, Nigel, 69
tindana (earth priest), 117, 121
"tiredness," 29
Tohaje (Red Warrior), 116
Tolouma, Richard, 62
Totope (Ghana), 3
Toussaint, Eric, 49
"Towards a Critical Theory of Third World Films" (Gabriel), 20
toxicity, 149; absorbed by African bodies, 11, 98; and electricity, 126; of

petroleum, 13; released by plastic production, 144; "toxic biographies," 11; of uranium, 6, 30–31; of waste dumps, 134, 136. See also oil industry; uranium extraction; waste
Tshilombo, Felix-Antoine Tshisekedi, 84

Ugochuku, 45n73
Un Homme Qui Crie (Haroun, 2010), 66
United Nations Framework Convention on Climate Change, 76
United States: and 1973 oil crisis, 48; oil imports from Africa, 1, 53
Untapped: The Scramble for Africa's Oil (Ghazvinian), 94
Up at Night (Makengo, 2019), 13, 80, 81, 84–87, 100–101; divergences of sound and image in, 85–86
uranium extraction, 5, 17–32; capital-intensive methods, 25; entangled temporality of breakdown, 21–22; France as consumer, 23–24; microparticles, 31; postcolonial sovereignty expressed by, 25; toxicity of, 6, 30–31; violence of, 12, 19; yellowcake, 22, 30. See also *Arlit, Deuxième Paris* (Mora-Kpai)

van der Veleden, Maja, 155n43
video films: development of, 108–11; digital video and software, 113–14, 118–19; hybrid-space composites, 118, 119, 121, 122; piracy, 110, 125; straight-to-video industry, 8–9, 13–14, 32, 111. See also cinema, African; Dagbani-language video production and exhibition; Nollywood films
Villiers, Jacques de, 20
violence: and debt equivalence, 77; duality of, 34; ecological, 159–60; ecological as inherent to development, 159–60; extractive, 6, 12, 17–19, 138; at multiple temporalities, 12, 18, 34; petroviolence, 41; scales of Anthropocenic, 34; security forces, 63–65; slow, 6, 12, 18–19, 32–33, 42–43; of uranium extraction, 12, 19; used to suppress citizen protest, 63–65. See also armed conflict
Vital Matter (Bennett), 121, 124
Viva Riva! (Wa Munga, 2011), 9, 13, 80, 87–92, 94, 99–101, 158; movement in, 89; opening montage, 89
Vogel, Susan Mullin, 148
Volta River, 107
Volta River Authority (VRA), 126n9

waiting, 12, 26–30; "culture of masculine," 29; modalities of, 21; "stuckedness," 26, 28; as type of labor, 29–30
Waiting for Happiness (2002), 157, 160–61
Walker, Lucy, 135
Wa Munga, Djo Tunda, 9, 80, 87–92, 99–101
waste, 6, 14; art discourse of, 130–31; electronic, 14; forms of labor and social relations generated by, 137; generated by video film production, 126; liveliness and vibrancy of plastic, 14, 129; plastic, 14, 129, 140–41; in uranium mining process, 18, 30; water sachets as source of, 140. See also Agbogbloshie waste dump (Accra, Ghana); art, African; art from waste; toxicity; *Welcome to Sodom* (2019)
Waste Land (Walker), 135
water sachet, 140
Watts, Michael, 36, 38
weapons sales, 48

Welcome to Sodom (2019), 14, 129, 131–42, 155n43; colonial narrative greenwashed by, 133–34; errors in, 131–32, 155n43; expertise of workers portrayed, 135, 137; global North consumer addressed by, 14, 133–35; household waste site images, 139; intertitles, 132, 137, 139; "Man" as subject hailed by, 134; moral rescue of garbage pickers as focus of, 134–35, 139, 148, 149; omission of Africans as agents, 134; plastic as hypervisible and unremarked, 139; single focus of as limitation, 137; soundscape of, 135–36; worker interviews, 135–36; worker request for more waste, 137; worker voices as "upcycled," 136
Wendy and Lucy (Reichardt), 29
Wengraf, Lee, 23, 53, 77n19
Wenzel, Jennifer, 6, 7, 36, 38–39, 101
"We Were Once Three Miles from the Sea" (Quarmyne), 3
What's New in African Cinema (*African Studies Review*), 157
Whissel, Kristen, 115, 119–20
Williams, James, 54
wind, 157–61; relationality of, 160–61
wind turbines, 148
Wishing Well, The (Clottey), 148–49

Wizard of Oz (1939), 147–48
women: embodied labor of, 72; feminist automobility, 82
Workers Leaving the Lumière Factory (Sortie des Usines Lumière à Lyon, 1895), 23
World Bank, 47, 49, 53, 54, 92, 111, 159; and Chad-Cameroon pipeline, 56–59, 61, 92–93; debt owed to citizens of Chad and Cameroon, 76; and Ghana National Electrification Program, 107
world cinemas, 9–10, 160
"worldliness," 4
World People's Conference on Climate Change and the Rights of Mother Earth, 76
"world risk" society, 18–19
World Trade Organization, 71
Wynter, Sylvia, 134

Ya Nmaha (*Nowhere Cool*, 1990), 108, 110
Yeboah, Ian, 140
Yellow Brick Road (*YBR*) (Clottey), 147–48
Yendi (Ghana), 107
Yusoff, Kathryn, 11

Zinder (Macky, 2021), 103n26

Carmela Garritano is Associate Professor in the Department of International Affairs and affiliated faculty in the Africana Studies program at Texas A&M University. She is author of *African Video Movies and Global Desires: A Ghanaian History*.

For Indiana University Press

Tony Brewer, Artist and Book Designer
Allison Chaplin, Acquisitions Editor
Gary Dunham, Editorial Director and Director
Sophia Hebert, Assistant Acquisitions Editor
Samantha Heffner, Marketing and Publicity Manager
Anna Garnai, Production Coordinator
Katie Huggins, Production Manager
Dave Hulsey, Associate Director and Director of Sales and Marketing
Nancy Lightfoot, Project Manager/Editor
Dan Pyle, Online Publishing Manager
Michael Regoli, Director of Publishing Operations
Pamela Rude, Senior Artist and Book Designer
Stephen Williams, Assistant Director of Marketing